Critical Essays on Langston Hughes

Critical Essays on Langston Hughes

Edward J. Mullen

G. K. Hall & Co. • Boston, Massachusetts

Library of Congress Cataloging in Publication Data

Main entry under title:

Critical essays on Langston Hughes.

(Critical essays on American literature)
Includes index.
1. Hughes, Langston, 1902–1967—Criticism and interpretation—Addresses, essays, lectures.
I. Mullen, Edward J., 1942– . II. Series.
PS3515.U274Z618 1986 818′.5209 85-16376
ISBN 0–8161–8697–9

This publication is printed on permanent/durable acid-free paper
MANUFACTURED IN THE UNITED STATES OF AMERICA

CRITICAL ESSAYS ON AMERICAN LITERATURE

This series seeks to anthologize the most important criticism on a wide variety of topics and writers in American literature. Our readers will find in various volumes not only a generous selection of reprinted articles and reviews but original essays, bibliographies, manuscript sections, and other materials brought to public attention for the first time. This volume by Edward Mullen contains forty-seven essays and reviews, the most comprehensive selection of materials available on Langston Hughes. Among the reprinted materials are reviews and articles by Countee Cullen, Alain Locke, Sterling Brown, Sherwood Anderson, Richard Wright, Saunders Redding, James Baldwin, and Arthur Davis. The introduction by Edward Mullen is itself a major contribution to Hughes studies in that it provides an overview of scholarship from the earliest reviews to the present. In addition, there are original essays by Melvin Tolson, Walter Daniel, R. Baxter Miller, and Richard K. Barksdale. We are confident that this volume will make a permanent and significant contribution to American literary study.

James Nagel, General Editor

Northeastern University

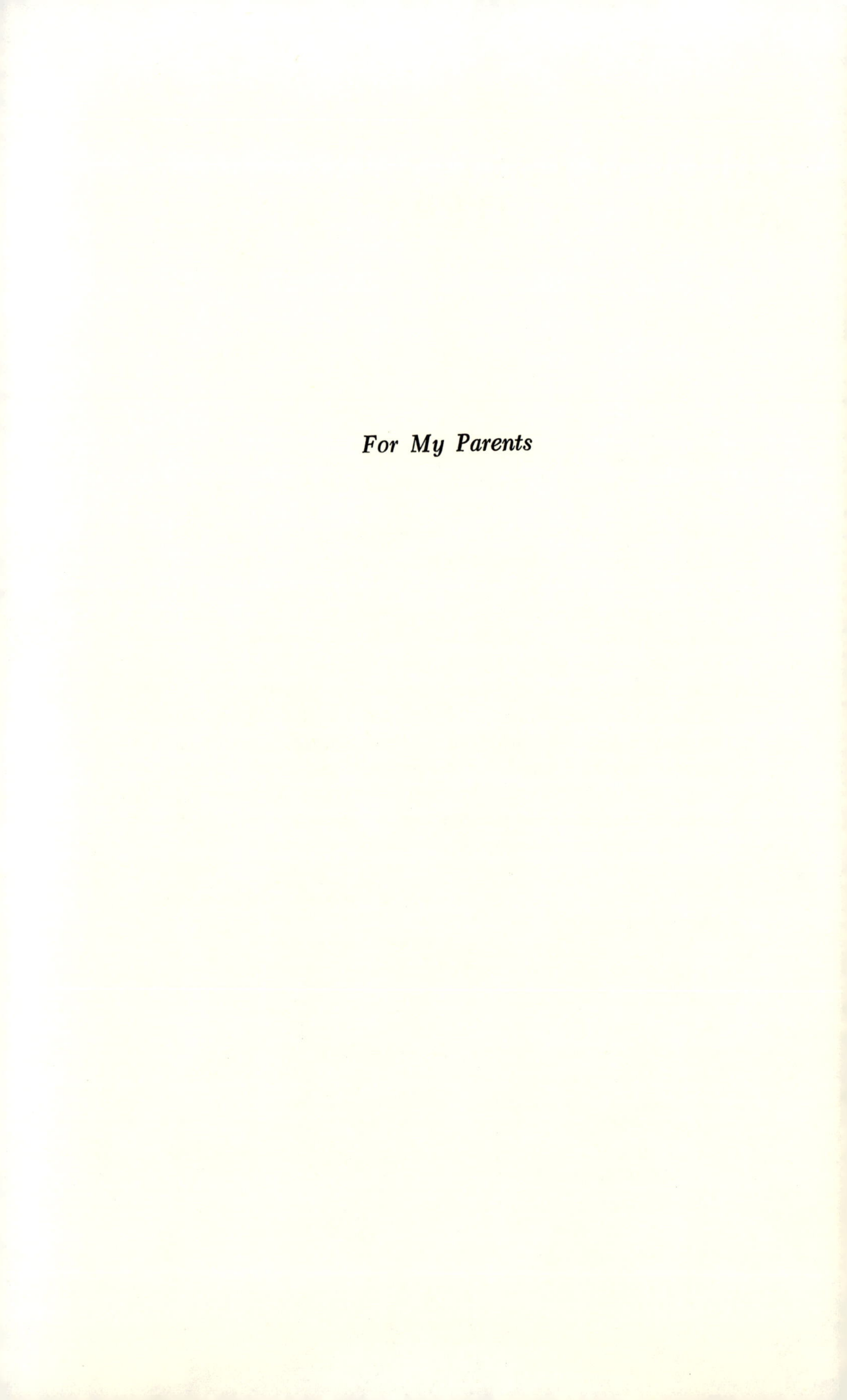

For My Parents

CONTENTS

INTRODUCTION

In selecting the contents of *Critical Essays on Langston Hughes*, I have attempted to choose works that would reflect both the evolution of Hughes's criticism from the 1920s to the present and strike a balance between documents of historical importance and more recent interpretive criticism. I have avoided reprinting material that is readily available in libraries and hence I have excluded the essays that appeared in Therman B. O'Daniel's excellent anthology, *Langston Hughes Black Genius: A Critical Evaluation* (1971). Given the extent of Hughes's production, this collection of essays focuses almost entirely on Hughes's literary production and omits from review his work as an anthologist, translator, and editor.

Langston Hughes was born in Joplin, Missouri, on 1 February 1902 and died in New York City on 22 May 1967. His first published work, "Mexican Games," appeared in the *Brownie's Book* in 1922, making his writing career of forty-five years among the longest of his contemporaries.[1] Yet in spite of a long, productive career and a considerable reputation outside of the United States, at the time of his death Hughes had barely entered the mainstream of American literature. An overview of the critical reaction to the work of Langston Hughes is therefore useful not only in gauging Hughes's own career but in considering the acceptance of the black writer within the traditional canon of American letters.

Commenting on the poetry of Langston Hughes, Onwuchekwa Jemie ventured the following: "Langston Hughes is quite possibly the most grossly misjudged poet of major importance in America."[2] This statement may seem startling at the onset since Hughes is today, at least in a popular sense, the most well-recognized black writer of the twentieth century. An examination, however, of his reception by American critics reveals that it was not until after his death that many critics began to take him seriously. Although he was labeled the "Dean of Black Letters," he has not been accorded the same stature in academic circles as Richard Wright, Ralph Ellison, or James Baldwin. This may be, as R. Baxter Miller has theorized, because Hughes produced no single work that achieved the status of a masterpiece such as Wright's *Native Son* or Ellison's *Invisible Man*.[3] The comments of Ernest Kaiser reflect this view: "Langston Hughes, if not capable of the rhetorical heights and lyrical intensity of a W. E. B. Du Bois, a Richard Wright or a James Baldwin, was a highly talented, extremely versatile, prolific journeyman writer who could turn his hand to many forms and types of writing as his varied output shows."[4] In sheer volume, however (it must be remembered that Hughes was a professional writer), Hughes's production dwarfed not only that of his immediate contemporaries (Countee Cullen, Claude McKay, Jean Toomer, and Zora Neale Hurston), but also the works of figures such as Wright, Ellison, and Baldwin, all of whom achieved prominence after the Harlem Renaissance proper. A prolific and versatile writer, Hughes authored more than forty books, edited or translated fourteen more, and contributed hundreds of reviews and essays to scores of anthologies, magazines, and newspapers. His literary and editorial production is so vast that even his serious critics fail to agree on exactly what he published. It may be that his wide-ranging genius, which made it difficult for Hughes to be identified primarily with one genre, has hampered his critical success. Another possible explanation has to do with the popular folk forms Hughes selected to serve as a vehicle for his art. As Sandra Y. Govan stated in an intriguing essay on Samuel R. Delany, critics of Afro-American literature have developed a critical astigmatism that prevents them from clearly seeing black writers who work outside established critical norms, especially those of popular literature.[5] Govan's statement is really an inversion of Charles F. Hockett's earlier formulation that "the discourses which the literary specialist values most highly tend to be the most despised by the layman."[6] Commenting on the difficulty in evaluating Hughes's work, Edward Margolies put it best when he wrote: "For Hughes's writing lies somewhere between folk material and 'literature' and the usual critical tools are not always applicable."[7] Another dynamic at play in the shaping of Hughesian criticism has to do with the role Langston played in the radical politics of the 1930s. Early in his career Margaret Larkin aptly identified him as a proletarian writer, a spokesman for the average black American.[8] It was this identification with race and class that was to underpin much of his writing and help shape the critical reaction to it. It may be helpful to bear these generalities in mind when reading the critical reaction to Hughes's work.

A BIBLIOGRAPHIC OVERVIEW

Thirteen book-length studies of Hughes have appeared since 1940, and he has been the subject of some twenty-one doctoral dissertations in American universities. Ironically, the first two studies were written in French. The first biographical study is that of the Haitian author René Piquion, *Langston Hughes: Un Chant Nouveau* (Port-au-Prince: Imprimérie de l'État, 1940). Hughes had met Piquion during a 1931 sojourn in Haiti and collaborated with him and Mercer Cook on a translation of Jacques Roumain's novel, *Gouverneurs de la rosée.* Piquion's study, which extols Hughes's sense of Negritude and posits him as a spokesman for the downtrodden, must be considered a piece of political polemic rather than a serious academic study.[9] The book also contains some poorly done translations of Hughes's verse into French. François Dodat's *Langston Hughes* (Paris: Seghers, 1964) is little more than a slight miscellany containing a short biographical introduction and translations of both verse and prose into French.

The first serious academic appraisal of Hughes's complete work is Donald C. Dickinson's *A Bio-Bibliography of Langston Hughes* (Hamden, Conn.: Archon, 1967; revised edition 1972).[10] The book, which is based on a 1964 doctoral dissertation at the University of Michigan, is divided between a long biographical essay and a bibliography of works by and about Hughes. Dickinson concludes that, although Hughes's work is uneven, he has produced some memorable interpretations of the American black and that except for passing mention Hughes has been neglected by literary historians. Although the Dickinson study was the first major bibliographic guide to Hughes, it offered little in the way of analysis and interpretation. In 1967 the poet-critic James A. Emanuel published the first book-length critical study of Hughes's life and works (*Langston Hughes* [New York: Twayne Publishers]). This brief well-written book was intended as a general introduction for American readers and as such it offers an overview of Hughes's life and work and concludes that he was the dean of American Negro writers. Emanuel finds Hughes's early blues poems to be an especially important contribution to American literature. That same year the editors of the Parisian francophone journal *Présence Africaine* (no. 64 [4th trimester 1967]) brought out an important issue in homage to Hughes that contains essays by Nicolás Guillén, Lamine Diakhate, François Dodat, Eldred Jones, and Andrew Salkey. In 1968 Milton Meltzer published *Langston Hughes: A Biography* (New York: Thomas Y. Crowell). This brief biography draws extensively on Hughes's autobiography *The Big Sea* (1940) and is of slight critical interest. Also in 1968 Ernest Kaiser published a "Selected Bibliography of the Published Writings of Langston Hughes" (*Freedomways* [Spring]:185–91) which corrected many of the minor errors in the Dickinson *Bio-Bibliography.* During the seventies, Hughes became the object of increased scrutiny. In 1970 two biographies for children appeared: Elizabeth Myers, *Langston Hughes: Poet of His People* (Champaign, Ill.: Garrard Pub. Co.) and Charlemae H. Rollins, *Black Trouba-*

dor: Langston Hughes (New York: Rand McNally). Comparable to Meltzer's earlier study, they offer sympathetic portraits of Hughes as a spokesman for all blacks.

The 1971 publication of Therman B. O'Daniel's *Langston Hughes Black Genius: A Critical Evaluation* (New York: William Morrow), which brought together fourteen essays on Hughes as well as an extensive selected classified bibliography, helped further the image of Hughes as the doyen of black American Letters. In 1975 Peter Mandelik and Stanley Schatt published a valuable *Concordance to the Poetry of Langston Hughes* (Detroit: Gale Research) which was followed in 1976 by Onwuchekwa Jemie's *Langston Hughes: An Introduction to the Poetry* (New York: Columbia University Press). Jemie's book, the first full-length study of Hughes's verse, is an introduction to the collected poems of Hughes from the dual perspective of Afro-American oral tradition (jazz and blues) and of the tradition of social protest.

In 1977 two volumes of significant bibliographic importance were published: Richard K. Barksdale's *Langston Hughes: The Poet and His Critics* (Chicago: American Library Association) and R. Baxter Miller's *Langston Hughes and Gwendolyn Brooks: A Reference Guide* (Boston: G. K. Hall). The former is an assessment of major critics' responses to Hughes's poetry, while the latter is a carefully annotated list of secondary literature from 1924 to 1977. Hughes's contact with the Hispanic world is the subject of Edward J. Mullen's *Langston Hughes in the Hispanic World and Haiti* (Hamden, Conn.: Archon, 1977) which offers the first bibliographic look at Hughes's Hispanic ties. A further barometer of serious interest in Hughes was the 1980 publication of Charles H. Nichols's edition *Arna Bontemps–Langston Hughes Letters, 1925–1967* (New York: Dodd Mead & Co.) which, in a lively introduction, places Hughes (and Bontemps) at the apex of Afro-American intellectual activity. Faith Berry's *Langston Hughes Before and Beyond Harlem* (Westport, Conn.: Lawrence Hill, 1983) is the most complete biography to date. Although it is not a complete study, since it traces Hughes's career only up to his permanent move to Harlem in the 1940s, it is a well-documented chronicle of the poet's early years, including his relationship with the literati of the Harlem Renaissance and the influence of Marxist aesthetics on his work. Because Berry focuses considerable attention on his sexual orientation (she maintains he was a homosexual) the book has been the object of considerable controversy.[11]

THE POETRY

There is general critical agreement that poetry was the genre in which Langston Hughes achieved his greatest artistic and popular successes and the form he used most adroitly to apprehend the condition of his people. Over his forty-five-year career as a writer, Hughes wrote some 571 poems that were published in fifteen separate volumes. Unlike his white contemporaries (John Dos Passos, William Carlos Williams, and Archibald MacLeish) Hughes's poetry received little if any formal academic criticism but was instead evaluated primarily in the pages of magazines and newspapers. It is also essential to understand that since Hughes was the member of the Harlem Renaissance movement most directly involved in the forging of an aesthetic of black folk expression, the critical response to his early books involved a response to a number of subtexts in American culture: folk art versus high art, propaganda versus literature, and black art versus white art.

Hughes's first volume of verse, *The Weary Blues* (New York: Knopf, 1926), took its title from a poem written about a piano player Hughes had known in Harlem and which first appeared in New York's *Amsterdam News* on 8 April 1923. Hughes called "The Weary Blues" his "lucky poem" since it received first prize in a literary contest sponsored by the National Urban League in 1925.

The awarding of the prize for "The Weary Blues" itself was from the onset a source of controversy. It was both prophetic and ironic. Prophetic in the sense that it anticipated the fame that Hughes was to one day garner and ironic because poems like "The Weary Blues" offended an important segment of the black intelligentsia who were laboring to present an image of blacks that reflected their own views of propriety and success. Thus in the work of Hughes and most particularly in his blues and jazz poems we see a curious synthesis of the cultural schizophrenia that underpinned the entire Harlem Renaissance movement. While a poem like Hughes's "The Negro Speaks of Rivers," which was inspired by the tradition of spirituals, was openly embraced by black critics as an artistic achievement, the blues poems were vehemently rejected by these same critics. In challenging the award of the prize to Hughes, Thomas Millard Henry wrote: "It lacks metaphor and poetic imagery so much in evidence in great poetry. It is jazz. . . . perhaps it is not bad to call such stuff doggerel. It is a product of the inferiority complex. Here in America it has acquired the nice name New Poetry."[12] A further protest was registered in the *New York Evening World* by Eugene F. Gordon, a black critic from Boston. Gordon contended that the selection of "The Weary Blues" for first place was evidence of a definite Nordic influence among the poetry judges who required Negroid poetry from Negroes.[13]

The race issue, propaganda versus real art, and Hughes's use of colloquial language quickly became the central issues in the critical reactions to *The Weary Blues*. In an anonymous review in the *Times Literary Supplement*, for example, he is contrasted with Countee Cullen and is dismissed as superficial.[14] The majority of the other reviews of this first book were generally favorable. The *New York Times*, for example, compared Hughes to a modern day François Villon, but expressed reservations about Hughes's use of jazz poems: "It is a mistake that Hughes' publisher should have placed the poet's inferior work, his jazz poems, in the forefront of the book and have permitted the book a title *Weary Blues* so exclusively connotative of this type of verse."[15] DuBose Heyward, a displaced Southerner who wrote *Porgy*, reviewed the book for the *New York Herald Tribune*.[16] While Heyward thought Hughes's use of syncopation in *The Weary Blues* was interesting, he found several of the short free verse poems superior in theme and execution. In short, Heyward conceived of Hughes in relationship to more established white writers such as Amy Lowell.

Although enthusiastic as well, Afro-American writers had their caveats. Jessie Fauset, the editorial assistant to W. E. B. Du Bois, who herself had produced a conventional image of black life in *There Is Confusion* (1925), characterized Hughes's poems as "warm, exotic, and shot through with color." She was clearly uncomfortable with his use of dialect ("I am no great lover of any dialect"), and tried to place his poetry in the context of standard American literature.[17] Countee Cullen, writing in *Opportunity*, was considerably more reserved. He, too, was struck by Hughes's "utter spontaneity and expression of a unique personality,"[18] but found the jazz poems to be interlopers in the company of the truly beautiful poems in other sections of the book. Cullen was quick to underscore the uncomfortable position in which Hughes's dialect verse placed him: "they tend to hurl this poet into the gaping pit that lies before all Negro writers, in the confines of which they become racial artists instead of artists pure and simple."[19] Alain Locke, writing in *Palms*, a little magazine founded by Idella Purnell Stone and Witter Bynner, offered perhaps the most cogent assessment of the book as a whole. He was among the first to recognize Hughes's debt to Afro-American music, particularly in the spiritual and secular jazz poems. Perhaps even more important was Locke's ability to see embedded in Hughes's verse the dialectical tension between the two worlds in which the black man lived. He wrote, "For the Negro experience rightly sensed even in the moods of the common folk is complex and paradoxical, like the Blues which Hughes has pointed out to be so characteristic, with their nonchalant humor against a background of tragedy."[20]

Published in February 1927, *Fine Clothes to the Jew* became a far more controversial text. In this collection Hughes incorporated some of the basic ideas from his essay "The Negro Artist and the Racial Mountain" which he had published in the *Nation* the previous June and where he exhorted black writers to abandon white aesthetic norms. Hughes personally liked this second volume, as he said in *The Big Sea*, because it was more impersonal and because it made use of the Negro folksong forms and included poems about work and problems of finding work.[21] The book was extensively reviewed in such important periodicals as *New Masses, Bookman*, the *New York Times*, the *New York Herald Tribune*, the *Saturday Review of Literature*, the *New Republic*, the *Nation*, and, of course, *Crisis* and *Opportunity*. Many of the poems in the book, especially those dealing with cabaret singers, street walkers, elevator boys, or other aspects of low life, alienated the black upper-middle class. In *The Big Sea* Hughes recalled that *Fine Clothes to the Jew* was well received by the literary magazines and the white press, but the Negro critics did not like it at all. The *Pittsburgh Courier* ran a headline across the top of a page, "Langston Hughes' Book of Poems Trash." A headline in the *New York Amsterdam News* read, "Langston Hughes, the Sewer Dweller." The *Chicago Whip* characterized Hughes as "the poet low-rate of Harlem." As Hughes wrote, "Others called the book a disgrace to the race, a return to the dialect tradition, and a parading of all our racial defects before the public."[22] J. A. Rogers's review in the *Pittsburgh Courier* accused Hughes of having written the book for a white audience, an obvious allusion to the poet's deliberate cultivation of a style associated with the stylized primitivism of the New Negro generation.[23] Eustace Gay wrote in the *Philadelphia Tribune* that it was "Bad enough to have white authors holding up our imperfections to public gaze. Our aim ought to be to present to the general public . . . our higher aims and aspirations."[24]

A closer examination of the critical reaction to this book is instructive since it tends to underscore a number of the cultural undercurrents operative during the Harlem Renaissance. The *Crisis* gave *Fine Clothes to the Jew* a fleeting but positive review and claimed that, like *The Weary Blues*, it possessed the fine qualities of force, passion, directness, and sensitive perception. The anonymous reviewer wrote: "There are extraordinarily beautiful bits here and there and while the poems distinctly confine themselves to lowly types, it is the human feeling and longing there that he [Hughes] emphasizes."[25]

Writing for the *New York Times Book Review*, Herbert S. Gorman found the collection uneven and flawed, but claimed that it did display "flashes of authentic inspiration and gives a vivid sensation of the Negro spirit."[26] DuBose Heyward was lukewarm in his reception of the book, failing to find in it anything that was really new. Heyward concluded, "But if this second book does not lift the art of the author to a new high level, it does appreciably increase the number of first-rate poems to the credit of Langston Hughes and it renews his high promise for the future."[27] Writing in the *Nation*, Harry Allan Potamkin saw in the book no visible progress beyond *The Weary Blues* and commented on its limited form and theme.[28] Julia Peterkin, who herself had won the Pulitzer Prize for *Scarlet Sister Mary*, a novel about blacks in the

South, located the book within the tradition of primitivism in vogue in the 1920s: "Langston Hughes . . . interprets the emotions of primitive types of American Negroes."[29] Much in the same vein were the comments of Babette Deutsch, who compared Hughes's verse to that of Ezra Pound, John Crowe Ransom, and Mark Van Doren; she concluded that "the verses of Langston Hughes are completely unliterary, often willfully illiterate, and as naively vital as any old ballad or folk song."[30]

There were, however, three important assessments of the book published that year. Margaret Larkin writing in *Opportunity* compared Hughes to Robert Burns and was the first to identify him as a proletarian poet. She wrote, "Perhaps Langston Hughes does not relish the title of proletarian poet but he deserves it just the same. 'Railroad Avenue,' 'Porter,' 'Saturday Night,' and 'The Songs from the Georgia Roads' all have their roots deep in the lives of workers. They give voice to the philosophy of men of the people, more rugged, more beautiful, better food for poetry than the philosophy of the middle class."[31]

In the *Carolina Magazine* Lewis Alexander praised Hughes for his view of art as social praxis and his use of nonconventional poetic forms. He wrote, "He is a real poet and at the rate he is going will develop into a genuine folk poet worthy of being called the spokesman of the black masses of America."[32]

It was his mentor Alain Locke, however, who was to give the book its most perspicacious and balanced review. Writing in the *Saturday Review of Literature*, Locke labeled the book "notable as an achievement in poetic realism in addition to its particular value as a folk study in verse of Negro life."[33] Locke astutely lifted Hughes's book out of the Harlem Renaissance polemic and compared him to other important American authors, such as Carl Sandburg and Edgar Lee Masters. Finally, he referred to "Mulatto" as a lyric condensation of the deepest tragedy of the race problem: "After this, there is nothing to be said about the finest tragedy always having to be Greek."[34]

Further evidence of the positive recognition of Hughes's contribution to the development of a new black folk idiom came from the black sociologist Charles S. Johnson, who served as the editor of *Opportunity* and was responsible for the promotion of literature by black authors during the years of the Harlem Renaissance. In an essay published in the *Carolina Magazine*, Johnson affirmed that "The poetry of Langston Hughes is without doubt the finest expression of this new Negro poetry. Like Sandburg he has shocked polite circles by daring to search for beauty in things and beings too commonplace for dignity and exaltation. . . ."[35]

In a telling essay published in the *Crisis* in 1928 by the senior black scholar, Allison Davis, Hughes's work was again criticized for projecting a faddish, simplistic portrait of blacks. Davis's essay is an important document inasmuch as it draws in and focuses on issues central to Hughes's early reception. The essay was not a review of the poetry of Hughes per se but rather a generalized denunciation of the New Negro movement and its attendant cult of primitivism:

> Our writers started almost ten years ago to capitalize on the sensational and sordid in Negro life, notably in Harlem, by making it appear that Negro life is distinctive for its flaming "color," its crude and primitive emotion. This facile acceptance of the old, romantic delusion of "racial literatures," which goes back beyond Taine all the way to Mme. de Stael, was a convenient mould for the energies of writers who had no tradition to guide them in treating Negro themes. What was more to the point, it interested the sophisticated reading public, at the height of the "jazz age" following the war, because it seemed to bring fresh and primitive forces to a jaded age.[36]

Davis was particularly piqued that Hughes had let himself be influenced by Carl Van Vechten, a white patron of Afro-American art who presented a somewhat sensationalized portrait of Harlem in *Nigger Heaven* (New York: Knopf, 1926): "Mr. Van Vechten disclaims any influence upon Mr. Hughes' first book, *The Weary Blues*. . . . The evident reply is that the drop from the best poems of this first book to any of those in *Fine Clothes to the Jew*, which Mr. Van Vechten undoubtedly *did* influence, is the real proof of his having finally misdirected Mr. Hughes."[37]

Fine Clothes to the Jew was Hughes's last book of verse written during the peak years of the Renaissance, for after the 1929 crash things changed dramatically for most black Americans. Writing by black writers hardly came to a halt at the end of the 1920s. After all there would be important work done during the 1930s by Arna Bontemps, Zora Neale Hurston, Wallace Thurman, and others, but the vogue of the New Negro was definitely passé among most white readers and publishers. Hughes, too, would temporarily abandon his blues and jazz poems (perhaps the most memorable documents written during the Renaissance) to take up the banner of social protest poetry. It would not be for fifteen years with his *Shakespeare in Harlem* (1942) that he would return to the idioms of popular music.

When the dust had settled on the immediate controversy surrounding the artistic merits of Harlem Renaissance writers, Hughes's first two books received a more impartial assessment. Melvin Tolson, an important post-Renaissance writer, in a 1940 Columbia University master's thesis, "The Negro Group of Harlem Writers" (chapter 4, "Langston Hughes," is reprinted in this volume), saw much to be praised in Hughes's verse and labeled him "the chief ballad-singer of proletarian upper Lenox Avenue."[38]

As early as 1947, Arna Bontemps, referring to Hughes's Renaissance publications, aptly labeled him a "chronicler of modern urbanization."[39] Similarly, Arthur Davis's essay, "The Harlem of Langston Hughes' Poetry" (reprinted in this volume), gives serious attention to Hughes's early poems about Harlem, thus dispelling the notion that they were exclusively portraits of hedonism.[40]

The first serious academic appraisal of Hughes's first two books would not appear until the 1962 publication of Jean Wagner's *Les Poètes nègres des États-Unis* (Paris: Librairie Ista) (translated into English as *Black Poets of the United States*). Wagner comments perceptively on Hughes's use of African motifs in *The Weary Blues* and was among the first to note Hughes's use of jazz as a rebellion motif. The most sustained and positive evaluation of *The Weary Blues* and *Fine Clothes to the Jew* is to be found in Jemie's *Langston Hughes: An Introduction to the Poetry* which presents impressive readings of many of these early poems in terms of the black aesthetic, which, according to Jemie, Hughes first articulated in "The Negro Artist and the Racial Mountain."

In *Langston Hughes: The Poet and His Critics* (1977), Richard K. Barksdale dedicates an entire chapter, "Blues, Jazz and Low-down Folks" (29–37), to a reassessment of Hughes's early books and concludes that "only Langston Hughes, master impressionist, could effectively depict black America's first great period of blues and jazz and low-down folks" (37). He also notes that taken together the poems have a certain architectonic unity and succeed in presenting a kaleidoscopic vision of the Harlem of the 1920s. Barksdale justly incorporates in his critical formulation the ideas of both Blyden Jackson and George Kent concerning Hughes's virtuosity with blues and jazz forms.[41]

If the dynamic of the Harlem Renaissance informed much of the critical reaction to Hughes's verse of the 1920s, then the critical reception to his poetry of the 1930s can be seen in many ways as a reaction to Hughes's involvement in Marxist political causes. During the 1930s there was little formal critical reaction to his poetry since most of it was not published in book form but rather in magazines such as *International Literature*, *New Masses*, *Crisis*, *Opportunity*, and *New Theatre*. These, too, were the years during which the poet traveled to the Soviet Union, China, and Spain where he served as a war correspondent for the Afro-American papers. Much of his poetry is a reaction to these experiences.

From 1931 to 1938 five books of verse were published: *Dear Lovely Death* (New York: Troutbeck Press, 1931), a twenty-page booklet privately printed and distributed by Amy Spingarn; *The Negro Mother* (New York: Golden Stair Press, 1931), another brief pamphlet; *The Dream Keeper and other poems* (New York: Knopf, 1932), a book of poems for children selected from *The Weary Blues* and *Fine Clothes to the Jew; Scottsboro Limited* (New York: Golden Stair Press, 1931), which contained a one-act play and four protest poems about the imprisonment and trial of four black youths in Alabama; and *A New Song* (New York: International Workers Order, 1938), a thirty-one-page booklet of social protest poems.

Formal reviews of his published verse from the thirties are scant. William Rose Benét and A. T. Eaton reacted with mild enthusiasm to the simple lyricism of *The Dream Keeper*,[42] but *Scottsboro Limited* and *A New Song* were met with either mute silence or outright rejection. The comments of Alain Locke regarding *Scottsboro Limited* are typical:

> Meanwhile, as the folk-school tradition deepens, Langston Hughes, formerly its chief exponent, turns more and more in the direction of social protest and propaganda; since *Scottsboro Limited* represents his latest moods, although *The Dream Keeper* and *Popo and Fifina* are also recent publications. The latter is a flimsy sketch, a local-color story of Haitian child life done in collaboration with Arna Bontemps, while *The Dream Keeper* is really a collection of the more lyrical of the poems in his first two volumes of verse, supplemented by a few unprinted poems—all designed to be of special appeal to child readers. The book is a delightful lyrical echo of the older Hughes, who sang of his people as "walkers with the dawn and morning," "loud-mouthed laughers in the hands of fate." But the poet of *Scottsboro Limited* is a militant and indignant proletarian reformer. . . .[43]

Another factor that affected Hughes's stature as a writer during the 1930s was the critical fallout from poems such as "Goodbye Christ" and "Christ in Alabama" which alienated important members of the black church. Walter C. Daniel discusses the implications of the controversy surrounding "Goodbye Christ" in "Langston Hughes versus the Black Preachers in the *Pittsburgh Courier* in the 1930s" (included in this volume).

It was critics from abroad, however, who were most receptive to Hughes's leanings toward poetry of social commitment. Nancy Cunard anthologized him in her *Negro Anthology* and in an important essay in *Left Review* called him "the travelling star of coloured America, the leader of the younger intellectuals."[44] In a classic Marxist reading of Hughes published in *International Literature*, Lydia Filatova asserted that "in his poems of 1931–32, he [Hughes] is a revolutionary poet who uses his writings as a weapon in the struggle against capitalism for the emancipation of toiling Negroes and toiling humanity in all countries."[45]

It was also during this period that Hughes was discovered by the francophone writers of the black diaspora such as Léopold Sédar Senghor, Paulette Nardal, and Etienne Léro, the founders of the Negritude school of ethnic consciousness. Sensitive to the contributions of black writers from North America, they translated the poetry of Hughes and published it in the pages of *La Revue de Monde Noir* (Paris) and *Légitime Défense* (Paris).[46] Because of Hughes's travels to Cuba, Haiti, Mexico, and Spain during this same time and due in some measure to his friendship with the Cuban poet, Nicolás Guillén, he was widely translated and eulogized in Spanish America for his celebration of blackness and the social criticism of the colonial mentality of the United States implicit in poems such as "I, too, Sing America." In September 1928, the Cuban journalist José Antonio Fernández de Castro published the first Spanish translation of a poem by Hughes, "Yo también honro América" ("I, too") in the Cuban journal *Social.* Hughes was subsequently translated by Jorge Luis Borges in *Sur* and by the Mexican Rafael Lozano in *Crisol*, a short-lived magazine of proletarian art. It was the journal *Contemporáneos* (1928–31), however, that played the most important role in Mexico in the introduction of black literature. For example, Xavier Villaurrutia published translations of four of Hughes's poems in *Contemporáneos* in the fall of 1931, and Ortiz de Montellano earlier published some short poems on black themes ("Motivos negros") in the same review in October 1928. The importance of the appearance of these materials in *Contemporáneos* cannot be overstated since *Contemporáneos* is widely recognized in the Hispanic world as one of the most important vanguard reviews.[47]

Recently a more dispassionate evaluation of the decade has taken place. In his *Langston Hughes: The Poet and His Critics*, Richard K. Barksdale summarizes most of the criticism of the period, dismissing much of it as myopic, and counters with a more dispassionate assessment of Hughes's writings during the 1930s. Faith Berry has been responsible for the most significant reassessment of this phase of Hughes's development. Her *Good Morning Revolution: Uncollected Social Protest Writings by Langston Hughes* (New York: Lawrence Hill, 1973) collects Hughes's most militant revolutionary pieces of social protest together with an essay that discusses the evolution of his ideological writings. Berry notes that Hughes's revolutionary prose and poetry was not limited to the 1930s but actually spanned his entire career; she also refutes the notion that Hughes was simply a "folk" poet.

During the 1940s Hughes returned to Harlem both in a physical and spiritual sense. He published three books of poetry during the decade—*Shakespeare in Harlem* (New York: Knopf, 1942), *Fields of Wonder* (New York: Knopf, 1947), and *One Way Ticket* (New York: Knopf, 1949)—as well as two patriotic protest pamphlets, *Freedom's Plow* (New York: Musette Publishing Co., 1943) and *Jim Crow's Last Stand* (Atlanta: Negro Publication Society of America, 1943).

The intense critical reception of the 1920s and the vehement reaction of the 1930s seem to have coalesced in the 1940s into a sense of disinterested stagnation. With *Shakespeare in Harlem* Hughes returned to the blues, jazz, and ballad motifs of the 1920s but, as Arthur Davis points out, the somber picture of Harlem is very different from that of *The Weary Blues.* Here Hughes captures something of the downbeat of ghetto life, a sense of its cynicism and violence. Mary Colum, reviewing for the *New York Times*, found the book sad and monotonous;[48] Owen Dodson writing for *Phylon* called it a "careless surface job";[49] and William Harrison in *Opportunity* lamented the presence of the most uprooted social types.[50] Reviews in *Poetry* and *Nation* were lukewarm.[51] The lone exception was Alfred Kreymborg who, writing for the *Saturday Review of Literature*, found the volume a subtle blending of tragedy and comedy.[52]

Fields of Wonder, a collection of mostly melancholy, lyrical evocation, received scant attention. Ruth Lechlitner found many poems "shallow, forced and contrived,"[53] while Hubert Creekmore complained in the *New York Times Book Review* of monotony and a "questionable logic."[54]

With *One Way Ticket*, Hughes returned to the somber nocturnal world of Harlem and again included poems in the blues and jazz modes. His critics were not kind. Saunders Redding called the book "stale, flat, and spiritless."[55] *Nation* referred to "a studied artlessness,"[56] while G. Lewis Chandler, writing in *Phylon*, expressed a sense of déjà vu about the book's selfsameness.[57] Harvey C. Webster's review in *Poetry* is a telling document inasmuch as it offers a curious synthesis of much of the previous criticism of Hughes's verse as too facile, repetitive, and dealing only with "the lighter aspect of the Negro experience."[58] In spite of the fact that Webster expresses a fondness for the saga of Madam Johnson, Alberta K, his final judgment is that Hughes is a limited reporter "of the surface of things."[59]

Hughes's last four books of poetry mark a paradoxical return to his original experimentation with black music and dialect forms. His last collections of verse were *Montage of a Dream Deferred* (New York: Henry Holt, 1951), *Selected Poems* (New York: Knopf, 1959), *Ask Your Mama: 12 Moods for Jazz* (New York: Knopf, 1961), and *The Panther and the Lash* (New York: Knopf, 1967).

Jean Wagner called *Montage* "The most ambitious experiment undertaken by Hughes in this domain."[60] In an important prefatory note Hughes explained the conceptual underpinnings of the poem: "In terms of Afro-American popular music and the sources from which it has progressed—jazz, ragtime, swing, blues, boogie-woogie, and be-bop—this poem on contemporary Harlem, like be-bop, is marked by conflicting changes, sudden nuances, sharp and impudent interjections, broken rhythms, and passages sometimes in the manner of the jam session, sometimes the popular song, punctuated by the riffs, runs, breaks, and disc-tortions of the music of a community in transition" (p. 2).

Saunders Redding, writing for the *New York Herald Tribune*, received the book with considerable more praise than he had accorded to *Shakespeare in Harlem.* Although Redding was cautious of "the jarring dissonances and broken rhythms of be-bop," he noted that Hughes had made a spiritually rewarding return to the days of the Harlem Renaissance.[61] John Parker in *Phylon* asserted that "With its freshness of approach, its powerful rhythm, and its moving quality, *Montage* further justifies its author's claim to the title . . . 'The Negro Poet Laureate.' "[62] Babette Deutsch, who had earlier labeled the verses of *Fine Clothes to the Jew* "completely illiterate," found the book marred by the limitations of folk art.[63] Rolfe Humphries, in the *Nation*, felt the message of *Montage* to be "oversimplified and theatrical."[64] More recent academic criticism points to a serious and positive reappraisal of *Montage.* Jean Wagner, Richard Barksdale, Theodore R. Hudson, and in particular Onwuchekwa Jemie, find *Montage* an exciting, artful example of how Hughes was able to adapt new black musical forms to mirror societal changes.

The 1959 publication of Hughes's *Selected Poems* by Knopf elicited predictably favorable but largely uncritical responses from periodicals such as *Crisis* and *Phylon* which had long monitored Hughes's career. The most significant and widely quoted review of *Selected Poems*, however, was that of James Baldwin, who, writing in the *New York Times*, concluded that the book was uneven: "This book contains a great deal which a more disciplined poet would have thrown into the wastebasket."[65] Clearly the subtext to this brief review (labeled by Barksdale as "the most disparaging and negative appraisals ever accorded Hughes's poetry" [105]) was that Hughes was a second-rate writer. Baldwin ends his brief assessment by asserting that Hughes has been unable to reconcile his role of black man writing out of a defined social context with his duty as an artist, a statement that echoes back to Alain Locke's earlier discourses on art versus propaganda.

Hughes's last and boldest experiment with fusing music and poetry, *Ask Your Mama: 12 Moods for Jazz* (New York: Knopf, 1961), received little immediate critical attention. It was in many ways his most unconventional book and the one that is most difficult to understand. Its physical appearance and typographical arrangement (it is printed entirely in capital letters and contains musical notations on the sides of the pages) become immediately apparent to the reader. Dudley Fitts called it "stunt poetry" and compared it to Vachel Lindsay's "Congo,"[66] while Rudi Blesh in the *New York Times Book Review* eulogized Hughes for his social awareness articulated through jazz rhythms [which] "hide . . . fire and steel."[67] Donald C. Dickinson, in his overview of Hughes's work, was less than laudatory: "In general, the results of this experimental technique seem less successful than Hughes' early blues rhythms. Even his wry sense of humor is less in evidence."[68]

Jean Wagner devoted considerable space to a reading of the book's multiple levels of structured meaning. Although he had some caveats, he was in general enthusiastic, viewing the book as an attempt by Hughes "to achieve a huge synthesis." He wrote, "From the thematic point of view, *Ask Your Mama* offers a striking summary of the American black world at this time, and even of the entire black world, for Hughes's technique enables us to sense their profound unity."[69] James Emanuel called it "a venturesome long poem updating Hughes's original efforts of the 1920's with a leap in technique that has outdistanced critical perceptions."[70] The most sustained evaluation of *Ask Your Mama* is found in Jemie's *Langston Hughes: An Introduction to the Poetry.* Jemie studied *Ask Your Mama* in relation to *Montage of a Dream Deferred* and labeled it "an avant-garde experiment." If cinematographic montage was the controlling mechanism in *Montage*, in *Ask Your Mama* it is free association of ideas. Jemie considers the latter to be the climax of Hughes's lifelong goal to fuse poetry and black music.

Although it was prepared by Hughes while he was living, *The Panther and the Lash* was published shortly after his death. Dedicated to Rosa Parks of Montgomery, Alabama, this last volume of verse seems to be a response to the racial and political tensions of the 1960s. Critical reception to this last volume was slim. Writing in the *New York Times*, Alden Whitman gave fleeting mention to the overall mood of the book ("a man lashing out at the indignities to which people of his race have been subjected"),[71] while Laurence Lieberman in *Poetry* quibbled with Hughes's politics ("The age demands intellectual commitment from its spokesmen").[72] Theodore Hudson, reviewing for the *CLA Journal*, found the book satisfying and its message valid, but felt the volume was "marred in places by the prosaic rather than the poetic."[73] W. Edward Farrison offered a longer, more balanced academic appraisal of the book, also in the *CLA Journal*, concluding that the collection was a fitting conclusion to Hughes's career and was a vital contribution to American poetry.[74] Onwuchekwa Jemie was more strongly enthusiastic, viewing the volume as a testimony to Hughes's "deep insight and enduring quality."[75]

THE PROSE

Although he would never garner a reputation as novelist or short story writer comparable to what he achieved as a poet, prose fiction was together with lecturing one of the vehicles by which Langston

Hughes earned his living. His output was impressive: two novels, three books of short stories, a two-volume autobiography, and five books centered around the character Jesse B. Semple. Although no book-length studies of Hughes's fiction have been published, it has been the subject of three doctoral dissertations.[76]

Hughes's first novel, *Not Without Laughter* (New York: Knopf, 1930), a semi-autobiographical account of a black boy growing up in the Midwest, received a mixed but generally lukewarm critical response. As James Emanuel wrote: "Praise was tempered with notice of structural defects and undramatic action."[77] It was barely mentioned in *Crisis*,[78] and Sterling Brown presented what amounted to a long plot summary in *Opportunity*.[79] V. F. Calverton's observation in the *Nation* offers a synthesis of the book's critical reception: "But 'Not Without Laughter' is significant despite these weaknesses. It is significant because even where it fails, it fails beautifully, and where it succeeds—namely, in its intimate characterizations and in its local color and charm—it succeeds where almost all others have failed."[80]

Two important critical reassessments were published in O'Daniel's *Langston Hughes Black Genius*. In "Not Without Laughter, Not Without Tears," W. Edward Farrison concludes that most of the previously published criticism "has generally overlooked the fact that it is an important social document as well as a literary work."[81] George Kent, in "Langston Hughes and Afro-American Folk and Cultural Tradition," studies *Not Without Laughter* within the context of Hughes's apprehension of black folk vision and tradition, noting that the novel's structure is controlled by a folk response to existence and that the book contains such forms as "blues, folk aphorisms, slave narratives and a slave tall story, dances and spirituals."[82] R. Baxter Miller subsequently located the image of home that unifies *Not Without Laughter* within a long tradition ranging from Homer to Baraka (Leroi Jones) in verse and from Charles Dickens to James Baldwin in prose.[83]

In 1934 Hughes published a collection of fourteen stories, *The Ways of White Folks* (New York: Knopf), which marked a change in direction from *Not Without Laughter*. Mirroring closely his ideological and aesthetic stance of the 1930s, these stories, which largely deal with race relations, received a positive critical response. Herschel Brickell, writing in the *North American Review*, called them "some of the best stories that have appeared in years."[84] Lewis Gannett called Hughes "a master of the storytelling art."[85] Vernon Loggins, in the *Saturday Review of Literature*, labeled *The Ways of White Folks* as Hughes's "strongest work,"[86] and E. C. Homes, reviewing for *Opportunity*, spoke of Hughes's superb irony, simplicity, and splendid craftsmanship.[87] Alain Locke, in *Survey Graphic*, called *The Ways of White Folks* "an important book," but expressed reservations about the role of sociology versus literature.[88]

Sherwood Anderson reviewed the book under the telling title, "Paying for Old Sins." He liked Hughes's style and approach and was quick to note the curious role reversal that Hughes had so effortlessly carried out here. Anderson wrote: "The Negro people in these stories of his are so alive, warm, and real and the whites are all caricatures, life, love, laughter, old wisdom all to the Negroes and silly pretense, fakiness, pretty much all to the whites. . . . Mr. Hughes, my hat off to you in relation to your own race but not to mine."[89] R. Baxter Miller was to later comment in *Langston Hughes and Gwendolyn Brooks: A Reference Guide* that "Of the many reviewers . . . over a half century of criticism, Anderson probably sensed Hughes's achievement most deeply. . . . Hughes created counter-culture and counter mythology, and Sherwood Anderson laughed at the recognition" (xii).

Martha Gruening, writing in *New Republic*, found a number of the stories in the book to be very good, but was clearly uncomfortable about the depiction of whites: "Octavus Roy Cohen finds colored people very funny, and Julia Peterkin finds them very quaint. Langston Hughes finds white people either sordid and cruel, or silly and sentimental. This indictment is perhaps largely, if not wholly, true. Nevertheless this collection of short stories suffers a little, as a whole, from being based on such a formula. Any formula is too cheap and easy for an artist of Hughes' caliber."[90] The review that appeared in *Crisis* highlighted the racial nature of the material and applauded Hughes's handling of it. The reviewers also noted that the book was uneven because many of the stories had been previously published in magazines and that none was "up to Hughes's standard."[91] More recently David Michael Nifong has studied Hughes's experimentation with narrative perspective in *The Ways of White Folks*. His conclusions along with the work of James Emanuel point to Hughes as a technical innovator in the field of the short story.[92]

In 1940 Hughes published the first part, *The Big Sea* (New York, Knopf), of an eventual two-part autobiography. Written with simple candor and considerable good humor, the book chronicled Hughes's life up to 1931 and offered a particularly good picture of the Harlem Renaissance. In general, it was well-received critically. Milton Rugoff (*New York Herald Tribune*),[93] Henrietta L. Herod (*Phylon*),[94] and Oswald Garrison Villard (*Saturday Review of Literature*)[95] all received the book sympathetically but had caveats about its structural organization and somewhat simplistic style. On the other hand, Ralph Ellison, writing for *New Masses*, chided Hughes for failing to follow Marxist aesthetic norms.

> Many *New Masses* readers will question whether this is a style suitable for the autobiography of a Negro writer of Hughes' importance; the national and class position of the writer should guide his

> selection of techniques and method, should influence his style. In the style of *The Big Sea* too much attention is apt to be given to the esthetic aspects of experience at the expense of its deeper meanings. Nor—this being a world in which few assumptions may be taken for granted—can the writer who depends upon understatement to convey these meanings be certain that they do not escape the reader. To be effective the Negro writer must be explicit; thus realistic; thus dramatic.[96]

Reviewers for *Crisis* and the *New York Times* were considerably more positive.[97] The most lavish praise was that accorded by Richard Wright, who, writing for *New Republic*, compared Hughes to Theodore Dreiser and spoke glowingly of Hughes's "humor, urbanity, and objectivity."[98] Recently the book has undergone an important critical reevaluation by scholars such as R. Baxter Miller, Kathleen A. Hauke, and Arnold Rampersad, all of whom view it as a document central to understanding Hughes's fictive and personal self.[99]

In 1952 Hughes brought out *Laughing To Keep From Crying* (New York: Henry Holt), a collection of short stories, many of which had been previously published. Reviewers noted the ease of telling, the universality of theme and lack of bitterness with which Hughes presented vignettes of racism in America and abroad, but they failed to respond to the book with the unabashed enthusiasm they had given to *Not Without Laughter*. Arna Bontemps, writing in *Saturday Review*, indirectly implied that the stories were somewhat facile when he wrote: "His stories like his poems, are for readers who will judge them with their hearts as well as their heads."[100] Stanley Cooperman, reviewing for *New Republic*, called it "a pleasant, relaxed book that gets its message across because it doesn't always insist on it."[101] Reviews by John Parker in *Phylon*,[102] William T. Hedden in the *New York Herald Tribune*,[103] and Bucklin Moon in the *New York Times*[104] were remarkably similar in tone, all noting Hughes's honest treatment of racial problems and suggesting that, although all the tales made good reading, they were not the best stories that Hughes had ever written.

In 1956 Hughes published *I Wonder As I Wander* (New York: Rinehart), a collection of autobiographical memoirs similar to *The Big Sea*. It covers the years 1931–37, which involved Hughes in travels to Russia, China, Spain, and Japan. Almost half the volume was devoted to his wanderings in the Soviet Union. For the most part it was received even less well than *The Big Sea*. Apart from Roi Ottley, who labeled it "excellent fare"[105] in *Saturday Review*, and James Emanuel, who classified it as the most interesting nonfiction of the 1950s,[106] critics appeared mildly indifferent to it. Saunders Redding wrote coyly in the *New York Herald Tribune* that "Hughes, it seems, did more wandering than wondering."[107] Luther Jackson in *Crisis* thought the book was marked by a "lack of reasoning of the whys and wherefores of race,"[108] and Nick Aaron Ford offered a lengthy list of shortcomings in his review in *Phylon*: "Despite the many favorable aspects, there are several shortcomings that cannot be ignored. First, the book is eighteen years too late. The material is topical, documentary, polemical, treated for the most part journalistically. If it had been published in 1938 or 1939 when it was written (or should have been) while the topical events were still fairly fresh, it could have had a powerful impact."[109]

Hughes was never particularly successful with book-length novels, and the 1958 publication of *Tambourines to Glory* (New York: John Day, 1958) is another case in point. Donald C. Dickinson put it this way: "If Hughes' second volume of autobiography was less adroit than his first, his second novel, *Tambourines to Glory*, did nothing to balance the scales."[110] Hughes had first elaborated the story of two Harlem women who start their own gospel church as a play in 1949. He labeled it "another Harlem folk piece" and felt it was funnier than the play.[111] Contemporary critical reception was mixed but generally mildly positive, stressing as usual Hughes's deft use of the folk idom of Harlem, his effortlessness of telling, and his skillful blend of irony and humor. Richard Gehaman in the *Saturday Review* concluded that it was a book that reaffirmed "its writer's talent."[112] James Ivy in a brief booknote in *Crisis* praised Hughes for his mastery of the Harlem idiom.[113] Arna Bontemps was more reserved, noting that the story was "as ribald, as effortless, and on the surface as artless as a folk ballad."[114] Gilbert Millstein's review in the *New York Times* seemed to synthesize the subtle negative undercurrents in the other reviews when he wrote: "In the end, the book is a minor effort, a side glance at a major phenomenon, with an industriously contrived climax."[115]

In 1963 a third and final collection of tales appeared under the title *Something in Common* (New York: Hill & Wang). Since this collection consisted largely of reprints of stories from *Laughing To Keep From Crying*, it received scant critical attention. In fact, the story which gave title to the book was first published in the *Chicago Defender* on 17 March 1934. Commenting on the collection for the *CLA Journal*, Richard A. Long took note of the wide disparity in theme, technique, and artistic merit of the stories brought together under this title: "In this selection of short stories written over a rather wide stretch of time, Langston Hughes displays his ability to handle a variety of styles and moods. There are thirty-seven stories in all, eleven of which appear for the first time in book form. Many are very skillful, some are weak."[116]

THE CREATION OF JESSE B. SEMPLE

In spite of the fact that Langston Hughes never achieved a significant name as a writer of novels and short stories, he did succeed in creating one of his most memorable characters through the medium of prose.

Hughes's most innovative and sustained contribution to prose fiction was the creation of the urban folk hero, Jesse B. Semple, who was introduced on 13 February 1943 in a newspaper column in the *Chicago Defender*. The fictional editorials that Hughes wrote for the *Defender* and a number of other black newspapers from 1943 to 1966 were eventually reworked and published in four separate books: *Simple Speaks His Mind* (New York: Simon & Schuster, 1950), *Simple Takes a Wife* (New York: Simon & Schuster, 1953), *Simple Stakes a Claim* (New York: Rinehart, 1957), and *Simple's Uncle Sam* (New York: Hill & Wang, 1965). A spiritual cousin to the Madam Alberta K. Johnson of "Madam to You," which appeared in *One Way Ticket* (1949) Semple (commonly known as Simple) served as fictive mouthpiece for Hughes for twenty-three years and captured a wide and faithful reading audience. Blyden Jackson maintains that "It is highly probable that Langston Hughes reached his most appreciative, as well as his widest, audience with a character whom he named, eponymously and with obvious relish Jesse B. Semple."[117] Most critics concur in that it was in Simple that Hughes achieved his greatest success in prose. Jemie calls him Hughes's "supreme creation,"[118] and Berry labeled him "his most enduring contribution to literature."[119] In spite of the difficulty in classifying them by traditional literary methodology (Emanuel notes reviewers placed the third Simple volume in twenty-one different categories)[120] the books were widely and enthusiastically reviewed.

Two themes surfaced in the reviews of *Simple Speaks His Mind* that would become central in all subsequent assessments of the Simple books: Hughes's handling of the race issue and the generic nature of these prose sketches. Saunders Redding, writing in the *New York Herald Tribune*, praised Hughes for opening "windows on a corner of life much publicized but little known."[121] Much in the same vein, G. Lewis Chandler in *Phylon* underscored the importance of Hughes's creation of a literary figure that "makes articulate what the average Negro experiences, mentally and physically, in a segregated society struggling for integration."[122] Hugh Smythe, writing for *Crisis*, seemed to synthesize the reception of black literary periodicals: "This is one of Langston Hughes' finest contributions: a combination book of humor, a sociological monograph, a piece of race relations literature, in short a *tour-de-force* in which he can take extreme pride, for he has produced a volume any and all can enjoy."[123] However, William Pfaff (*Commonweal*) called the effect of the book "more polemical than artistic,"[124] and William Gardner Smith in *New Republic* noted that white readers unfortunately would not be able to understand all the humor in the book.[125]

Simple Takes a Wife, Hughes's second Simple collection, was a more serious book and one with a greater sense of continuity—a fact noted by most of its critics. Arna Bontemps, writing in the *New York Herald Tribune*, remarked that the book was superior to the first volume and that it had "too much bite to be just funny."[126] Carl Van Vechten, reviewing for the *New York Times*, asserted that it was "more brilliant, more skillfully written, funnier, and perhaps just a shade more tragic than its predecessor."[127] Abner Berry, a Marxist critic for *New Masses*, wrote that "by portraying the richness of Negro life, Hughes' work sharply opposes the 'arty' degeneracy of writers like Richard Wright and Ralph Ellison."[128]

Hughes's ability to rework his Simple columns into books appears to have improved with time. John Parker in *Phylon* labeled *Simple Stakes a Claim* "a fresh and vital collection of short pieces" and suggested comparison of Simple to other folk characters such as Uncle Remus or Mr. Dooley.[129] In a long review in *Crisis*, Luther Jackson praised *Simple Stakes a Claim* as both an artistic and commercial success, stressing the fact that here Hughes reaches "new glorious heights of racial indignation and disgust."[130] Gilbert Millstein (*New York Times Book Review*) likewise found the book to be "funny, sharp, indignant and tolerant—even of whites."[131]

Hughes's last Simple volume—*Simple's Uncle Sam*—is clearly a more serious, sardonic, and less comic view of life in an urban ghetto. W. Edward Farrison, writing in the *CLA Journal*, took cognizance of this fact and concluded that *Simple's Uncle Sam* was an "excellent continuation of his [Hughes's] reading—his criticism of life."[132] Reviews in the *New York Times* and *Library Journal* affirmed the book's appeal to a wide range of readers and praised Hughes's deft use of satire to study race relations in America.[133]

Apart from an early essay by Arthur Davis, which highlighted just how Simple typified "the thinking of the average Negro,"[134] it was not until after Hughes's death that the figure of Jesse B. Semple became the object of serious academic criticism. *Langston Hughes: Black Genius*, for example, contains three essays on the Simple books. Of particular note is Harry L. Jones's "Rhetorical Embellishment in Hughes's Simple Stories," one of the earliest efforts to explain Hughes's artistic use of language in the Simple stories.[135] In 1971, Lucia Shelia Hawthorne completed a doctoral dissertation entitled "A Rhetoric of Human Rights as Expressed in the 'Simple Columns' " (Pennsylvania State University) which further analyzed Hughes's use of persuasive discourse. Julian C. Carey, in an essay published that same year, examined

Simple in the context of *Négritude*, rejecting some of the claims Arthur Davis had made earlier concerning the racial dynamic through which the character Jesse B. Semple functioned.[136] More recent criticism evinces a movement away from the issue of race and a greater concern with the narrative strategies that gave the Simple books such universal appeal. The artistic devices used by Hughes, which were responsible for the enormous popularity of the tales, are well studied by Phyllis R. Klotman in "Jesse B. Semple and the Narrative Art of Langston Hughes" (reprinted in this volume). Klotman maintains that as a writer Hughes not only knew his medium but also knew the people whom he addressed through that medium. Further evidence of the unrestricted versatility of the Simple tales is Susan L. Blake's "Old John in Harlem: The Urban Folktales of Langston Hughes" (reprinted in this volume) which studies the creation of Jesse B. Semple within the context of black folk tradition. According to Blake, in the Simple stories Hughes redefined the notion of black folk tradition by positing the notion of a dynamic folk tradition, the goal of which was social change in a real world.

So close was the identification between Hughes and the figure of Simple that shortly after Hughes's death a brief column appeared in *Newsweek* labeled "The Death of Simple" which spoke eloquently of the role that the ironic, garrulous Jesse B. Semple played in American culture.[137]

THE DRAMA

Although Langston Hughes's contributions in the area of poetry and prose fiction have received the most critical attention, his work in the theater was extraordinarily rich and varied and meant a great deal to him personally. Although he never achieved the reputation of a major American playwright, his output was considerable. He wrote nine full-length plays (*Mulatto, Little Ham, Troubled Island, When the Jack Hollers, Joy to My Soul, Front Porch, The Sun Do Move, Simply Heavenly,* and *Tambourines to Glory*), two one-act plays (*Soul Gone Home* and *Don't You Want to Be Free?*), four gospel song-plays (*Gospel Glow, Black Nativity, Jericho-Jim Crow,* and *The Prodigal Son*), and more than twenty other scripts for opera, radio, and film.

In spite of the lukewarm critical reception of many of his plays and a seemingly endless series of personal traumas associated with his work in the theater (especially the rift with Zora Neale Hurston over the authorship of *Mule Bone* and the legal entanglements related to the production of *Mulatto*),[138] Hughes did achieve a number of real commercial successes.

Langston's interest in the theater began early in his youth; while living in Topeka, Kansas, his mother took him to plays such as *Buster Brown*, *Under Two Flags*, and *Uncle Tom's Cabin*. As Faith Berry reports, "When most pre-teen boys in Lawrence were playing ball, Langston Hughes was going to the theater. The interest in plays, which he had acquired from his mother, soon developed into a favorite diversion."[139] His apprenticeship in the theater was a long one stretching back to the summer of 1926 when he wrote lyrics for a projected revue, *O Blues*, which, although it never materialized, provided Hughes with invaluable experience in theater production and put him in touch with important practitioners of the art. That same year in "The Negro Artist and the Racial Mountain," he spoke directly about the emergence of a black theater: "Now I await the rise of the Negro theater. Our folk music, having achieved world-wide fame, offers itself to the genius of the great individual American Negro composer who is to come. And within the next decade I expect to see the work of a growing school of colored artists who paint and model the beauty of dark faces and create with new technique the expressions of their own soul-world. And the Negro dancers who will dance like Flame and the singers who will continue to carry our songs to all who listen—they will be with us in even greater numbers tomorrow."[140]

His work in theater paralleled his activities in other areas, and he frequently borrowed thematic material from his poems, short stories, and novels and rewrote it as plays. *Mulatto* and *Tambourines to Glory* are cases in point. His first play, entitled *The Gold Piece*, appeared in 1921 in *The Brownie's Book*, a magazine for children established by W. E. B. Du Bois and the editors of *Crisis*. In addition to writing plays, Hughes also founded three important dramatic groups: the Suitcase Theater in Harlem, the Negro Art Theater in Los Angeles, and the Skyloft Players in Chicago.

Critical reaction to Hughes's work as a dramatist is sketchy and, when compared to his work in other genres, appears almost nonexistent. This may be explained by the fact that, until the appearance of Webster Smalley's 1963 edition of *Five Plays by Langston Hughes* (Bloomington: Indiana University Press), no printed versions of his plays were available. Smalley's edition contains the texts of five plays: *Mulatto, Soul Gone Home, Little Ham, Simply Heavenly*, and *Tambourines to Glory*. Smalley's introduction, although not a book-length critical study, effectively highlights Hughes's role as one of the premier interpreters of black urban life in North America. Although Hughes's work did not have the full impact of a text like Wright's *Native Son*, it nonetheless conveyed in a powerful and direct way a sense of life in black urban America.

It is important to note that five of Hughes's plays were written during the thirties—a turbulent period in his life and a time when he received few accolades from white or black critics. His first play, *Mulatto*, based on the miscegenation theme and on Hughes's short story, "Father and Son," was a commercial but not an artistic success. It opened on Broadway on 24 October 1935 and had the longest run of any play by a black author until the production of Lorraine Hansberry's *A Raisin in the Sun* broke the record in 1959. Initial critical response was spotty and Hughes was frequently accused of artlessness. Brooks Atkinson's review of *Mulatto* for the *New York Times* is a telling document: "To judge by *Mulatto* Mr. Hughes has little of the dramatic strength of mind that makes it possible for a writer to tell a coherent, driving story in the theatre. His ideas are seldom completely expressed; his play is pretty thoroughly defeated by the grim mechanics of the stage. What gives it a sobering sensation in spite of its artlessness is the very apparent earnestness of Mr. Hughes's state of mind. He is writing about the theme that lies closest to his heart."[141]

Edith J. R. Isaacs, writing in *Theatre Arts Monthly*, echoed much the same view:

> More, too, might have been expected of *Mulatto*, a drama by Langston Hughes, who is a good poet and a leader in negro [*sic*] affairs. In this first play he is concerned with the state of the negro [*sic*] in the south today—a problem that welcomes restatement by a man who knows his subject through training and sympathies. Unquestionably negro [*sic*] life in the south is today little less complex than it ever was; the negroes [*sic*] in *Mulatto* are, as they have ever been, "someone to rape or to lynch," "good for workin' and lovin' "—good for nothing else. So far, the picture is searing; what destroys its effectiveness is Mr. Hughes' weak, amateurish writing, and the unvarnished fact that the negro [*sic*] protagonist is as ingrate and obnoxious as the villainous whites believe. When Mr. Hughes has his next play produced, he should make sure that Rose McClendon is again present. After what seemed like a heedless beginning—actually a thoughtful statement of the character's submissive, selfless quality—Miss McClendon's rare sensitivity and beautiful voice made her scenes glow like bright lights in shoddy surroundings.[142]

In his *Black Drama* Loften Mitchell described the opening of the play in the following terms: "Teeth gnashed and people squirmed when Langston Hughes' *Mulatto* opened on Broadway in 1934. Many critics complained that the play was too realistic, too bitter and too hostile. Nevertheless, audiences flocked to it, and the play enjoyed a long run."[143]

More recent critical reaction is mixed. Darwin Turner considers that the play is "weak artistically in plot, structure, language, and thought,"[144] and Webster Smalley warns readers that *Mulatto* "is very much a play of the thirties, an era when sociopolitical plays dominated American drama."[145] Doris E. Abramson is considerably more sympathetic, noting that "there is a universality about *Mulatto* that other plays of the period lack."[146] In an engaging comparison of Hughes's play with Edward Sheldon's *The Nigger* ("Miscegenation on Broadway: Hughes' *Mulatto* and Edward Sheldon's *The Nigger*," reprinted in this volume), Richard K. Barksdale adds another link in the chain of evidence supporting a critical reappraisal of *Mulatto* as a play rich in psychological nuances.

Don't You Want to Be Free?, a folk pageant that traced the history of the American black from slavery to the depression, was Hughes's second most successful drama of the 1930s. Produced by the Harlem Suitcase Theater (1937–38), it was performed 135 times in two years, making it one of the longest running plays in Harlem during Hughes's lifetime. In 1938 Edward Lawson spoke of it enthusiastically as an "interesting compendium of poetry, song, and drama combined in a manner that is engagingly new."[147] His views were not shared by contemporary critics. Hilda Lawson felt that Hughes overstated the facts of black life in order to support his thesis that "the overseer of slave days still confronts the Negro in every phase of his present life,"[148] and Norman MacLeod concluded that "Unfortunately, however, *Don't You Want to Be Free*—even as a sustained piece of 'agit-prop' writing does not reach the level of Langston Hughes' best work or approximate the excellence we have come to expect of him."[149]

Although Darwin Turner concedes that "in language and in thought the play was the most artistic which Hughes had written, its obvious aiming at a Negro audience made it unsuitable for commercial production on Broadway."[150] Doris E. Abramson is considerably more positive, crediting Hughes's blending of poetry and drama with raising "agit-prop" "to a rare level of literary value."[151]

One other play from this period merits review—*Emperor of Haiti*. First presented as *Drums of Haiti* (1936), Hughes rewrote it as an opera, *Troubled Island*, and further revised it in 1963 as *Emperor of Haiti*. Turner noted that the play has both artistic and historical flaws: "As in much of Hughes's drama, low comic relief is overworked while plot lags."[152] Hughes's reputation as a dramatist was heightened by Helene Keyssar's detailed reevaluation of this play. In her study, *The Curtain and The Veil: Strategies in Black Drama* (New York: Burt Franklin & Co., 1981), she expanded upon and refined some of Darwin Turner's earlier assessments of *The Emperor of Haiti*. Keyssar argued that, by employing one of the oldest tricks of drama, that of historical distance, Hughes was able in *The Emperor of Haiti* to confront a complex of issues that no contemporary American location could contain. He was thus able to seduce both black and white viewers to a recognition of persons who might otherwise have been dismissed as abhorrent, unbelievable, or both.

Evelyn Quita Craig further enriched Hughes's reputation as a dramatist through the discovery of a script entitled *Troubled Island* that Hughes had submitted to the Federal Theater. An examination of scripts indicates that it is based on *Emperor of Haiti* (originally *Drums of Haiti*) and that it is "a brilliantly polished version of the former."[153] Craig writes, "*Troubled Island* flows more smoothly, concentrates more sharply on essentials, and is usually more brilliantly, wittily, or poetically phrased than *Emperor of Haiti.*"[154]

In the last two decades of his life Hughes turned away from serious drama and concentrated on musicals, often rewriting and adapting his fiction to the popular stage. For example, *Simple Takes a Wife* was transformed into *Simply Heavenly*, which enjoyed a brief run on Broadway in 1957. Similarly, *Tambourines to Glory*, based on the novel of the same name, had a short run at New York's Little Theater in November 1963. Although Turner considers *Tambourines* to be one of Hughes's stronger plays, it was unfavorably reviewed in the popular press.[155] Hughes's greatest success appears to have been the gospel song-play, a genre that permitted him greater flexibility as a writer and allowed him to use poetry. *Black Nativity* (1961), a gospel song-play first performed at New York's 41st Street Theater, was extraordinarily successful both in the United States and Europe. Writing in the *Nation*, Robert Shelton reported: "*Black Nativity* has taken the volcanic energy of Negro gospel music and channeled it skillfully toward theatrical ends. It has already introduced new audiences to gospel music in Spoleto, London and seven other European centers. It will return to the Continent for six months and tour the United States for forty weeks. There is even some talk of taking it to Russia and Eastern Europe."[156]

For a complex set of reasons, such as the state of the black theater in the twenties and thirties, the explosive nature of the race question itself, and his inability to adapt forms that had originated as poems or short stories (*Mulatto* and *Scottsboro Limited* are cases in point), Hughes never achieved the same critical acclaim for his playwriting that he did for his poetry and prose fiction. In addition, there is the question of his reputation as a poet, which seemed to haunt him critically. Thought of primarily as a poet, his work in other genres seemed necessarily to pale in comparison. Once during the production of *Tambourines to Glory* in 1963 he remarked to Lewis Nichols, drama critic for the *New York Times*, that "I keep going back to poetry to make a living."[157]

Despite their reservations, however, Hughes's critics have noted the enormous variety of dramatic form and situation in his plays and credit him with being one of the fountainheads for what was to be called in the 1970s "Black Theater." In his 1971 doctoral dissertation, "Langston

Hughes as American Dramatist," Edwin Leon Coleman offered the following assessment:

> Hughes' contribution to the theatre, then, lies in the fact that his plays, while representing a personal growth, also parallel the development of the Civil Rights movement in the United States and the flowering of the black cultural philosophy. Besides his dual role as the progenitor for many black artists today and spokesman for his race, Hughes has served as an educator for white audiences who are unfamiliar with the world of the ghetto. He has given to all a realistic portrait of a segment of America, and in a pluralistic society it is vital that each part know what the other is thinking and feeling and wanting. This was Hughes' gift. (175–76)

CONCLUSION

A survey of the critical reaction to the writings of Langston Hughes reveals that Hughes was engaged for much of his career as a writer in a critical debate with his interpretive audience, an audience that spent most of its time dealing with issues other than the artistic worth of what he produced. His reputation as a writer was judged for most of his career by the judicial critics of the mass print media (newspapers and magazines) who had great difficulty evaluating the writings of a writer who worked so clearly out of the mainstream aesthetic. Typical of the early critical obfuscation of his work was the obsession of many in comparing him to the more universalist Countee Cullen.[158] In this regard the comments of Arnold Rampersad are particularly illuminating:

> As the history of black poetry demonstrates, to turn away from received notions of the universal is a radical and even sometimes a revolutionary act; the dissenting writer and critic risk the censure of those who claim to have created the universal, as well as those of their own group unable to confront the paradox between their abused social and material state and the advertised standards of the culture into which they have been indoctrinated. The work of the dissenter is dismissed either summarily or with condescension—it is often called "protest" literature and consigned to the literary attic. Neither literature nor literary criticism can flourish under such conditions.[159]

It is also true that Hughes was never anxious to be accepted by mainstream tradition. That is not to say that he was not sensitive to the criticism of his works but that early in his writing career he realized that once a writer begins making concessions, even slight ones, to anyone's conditions and demands he loses his independence and integrity. Hence at the height of the depression he gave up the support of Charlotte Mason, a wealthy patron of the arts, to follow his own artistic inclinations. By rejecting the dominant, universalist aesthetic, Hughes was able to portray more effectively the cultural schizophrenia of American life and to articulate the voice of that other America, those who lived "separate but equal" lives in America's urban centers, and to their slow, painful entrance into the mainstream of American life.

The irony is, of course, that whereas in writers such as Cullen there is no essential progress in form or complexity, the work of Hughes is one of constant rebirth and rediscovery. In the 1920s Hughes introduced blues and jazz to poetry, in the 1940s he caught the darker side of urban America, in the 1950s he produced the genial Jesse B. Simple, and in his last years he returned to the theater, fusing music, poetry, and drama in the gospel song-play.

In the last decade Hughes has undergone an important critical reevaluation. Although admittedly much of what was published immediately after his death was panegyric, one notes a gradual shift toward serious examination of text and sign in his work. Critics such as Richard K. Barksdale, R. Baxter Miller, Blyden Jackson, James Emanuel, Therman B. O'Daniel, and Onwuchekwa Jemie, among others, have begun to illuminate the vast oeuvre of one of the most important writers of twentieth-century America. Also, the founding of the Langston Hughes Society in 1981 and the publication of the society's journal, the *Langston Hughes Review*, is but another indication of the growing critical interest in his work in both North American and world literary circles. Thus, the editors of the *Langston Hughes Review* regard Hughes "as one of the most representative writers in the history of Afro-American literature, and as the seminal creator of what has come to be called *Negritude* and the Black aesthetic."

It is worth noting that one of the most productive areas of research on Hughes, exemplified in books such as Martha Cobb's *Harlem Haiti, and Havana: A Comparative Critical Study of Langston Hughes, Jacques Roumain, and Nicolás Guillén* (Washington, D.C.: Three Continents Press, 1979), lies in the study of the coextensive relationship of Hughes's work with the Africanist poetics of other black writers in the Caribbean and the Latin American mainland. This is but one example of the direction that criticism on Hughes is taking. Although much has been written on Langston Hughes, more work needs to be done. Recent trends indicate that Langston Hughes is now undergoing a long-deserved critical renaissance.

The editor wishes to thank the authors and holders of copyright for their permission to reprint the materials included in this volume. The editor also recognizes the important contributions of scholars such as Donald C. Dickinson, George Bass, Faith Berry, Richard K. Barksdale,

R. Baxter Miller, Therman B. O'Daniel, and Arnold Rampersad, whose earlier scholarship provided the basis for this book. I would also like to express my appreciation to Blyden Jackson for his careful reading of my introductory essay and to Linda Dowell for her meticulous typing of the final manuscript.

I gratefully acknowledge the support of the University of Missouri–Columbia for granting me a Research Leave, which enabled me to complete this work.

EDWARD J. MULLEN

Notes:

1. See Donald C. Dickinson, "Langston Hughes and the *Brownie's Book*," *Negro History Bulletin* 31 (December 1968):8–10.

2. Onwuchekwa Jemie, *Langston Hughes: An Introduction to the Poetry* (New York: Columbia University Press, 1976), 187.

3. R. Baxter Miller, "'No Crystal Stair': Unity, Archetype and Symbol in Langston Hughes's Poems on Women," *Negro American Literature Forum* 9 (Winter 1975):109.

4. Ernest Kaiser, "Selected Bibliography of the Published Writings of Langston Hughes," *Freedomways* 8 (Spring 1968):185.

5. Sandra Y. Govan, "The Insistent Presence of Black Folk in the Novels of Samuel R. Delany," *Black American Literature Forum* 18 (Summer 1984):43.

6. Cited in Robert A. Hall, Jr., "Once More—What Is Literature," *Modern Language Journal* 63 (March 1979):92.

7. Edward Margolies, review of *Langston Hughes*, by James A. Emanuel, *Library Journal* 92 (August 1967):2778.

8. Margaret Larkin, "A Poet of the People—A Review," *Opportunity* 5 (March 1927):84–85.

9. See Mercer Cook's review of *Langston Hughes: Un Chant Nouveau*, by René Piquion, *Phylon* 4 (1940):300.

10. Two early bibliographies of Hughes are Inez Johnson Babb's *Bibliography of Langston Hughes: Negro Poet* (M.A. thesis, Pratt Institute, 1947), and Therman B. O'Daniel's "A Langston Hughes Bibliography," *CLA Bulletin* 7, no. 2 (1951). See also O'Daniels's "Langston Hughes: An Updated Selected Bibliography," *Black American Literature Forum* 15 (Fall 1981):104–7. Also of importance is Blyden Jackson's bibliographical essay on Hughes in *Black American Writers: Bibliographical Essays*, ed. M. Thomas Inge, Maurice Duke, and Jackson R. Bryer, vol. 1 (New York: St. Martin's Press, 1978).

11. See Ted Joans, "Getting Off the A Train," *American Book Review* 6 (May–June 1984):14.

12. Thomas Millard Henry, "Letter to the Editor," *Messenger* 7 (June 1925):239.

13. Eugene F. Gordon, "At Random," *Opportunity* 3 (July 1925):219.

14. Review of *The Weary Blues, Times Literary Supplement,* 29 July 1926, 515.

15. "Five Silhouettes on the Slope of Mount Parnassus," *New York Times Book Review,* 21 March 1926, 6, 16.

16. DuBose Heyward, "The Jazz Band's Sob," *New York Herald Tribune,* 1 August 1926, 4.

17. Jesse Fauset, review of *The Weary Blues, Crisis* 30–31 (March 1926):239.

18. Countee Cullen, "Poet on Poet," *Opportunity* 4 (March 1926):73.

19. Ibid.

20. Alain Locke, "The Weary Blues," *Palms* 4 (1926–27):27–28.

21. *The Big Sea* (New York: Knopf, 1940), 263.

22. Ibid., 265–66.

23. J. A. Rogers, review of *Fine Clothes to the Jew, Pittsburgh Courier,* 12 February 1927, sec. 2, p. 4.

24. Eustace Gay, review of *Fine Clothes to the Jew, Philadelphia Tribune,* 8 March 1927, 4.

25. Review of *Fine Clothes to the Jew, Crisis* 34 (March 1927):20.

26. Herbert S. Gorman, "Tradition and Experiment in Modern Poetry," *New York Times Book Review,* 27 March 1927, 2.

27. DuBose Heyward, "Sing A Soothin' Song," *New York Herald Tribune Books,* 20 February 1927, 5.

28. Harry Allan Potamkin, "Old Clothes," *Nation* 124 (13 April 1927):403–4.

29. Julia Peterkin, "Negro Blue and Gold," *Poetry* 31 (1927–28):44.

30. Babette Deutsch, "Four Poets," *Bookman* 65 (April 1927):221.

31. Margaret Larkin, "A Poet of the People," *Opportunity* 5 (March 1927):84.

32. Lewis Alexander, review of *The Weary Blues, Carolina Magazine* 57 (May 1927):44.

33. Alain Locke, "Common Clay and Poetry," *Saturday Review of Literature* 3 (9 April 1927):712.

34. Ibid.

35. Charles S. Johnson, "Jazz Poetry and Blues," *Carolina Magazine* 58 (May 1928):18.

36. Allison Davis, "Our Negro Intellectuals," *Crisis* 35 (August 1928):268.

37. Ibid., 269.

38. Melvin Tolson, "The Harlem Group of Negro Writers" (M.A. thesis, Columbia University, 1940), 36.

39. Arna Bontemps, "The Harlem Renaissance," *Saturday Review of Literature* 30 (22 March 1947):13.

40. Arthur Davis, "The Harlem of Langston Hughes' Poetry," *Phylon* 13 (4th Quarter 1952):276–83.

41. See Blyden Jackson, "From One 'New Negro' to Another," in *Black Poetry in America: Two Essays on Historical Interpretation,* (Baton Rouge: Louisiana State University Press, 1974), 51–58, and George Kent, "Langston Hughes and the Afro-American Folk and Cultural Tradition," in *Langston Hughes: Black Genius,* ed. Therman O'Daniel (New York: William Morrow, 1971), 183–210.

42. William Rose Benét, "Round About Parnassus," *Saturday Review of Litera-*

ture 9 (12 November 1932):241, and Anne T. Eaton, "The New Books for Children," *New York Times Book Review,* 17 July 1932, 13.

43. Alain Locke, "Outstanding Books of 1932," *Opportunity* 11 (January 1933): 14–18.

44. Nancy Cunard, "Three Negro Poets," *Left Review* 3 (September 1937):530.

45. Lydia Filatova, "Langston Hughes: American Writer," *International Literature* 1 (1933):99.

46. See Thomas A. Hale, "From Afro-America to Afro-France: The Literary Triangle Trade," *French Review* 49 (May 1976):1089–96.

47. See Edward J. Mullen, *Langston Hughes in the Hispanic World and Haiti* (Hamden, Conn.: Archon, 1977), 19–20.

48. Mary Colum, "The New Books of Poetry," *New York Times Book Review,* 22 March 1942, 9.

49. Owen Dodson, "Shakespeare in Harlem," *Phylon* 11 (Fall 1942):337.

50. William Harrison, review of *Shakespeare in Harlem, Opportunity* 19 (July 1942):219.

51. See H. R. Hays, "To be Sung or Shouted," *Poetry* 60 (April–September 1942):223–24, and the anonymous review of *Shakespeare in Harlem* in the *Nation* 155 (15 August 1942):119.

52. Alfred Kreymborg, "Seven American Poets," *Saturday Review* 25 (April 1942):9.

53. Ruth Lechlitner, "Stevens, Cullen, Hughes, Bynner, Greenberg," *New York Herald Tribune Book Review,* 31 August 1947, 4.

54. Hubert Creekmore, review of *Fields of Wonder, New York Times Book Review,* 4 May 1947, 10.

55. Saunders Redding, review of *One Way Ticket, Saturday Review of Literature* 32 (22 January 1949):24.

56. Rolfe Humphries, "Verse Chronicle," *Nation* 168 (15 January 1949):80.

57. G. Lewis Chandler, "Selfsameness and a Promise," *Phylon* 10 (Summer 1949):189–91.

58. Harvey C. Webster, "One-Way Poetry," *Poetry* 75 (October 1949–March 1950):300.

59. Ibid., 302.

60. Jean Wagner, *Black Poets in the United States* (Urbana: University of Illinois Press, 1973), 414.

61. Saunders Redding, "What It Means to be Colored," *New York Herald Tribune Book Review,* 11 March 1951, 5.

62. John Parker, review of *Montage of a Dream Deferred, Phylon* 12 (Summer 1951):197.

63. Babette Deutsch, "Waste Land of Harlem," *New York Times Book Review,* 6 May 1951, 23.

64. Rolfe Humphries, "Verse Chronicle," *Nation* 72 (17 March 1951):256.

65. James Baldwin, "Sermons and Blues," *New York Times Book Review,* 29 March 1959, 6.

66. Dudley Fitts, "A Trio of Singers in Varied Keys," *New York Times Book Review,* 29 October 1961, 16.

67. Rudi Blesh, "Jazz as a Marching Jubilee," *New York Herald Tribune*, 26 November 1961, 4.

68. Dickinson, *A Bio-bibliography*, 95.

69. Wagner, *Black Poets*, 468.

70. James Emanuel, "The Literary Experiments of Langston Hughes," in *Langston Hughes: Black Genius*, ed. O'Daniel, 171.

71. Alden Whitman, "End Papers," *New York Times*, 1 June 1968, 25.

72. Laurence Lieberman, "Poetry Chronicle," *Poetry* 112 (August 1968):339; reprinted in Lieberman's *Unassigned Frequencies: American Poetry in Review: 1964–1977* (Urbana: University of Illinois Press, 1977).

73. Theodore Hudson, "Langston Hughes' Last Volume of Verse," *CLA Journal* 11 (June 1968):348.

74. W. Edward Farrison, review of *The Panther and The Lash*, *CLA Journal* 11 (March 1968):259–61.

75. Jemie, *Langston Hughes: An Introduction to the Poetry*, 124.

76. See Elwyn Ellison Breaux, "Comic Elements in Selected Prose Works by James Baldwin, Ralph Ellison, and Langston Hughes" (Ph.D. diss., Oklahoma State University, 1971); David Dobbs Britt, "The Image of the White Man in the Fiction of Langston Hughes, Richard Wright, James Baldwin, and Ralph Ellison" (Ph.D. diss., Emory University, 1968); James Emanuel, "The Short Stories of Langston Hughes" (Ph.D. diss., Columbia University, 1962); and George E. Franklin, "Recurrent Themes in the Novels and Short Fiction of Langston Hughes" (Ph.D. diss., University of Utah, 1975).

77. James Emanuel, *Langston Hughes* (New York: Twayne Publishers, 1967):33.

78. "The Browsing Reader," *Crisis* 37 (September 1930):321.

79. Sterling Brown, review of *Not Without Laughter*, *Opportunity* 8 (September 1930):279–80.

80. V. F. Calverton, review of *Not Without Laughter*, *Nation* 131 (6 August 1930):157–58.

81. W. Edward Farrison, "Not Without Laughter, Not Without Tears," in *Langston Hughes*, ed. O'Daniel, 108.

82. George Kent, "Langston Hughes and Afro-American Folk and Cultural Tradition," in ibid., 196–97.

83. R. Baxter Miller, " 'Done Made Us Leave Home': Langston Hughes's *Not Without Laughter*—Unifying Image and Three Dimensions," *Phylon* 37 (Winter 1976):362–69.

84. Herschel Brickell, "Good Short Stories," *North American Review* 238 (September 1934):286.

85. Lewis Gannett, "Books and Things," *New York Herald Tribune*, 27 June 1934, 15.

86. Vernon Loggins, "Jazz Consciousness," *Saturday Review of Literature* 10 (14 July 1934):805.

87. E. C. Holmes, review of *The Ways of White Folks*, *Opportunity* 12 (September 1934):283–84.

88. Alain Locke, "Negro Angle," *Survey Graphic* 23 (November 1934):565.

89. Sherwood Anderson, "Paying for Old Sins," *Nation* 139 (11 July 1934):49–50.

90. Martha Gruening, "White Folks are Silly," *New Republic* 80 (September 1934):108–9.

91. George Streator, "A Nigger Did It," *Crisis* 41 (July 1934):216.

92. David Michael Nifong, "Narrative Technique and Theory in *The Ways of White Folks*," *Black American Literature Forum* 15 (Fall 1981):93–96.

93. Milton Rugoff, "Negro Writer's Heap of Living," *New York Herald Tribune Books*, 25 August 1940, 5.

94. Henrietta L. Herod, review of *The Big Sea*, *Phylon* 2 (Spring 1941):94–96.

95. Oswald Garrison Villard, review of *The Big Sea*, *Saturday Review of Literature* 22 (31 August 1940):12.

96. Ralph Ellison, "Stormy Weather," *New Masses* 37 (September 1940):20.

97. Theophilus Lewis, "Adventurous Life," *Crisis* 47 (December 1940):395–96; Catherine Woods, "A Negro Intellectual Tells His Life Story," *New York Times Book Review*, 25 August 1940, 5.

98. Richard Wright, "Forerunner and Ambassador," *New Republic* 103 (July–December 1940):600–601.

99. R. Baxter Miller, " 'Even After I Was Dead': The Big Sea—Paradox, Preservation and Holistic Time," *Black American Literature Forum* 11 (Summer 1977):39–45; Kathleen A. Hauke, "A Self Portrait of Langston Hughes," (Ph.D. diss., University of Rhode Island, 1982); Arnold Rampersad, "Biography, Autobiography, and Langston Hughes," unpublished.

100. Arna Bontemps, "Black and Bubbling," *Saturday Review of Literature* 35 (5 April 1952):17.

101. Stanley Cooperman, "Fiction before Problems," *New Republic* 126 (May 1952):2.

102. John Parker, "Literature of the Negro Ghetto," *Phylon* 13 (Fall 1952):257–58.

103. William T. Hedden, "Laughter and Tears Across the Barriers," *New York Herald Tribune Books*, 30 March 1952, 2.

104. Bucklin Moon, "Laughter, Tears, and the Blues," *New York Times Book Review*, 23 March 1952, 4.

105. Roi Ottley, "Politics, Poetry, and Peccadillos," *Saturday Review of Literature* 39 (17 November 1956):35.

106. Emanuel, *Langston Hughes*, 46.

107. Saunders Redding, "Travels of Langston Hughes," *New York Herald Tribune Books*, 23 December 1956, 7.

108. Luther Jackson, "Review of *I Wonder As I Wander*," *Crisis* 64 (February 1957):119–20.

109. Nick Aaron Ford, "Odyssey of a Literary Man," *Phylon* 18 (Spring 1957): 88–89.

110. Dickinson, *A Bio-bibliography*, 109.

111. *Arna Bontemps and Langston Hughes: Letters 1925–1967*, ed. Charles H. Nichols (New York: Dodd & Mead, 1980), 345.

112. Richard Gehaman, "Free, Free Enterprise," *Saturday Review of Literature*, 41 (22 November 1958):20.

113. James Ivy, review of *Tambourines to Glory*, *Crisis* 66 (January 1959):59.

114. Arna Bontemps, "How the Money Rolled In!," *New York Herald Tribune*, 7 December 1958, 4.

115. Gilbert Millstein, "Laura and Essie Belle," *New York Times*, 23 November 1958, 51.

116. Richard A. Long, review of *Something in Common and Other Stories, CLA Journal* 7 (December 1963):117.

117. Blyden Jackson, "A Word About Simple," *CLA Journal* 11 (June 1968):310.

118. Jemie, *Langston Hughes: An Introduction to the Poetry*, 27.

119. Faith Berry, *Langston Hughes: Before and Beyond Harlem* (Westport, Conn.: Lawrence Hill, 1983), 309.

120. Emanuel, *Langston Hughes*, 160.

121. Saunders Redding, "What It Means to be Colored," *New York Herald Tribune Books*, 11 June 1950, 13.

122. G. Lewis Chandler, "For Your Recreation and Reflection," *Phylon* 12 (Spring 1951):94–95.

123. Hugh Smythe, "Hughesesque Insight," *Crisis* 57 (June 1950):378.

124. William Pfaff, review of *Simple Speaks His Mind, Commonweal* 52 (26 May 1950):181.

125. William Gardner Smith, "Simple's Dialogues," *New Republic* 123 (September 1950):20.

126. Arna Bontemps "That Not So Simple Sage, Mr. Simple," *New York Herald Tribune Books*, 14 June 1953, 12.

127. Carl Van Vechten, "In the Heart of Harlem," *New York Times*, 31 May 1953, 5.

128. Abner Berry, "Not So Simple," *New Masses* 6 (September 1953): 55–58.

129. John Parker, "The Remarkable Mr. Simple Again," *Phylon* 18 (Winter 1957):435.

130. Luther Jackson, review of *Simple Stakes A Claim, Crisis* 64 (May 1957): 119–20.

131. Gilbert Millstein, "Negro Everyman," *New York Times Book Review*, 29 September 1957, 41.

132. W. Edward Farrison, review of *Simple's Uncle Sam, CLA Journal* 9 (March 1966):300.

133. Charles Poore, "Satire is the Eternal Vaudeville of Morality," *New York Times*, 11 November 1963, 45; Francis D. Campbell, "Review of *Simple's Uncle Sam*," *Library Journal* 90 (November 1965):4806.

134. Arthur Davis, "Jesse B. Semple: Negro American," *Phylon* 15 (1st Quarter 1954):21–28.

135. Harry L. Jones, "Rhetorical Embellishment in Hughes's Simple Stories," in *Langston Hughes*, ed. O'Daniel, 132–44.

136. Julian C. Carey, "Jesse B. Semple Revisited and Revised," *Phylon* 32 (December 1971):158–63.

137. "The Death of Simple," *Newsweek* 69 (5 June 1967):104.

138. See *The New York Times*, 14 January 1936, sec. 9, col. 4, p. 25.

139. Berry, *Langston Hughes: Before and Beyond Harlem*, 10.

140. "The Negro Artist and the Racial Mountain," *Nation* 122 (June 1926):692–94.

141. Brooks Atkinson, review of *Mulatto, New York Times*, 25 October 1935, 25.

142. Edith J. R. Isaacs, *Theatre Arts Monthly* 19 (December 1935):902.

143. Loften Mitchell, *Black Drama: The Story of the American Negro in the Theatre* (New York: Hawthorne, 1967), 97.

144. Darwin Turner, "Langston Hughes as Playwright," *CLA Journal* 11 (June 1968):299.

145. Webster Smalley, *Five Plays by Langston Hughes* (Bloomington: Indiana University Press, 1963), xi.

146. Doris E. Abramson, *Negro Playwrights in the American Theatre 1925–1959* (New York: Columbia University Press, 1969), 87.

147. Edward Lawson, "Theatre in a Suitcase," *Opportunity* 26 (December 1938):360.

148. Hilda Josephine Lawson, "The Negro in American Drama" (Ph.D. diss., University of Illinois, 1939), 106–7.

149. Norman MacLeod, "The Poetry and Argument of Langston Hughes," *Crisis* 46 (1938):359.

150. Turner, "Langston Hughes as Playwright," 304.

151. Abramson, *Negro Playwrights*, 83.

152. Turner, "Langston Hughes as Playwright," 307.

153. Evelyn Quita Craig, *Black Drama of the Federal Theatre Era* (Amherst: University of Massachusetts Press, 1980), 163.

154. Ibid.

155. "Gospel Truth," *Newsweek* 62 (18 November 1957):72.

156. Robert Shelton, "Theatre," *Nation* 196 (January 1963):20.

157. See Lewis Nichols, "Langston Hughes Describes the Genesis of His *Tambourines to Glory*," *New York Times*, 27 October 1963, sec. 2, p. 3.

158. See among others Bontemps, "The Harlem Renaissance," 12; Lechlinter, "Stevens, Cullen, Hughes, Greenberg," 4; and Tolson, "The Harlem Group of Negro Writers," 27–40.

159. Arnold Rampersad, "The Universal and the Particular in Afro-American Poetry," *CLA Journal* 25 (September 1981):16–17.

REVIEWS

Poet on Poet

Countee Cullen*

Here is a poet with whom to reckon, to experience, and here and there, with that apologetic feeling of presumption that should companion all criticism, to quarrel.

What has always struck me most forcibly in reading Mr. Hughes' poems has been their utter spontaneity and expression of a unique personality. This feeling is intensified with the appearance of his work in concert between the covers of a book. It must be acknowledged at the outset that these poems are peculiarly Mr. Hughes' and no one else's. I cannot imagine his work as that of any other poet, not even of any poet of that particular group of which Mr. Hughes is a member. Of course, a microscopic assiduity might reveal derivation and influences, but these are weak undercurrents in the flow of Mr. Hughes' own talent. This poet represents a transcendently emanicipated spirit among a class of young writers whose particular battle-cry is freedom. With the enthusiasm of a zealot, he pursues his way, scornful, in subject matter, in photography, and rhythmical treatment, of whatever obstructions time and tradition have placed before him. To him it is essential that he be himself. Essential and commendable surely; yet the thought persists that some of these poems would have been better had Mr. Hughes held himself a bit in check. In his admirable introduction to the book, Carl Van Vechten says the poems have a "highly deceptive air of spontaneous improvisation." I do not feel that the air is deceptive.

If I have the least powers of prediction, the first section of this book, *The Weary Blues*, will be most admired, even if less from intrinsic poetical worth than because of its dissociation from the traditionally poetic. Never having been one to think all subjects and forms proper for poetic consideration, I regard these jazz poems as interlopers in the company of the truly beautiful poems in other sections of the book.

*Reprinted from *Opportunity* 4 (4 March 1926):73–74, by permission of the journal.

They move along with the frenzy and electric heat of a Methodist or Baptist revival meeting, and affect me in much the same manner. The revival meeting excites me, cooling and flushing me with alternate chills and fevers of emotion; so do these poems. But when the storm is over, I wonder if the quiet way of communing is not more spiritual for the God-seeking heart; and in the light of reflection I wonder if jazz poems really belong to that dignified company, that select and austere circle of high literary expression which we call poetry. Surely, when in *Negro Dancers* Mr. Hughes says

Me an' ma baby's
Got two mo' ways,
Two mo' ways to do de buck!

he voices, in lyrical, thumb-at-nose fashion the happy careless attitude, akin to poetry, that is found in certain types. And certainly he achieves one of his loveliest lyrics in *Young Singer.* Thus I find myself straddling a fence. It needs only *The Cat and The Saxaphone*, however, to knock me over completely on the side of bewilderment, and incredulity. This creation is a *tour de force* of its kind, but is it a poem:

EVERYBODY
Half-pint,–
Gin?
No, make it
LOVES MY BABY
corn. You like
don't you, honey?
BUT MY BABY . . . .

In the face of accomplished fact, I cannot say *This will never do*, but I feel that it ought never to have been done.

But Mr. Hughes can be as fine and as polished as you like, etching his work in calm, quiet lyrics that linger and repeat themselves. Witness *Sea Calm*:

How still,
How strangely still.
The water is today.
It is not good
For water
To be so still that way.

Or take *Suicide's Note*:

The Calm,
Cool face of the river
Asked me for a kiss.

Then crown your admiration with *Fantasy in Purple*, this imperial swan-song that sounds like the requiem of a dying people:

Beat the drums of tragedy for me,
Beat the drums of tragedy and death.
And let the choir sing a stormy song
To drown the rattle of my dying breath.

Beat the drums of tragedy for me,
And let the white violins whir thin and slow,
But blow one blaring trumpet note of sun
To go with me to the darkness where I go.

Mr. Hughes is a remarkable poet of the colorful; through all his verses the rainbow riots and dazzles, yet never wearies the eye, although at times it intrigues the brain into astonishment and exaggerated admiration when reading, say samething like *Caribbean Sunset*:

God having a hemorrhage,
Blood coughed across the sky,
Staining the dark sea red:
That is sunset in the Caribbean

Taken as a group the selections in this book seem one-sided to me. They tend to hurl this poet into the gaping pit that lies before all Negro writers, in the confines of which they become racial artists instead of artists pure and simple. There is too much emphasis here on strictly Negro themes; and this is probably an added reason for my coldness toward the jazz poems—they seem to set a too definite limit upon an already limited field.

Dull books cause no schisms, raise no dissensions, create no parties. Much will be said of *The Weary Blues* because it is a definite achievement, and because Mr .Hughes, in his own way, with a first book that cannot be dismissed as merely *promising*, has arrived.

[Review of *The Weary Blues*] **Jessie Fauset***

Very perfect is the memory of my first literary acquaintance with Langston Hughes. In the unforgettable days when we were publishing *The Brownies' Book* we had already appreciated a charming fragile conceit which read:

*Reprinted from *Crisis* 30–31 (March 1926):239, by permission of the journal.

Out of the dust of dreams,
Fairies weave their garments;
Out of the purple and rose of old memories,
They make purple wings.
No wonder we find them such marvelous
things.

Then one day came "The Negro Speaks of Rivers." I took the beautiful dignified creation to Dr. Du Bois and said: "What colored person is there, do you suppose, in the United States who writes like that and yet is unknown to us?" And I wrote and found him to be a Cleveland high school graduate who had just gone to live in Mexico. Already he had begun to assume that remote, so elusive quality which permeates most of his work. Before long we had the pleasure of seeing the work of the boy, whom we had sponsored, copied and recopied in journals far and wide. "The Negro Speaks of Rivers" even appeared in translation in a paper printed in Germany.

Not very long after Hughes came to New York and not long after that he began to travel and to set down the impressions, the pictures, which his sensitive mind had registered of new forms of life and living in Holland, in France, in Spain, in Italy and in Africa.

His poems are warm, exotic and shot through with color. Never is he preoccupied with form. But this fault, if it is one, has its corresponding virtue, for it gives his verse, which almost always is imbued with the essence of poetry, the perfection of spontaneity. And one characteristic which makes for this bubbling-like charm is the remarkable objectivity which he occasionally achieves, remarkable for one so young, and a first step toward philosophy. Hughes has seen a great deal of the world, and this has taught him that nothing matters much but life. Its forms and aspects may vary, but living is the essential thing. Therefore make no bones about it,—"make the most of what you too may spend."

Some consciousness of this must have been in him even before he began to wander for he sent us as far back as 1921:

Shake your brown feet, honey,
Shake your brown feet, chile,
Shake your brown feet, honey,
Shake 'em swift and wil'— . . .
Sun's going down this evening—
Might never rise no mo'.
The sun's going down this very night—
Might never rise no mo'—
So dance with swift feet, honey,
(The banjo's sobbing low) . . .

The sun's going down this very night—
Might never rise no mo'.

Now this is very significant, combining as it does the doctrine of the old Biblical exhortation, "eat, drink and be merry for tomorrow ye die," Horace's "Carpe diem," the German "Freut euch des Lebens" and Herrick's "Gather ye rosebuds while ye may." This is indeed a universal subject served Negro-style and though I am no great lover of any dialect I hope heartily that Mr. Hughes will give us many more such combinations.

Mr. Hughes is not always the calm philosopher; he has feeling a-plenty and is not ashamed to show it. He "loved his friend" who left him and so taken up is he with the sorrow of it all that he has no room for anger or resentment. While I do not think of him as a protagonist of color,—he is too much the citizen of the world for that—, I doubt if any one will ever write more tenderly, more understandingly, more humorously of the life of Harlem shot through as it is with mirth, abandon and pain. Hughes comprehends this life, has studied it and loved it. In one poem he has epitomized its essence.

Does a jazz-band ever sob?
They say a jazz-band's gay.
Yet as the vulgar dancers whirled
And the wan night wore away,
One said she heard the jazz-band sob
When the little dawn was grey.

Harlem is undoubtedly one of his great loves; the sea is another. Indeed all life is his love and his work a brilliant, sensitive interpretation of its numerous facets.

Review of *The Weary Blues* — Anonymous*

Mr. Hughes, we are told in the introduction to this volume, is a negro poet of twenty-three who has enjoyed an extraordinarily picturesque and rambling existence. His verses certainly reflect the headlong zest which has characterized his life, of which the rhythm has been, in his own words, "a jazz rhythm." To be "caged in the circus of civilization" while "all the tom-toms of the jungles beat in my blood" may provoke fine poetry, as Mr. Cullen has proved. But in Mr. Hughes the conflict has been superficial. His soul has not, as he claims, "grown

*Reprinted from the *Times Literary Supplement*, 29 July 1926, 5.

deep like the rivers." Where it expresses itself at all it is in such verses as "Aunt Sue's Stories," in which the negro feels himself back into the toil and sorrow or the primitive delight of his race. Civilization merely excites his senses, and he becomes the poet, flamboyant or sentimental, of the cabaret, while the conflict between two strains of blood, which Mr. Cullen interpreted so poignantly, issues at best in such a whimsey as the following:—

My old man's a white old man
And my old mother's black.
If ever I cursed my white old man
I take my curses back.

If ever I cursed my black old mother
And wished she were in hell,
I'm sorry for that evil wish
And now I wish her well.

My old man died in a fine big house,
My ma died in a shack.
I wonder where I'm gonna die,
Being neither white nor black?

The Jazz Band's Sob

DuBose Heyward*

A little over a year ago the brilliant Negro journal *Opportunity* awarded a prize for a poem, "The Weary Blues," by Langston Hughes. Shortly thereafter the *Forum* reprinted the poem. Previous to the appearance of this poem very few were aware of the existence of the author, although he had been writing for seven years; an apprenticeship the results of which are evident in the pages of this volume, to which his prize poem gives its name.

"The Weary Blues" challenges more serious consideration than that generally accorded a "first book." Langston Hughes, although only twenty-four years old, is already conspicuous in the group of Negro intellectuals who are dignifying Harlem with a genuine art life. And, too, his use of syncopation in his prize poem suggested the possibility of a conflict in the rhythms of poetry paralleling that which is taking place between the spiritual and jazz exponents of Negro music.

Let it be said at once then that this author has done nothing particularly revolutionary in the field of rhythm. He is endowed with too subtle

*Reprinted from the *New York Herald Tribune Books*, 1 August 1926, sec. 6, pp. 4–5.

a musical sense to employ the banjo music of Vachel Lindsay, but he is close kin to Carl Sandburg in his use of freer, subtler syncopation. In fact, he has wisely refused to be fettered by a theory and has allowed his mood to select its own music. Several of the short free verse poems might have been written by Amy Lowell.

But if he derives little that is new in rhythm from his "Blues" he has managed to capture the *mood* of that type of Negro song, and thereby has caught its very essence. When he is able to create a minor, devil-may-care music, and through it to release a throb of pain, he is doing what the Negroes have done for generations, whether in the "Blues" of the Mississippi region or a song like "I Can't Help from Cryin' Sometimes," as sung by the black folk of the Carolina low country.

As he says in his "Cabaret":

Does a jazz band ever sob?
They say a jazz band's gay.
Yet as the vulgar dancers whirled
And the wan night wore away,
One said she heard the jazz band sob
When the little dawn was gray.

That Langston Hughes has not altogether escaped an inevitable pitfall of the Negro intellectual is to be regretted. In one or two places in the book the artist is obscured by the propagandist. Pegasus has been made a pack-horse. It is natural that the Negro writer should feel keenly the lack of sympathy in the South. That the South is a great loser thereby brings him small comfort. In the soul of a poet, a revolt so born may be transmuted through the alchemy of art into poetry that, while it stings the eyes with tears, causes the reader to wonder.

But far more often in the volume the artist is victor:

We have to-morrow
Bright before us
Like a flame.

Yesterday
A night-gone thing.
A sun-down name.

And dawn to-day
Broad arch above the road we came.

And in "Dream Variation" youth triumphs:

To fling my arms wide
In some place of the sun,
To whirl and to dance
Till the white day is done.

Then rest at cool evening
Beneath a tall tree
While the night comes on gently,
Dark like me—
That is my dream!

It is, however, as an individual poet, not as a member of a new and interesting literary group, or as spokesman for a race, that Langston Hughes must stand or fall, and in the numerous poems in *The Weary Blues* that give poignant moods and vivid glimpses of seas and lands caught by the young poet in his wanderings I find an exceptional endowment. Always intensely subjective, passionate, keenly sensitive to beauty and possessed of an unfaltering musical sense, Langston Hughes has given us a "first book" that marks the opening of a career well worth watching.

[Review of *The Weary Blues*]

Alain Locke*

I believe there are lyrics in this volume which are such contributions to pure poetry that it makes little difference what substance of life and experience they were made of, and yet I know no other volume of verse that I should put forward as more representatively the work of a race poet merely because he writes in many instances of Negro life and consciously as a Negro; but because all his poetry seems to be saturated with the rhythms and moods of Negro folk life. A true "people's poet" has their balladry in his veins; and to me many of these poems seem based on rhythms as seasoned as folk songs and on moods as deep-seated as folk-ballads. Dunbar is supposed to have expressed the peasant heart of his people. But Dunbar was the showman of the Negro masses; here is their spokesman. The acid test is the entire absence of sentimentalism; the clean simplicity of speech, the deep terseness of mood. Taking these poems too much merely as the expressions of a personality, Carl Van Vechten in his debonair introduction wonders at what he calls "their deceptive air of spontaneous improvization." The technique of folk song and dance are instinctively there, giving to the individual talent the bardic touch and power. Especially if Hughes should turn more and more to the colloquial experiences of the common folk whom he so intimately knows and so deeply loves, we may say that the Negro masses have found a voice, and promise to add to their

*Reprinted from *Palms* 1 (1926–27):25–27.

natural domain of music and the dance the conquest of the province of poetry. Remember—I am not speaking of Negro poets, but of Negro poetry.

Poetry of a vitally characteristic racial flow and feeling then is the next step in our cultural development. Is it to be a jazz-product? The title poem and first section of *The Weary Blues* seem superficially to suggest it. But let us see.

> And far into the night he crooned that tune.
> The stars went out and so did the moon.

Or this:

> Sing your Blues song,
> Pretty baby
> You want lovin'
> And you don't mean maybe.
>
> Jungle lover . . . .
> Night-black boy . . . .
> Two against the moon
> And the moon was joy.

Here,—I suspect yet uncombined, are the two ingredients of the Negro poetry that will be truly and beautifully representative: the rhythm of the secular ballad but the imagery and diction of the Spiritual. Stranger opposites than these have fused to the fashioning of new beauty. Nor is this so doctrinaire a question as it seems, when considering a poet who has gone to the cabaret for some of his rhythms and to the Bible for others.

In the poems that are avowedly racial, Hughes has a distinctive note. Not only are these poems full of that passionate declaration and acceptance of race which is a general characteristic of present day Negro poets, but there is a mystic identification with the race experience which is, I think, instinctively deeper and broader than any of our poets has yet achieved.

The Negro Speaks of Rivers catches this note for us most unmistakeably:

> I've known rivers;
> I've known rivers ancient as this world and older than
> the flow of human blood in human veins.
>
> My soul has grown deep like the rivers.
>
> I bathed in the Euphrates when dawns were young.
> I built my hut near the Congo and it lulled me to sleep.
> I looked upon the Nile and raised the pyramids above it.

I heard the singing of the Mississippi when Abe Lincoln
went down to New Orleans, and I've seen its muddy
bosom turn all golden in the sunset.

I've known rivers;
Ancient, dusky rivers.

My soul has grown deep like the rivers.

Remembering this as the basic substratum of this poetry, we may discriminatingly know to what to attribute the epic surge underneath its lyric swing, the primitive fatalism back of its nonchalance, the ancient force in its pert colloquialisms, the tropic abandon and irresistableness of its sorrow and laughter.

No matter how whimsical or gay the poet may carry his overtones after this, or how much of a bohemian or happy troubadour he may assume to be, we will always hear a deep, tragic undertone pulsing in his verse. For the Negro experience rightly sensed even in the moods of the common folk is complex and paradoxical like the Blues which Hughes has pointed out to be so characteristic, with their nonchalant humor against a background of tragedy; there is always a double mood, mercurial to the artist's touch like an easily improvised tune. As our poet himself puts it:

In one hand
I hold tragedy
And in the other
Comedy,—
Masks for the soul.

Laugh with me.
You would laugh!
Weep with me,
Would you weep!

Tears are my laughter.
Laughter is my pain.
Cry at my grinning mouth,
If you will.
Laugh at my sorrow's reign.

[Review of *Fine Clothes to the Jew*] **J. A. Rogers***

The fittest compliment I can pay this latest work by Langston Hughes is to say that it is, on the whole, about as fine a collection of piffling trash as is to be found under the covers of any book. If *The Weary Blues* made readers of a loftier turn of mind weary, this will make them positively sick.

For instance, this so-called poem, the first in the book:

HEY

Sun's a settin'
This is what I'm gonna sing.
Sun's a settin'
This is what I'm gonna sing:
I feels de blues a comin',
Wonder what de blues'll bring.

If this is poetry then verily Shakespeare, Keats, Poe, Dunbar, McKay, were Ainus or Australian Bushmen. But, of course, this book, like *The Weary Blues*, is designed for white readers, with their preconceived notions about Negroes.

Here's another:

RED SILK STOCKINGS

Put on yo' red silk stockings,
Black gal.
Go out an' let de white boys
Look at yo' legs.

Ain't nothin' to do for you, nohow,
Round this town,—
You's too pretty.
Put on yo' red silk stockings, gal
An' tomorrow's chile'll
Be a high yaller.

Go out an' let de white boys
Look at yo' legs.

And the pity of it is that Mr. Hughes is capable of producing other than such degenerate stuff as this. He is capable of finer, loftier expression. The fact that he writes of Negroes in the humbler walks of life has nothing to do with it. With Mr. Hughes, it is indeed a case of "Fine Clothes to the Jew"; of selling his best clothes to the ragman.

Nor must the blame for this prostitution of talent be laid wholly on

*Reprinted from the *Pittsburgh Courier*, 12 February 1927, sec. 2, p. 4, by permission of the *Pittsburgh Courier*.

Mr. Hughes. The Negro group is even more to blame in that it has made absolutely no provision for its writers, expecting the Nordic to do it. Poets, like ladies, must live, and if they are to get along they must put their feet under the white man's kitchen table or starve. And when one sits to another's table he can't very well dictate the dishes.

What is aimed at in America is the social degradation of the Negro to a stage where his labor can be had in the cheapest market. The rage over books like this and the vogue of the spirituals among white people is but a red herring drawn across the trail. When it comes to books or articles that vitally affect the question then these same folk will be found, generally, to be the rankest kind of conservatives. Recently George S. Schuyler sent some of his Southern snapshots to the New Masses, a Communist paper, and after the editor had finished trimming it, it looked as if the Imperial Wizard, bitterest foe of the Communists, had been through it, instead.

This book, while it has some modicum of truth and beauty, is plainly an attempt to exploit the jazzy, degenerate, infantile and silly vogue inspired by the success of such plays as "Lulu Belle." It has 89 pages, and it is safe to say that the matter in the whole could be held in sixteen pages.

Fine Clothes to the Jew is unworthy both of Mr. Hughes and Messrs. Knopf, the publishers. I would very much rather have said a good word for both, especially as Knopf is publisher of *The Fire in the Flint*. But a reviewer owes a duty both to himself and his readers, for, in proportion as one praises the bad he detracts from the good. We have had enough of Mr. Hughes in this vein,—too much in fact—and the Negro public, if it will not help Mr. Hughes to publish his worthy poems, can do at least this, it can discourage the marketing of such books, books that help but to tighten the chains of social degradation.

Sing A Soothin' Song

DuBose Heyward*

When Langston Hughes published his first volume less than a year ago under the title of *The Weary Blues* he sounded a new note in contemporary American poetry. Like practically all first books of lyric poetry the quality was uneven. At its worst it was interesting, because it was spontaneous and unaffected. At its best the poems contained flashes of passionate lyrical beauty that will probably stand among the finest examples of the author's work. This irregularity of quality is to

*Reprinted from the *New York Herald Tribune Books*, 20 February 1927, 5.

be expected in a volume that is in a way a spiritual biography of the poet. Writing has been an escape; it has registered the depths, and it has caught the fire of the emotional crises through which its author has passed. Because Langston Hughes had suffered with intensity and rejoiced with abandon and managed to capture his moods in his book he sounded an authentic note.

Unfortunately, writing poetry as an escape and being a poet as a career are two different things, and the latter is fraught with dangers. In *Fine Clothes to the Jew* we are given a volume more even in quality, but because it lacks the "high spots" of *The Weary Blues* by no means as unforgettable as the first book. The outstanding contribution of the collection now under review is the portraiture of the author's own people. Langston Hughes knows his underworld. He divines the aspirations and the tragic frustrations of his own race, and the volume is a processional of his people given in brief, revealing glimpses. Here is a boy cleaning spittoons, who sings of his work. "A bright bowl of brass is beautiful to the Lord." And here is the psychology of the Negro bad man in a single stanza:

I'm a bad, bad man
'Cause everybody tells me so
I'm a bad, bad man.
Everybody tells me so
I takes ma meanness and ma licker
Everywhere I go

In "The Death of Do Dirty," "The New Cabaret Girl," "Prize Fighter," "Ballad of Gin Mary," "Porter," "Elevator Boy" and the several poems bearing the sadness of the Negro prostitute, we are given sharply etched impressions that linger in the memory.

The "Glory Hallelujah" section of the book contains a number of devotional songs which have the folk quality of the spiritual. A lovely example is the "Feet o' Jesus"

At de feet o' Jesus,
    Sorrow like a sea
Lordy, let yo' mercy
    Come driftin' down on me.

At de feet o' Jesus,
    At yo' feet I stand
Oh, ma little Jesus
    Please reach out yo' hand.

From the section "From the Georgia Roads" tragedy emerges in the poignant, "Song for a Dark Girl."

Way down South in Dixie,
    (Break the heart of me)

They hung my black young lover
    To a cross roads tree.

Way down South in Dixie,
    (Bruised body high in air)
I asked the white Lord Jesus
    What was the use of prayer.

    Way down South in Dixie,
    (Break the heart of me),
Love is a naked shadow
    On a gnarled and naked tree.

Fine Clothes to the Jew contains much of beauty, and in most of the poems there is the same instinctive music and rhythm that distinguished the poet's best earlier work. Against this must be set what appears to me to be an occasional conscious striving for originality, as in the title, and the employment in one or two of the poems of a free verse that invades the territory of prose. But if this second book does not lift the art of the author to a new high level it does appreciably increase the number of first-rate poems to the credit of Langston Hughes, and it renews his high promise for the future.

A Poet for the People

Margaret Larkin*

In casting about for a precise category in which to identify the work of Langston Hughes, I find that he might be acclaimed a new prophet in several fields, and very likely he does not think of himself as belonging to any of them.

There is still a great deal of talk about "native American rhythms" in poetic circles, and the desirability of freeing poetry from the stiff conventions which Anglo Saxon prosody inflicted upon it. In turning to the rhythm pattern of the folk "blues," Langston Hughes has contributed something of great value to other poets, particularly since he uses the form with variety and grace.

De po' house is lonely,
An' de grave is cold.
O, de po' house is lonely,
De graveyard grave is cold.
But I'd rather be dead than
To be ugly an' old.

*Reprinted from *Opportunity* 5 (March 1927):84–85, by permission of the journal.

This apparently simple stuff is full of delicate rhythmic variety through which the long ripple of the form flows boldly. The "blues" are charming folk ballads and in the hands of this real poet present great possibilities for beauty.

Ever since I first heard Langston Hughes read his verse, I am continually wanting to liken his poems to those of Bobby Burns. Burns caught three things in his poems: dialect, speech cadence, and character of the people, so that he seems more Scotch than all of bonnie Scotland. It is a poet's true business to distill this pure essence of life, more potent by far than life ever turns out to be, even for poets. I think that Hughes is doing for the Negro race what Burns did for the Scotch—squeezing out the beauty and rich warmth of a noble people into enduring poetry.

In hearing a group of young poets reading their new poems to each other recently, I was struck with their common tendency to intricacy, mysticism, and preoccupation with brilliant technique. Their poems are competent and beautiful, and the antithesis of simple. To any but other poets, skilled in the craft, they are probably as completely mysterious as though in a foreign tongue. The machine age and the consequent decline of the arts has driven many poets and artists into the philosophy that art is the precious possession of the few initiate. Poets now write for the appreciation of other poets, painters are scornful of all but painters, even music, most popular of all the arts, is losing the common touch. Perhaps this is an inevitable development. Yet the people perish. Beauty is not an outworn ideal, for they still search for it on Fourteenth street. While the poets and artists hoard up beauty for themselves and each other, philosophizing upon the "aristocracy of art," some few prophets are calling for art to come out of rich men's closets and become the "proletarian art" of all the people.

Perhaps Langston Hughes does not relish the title of Proletarian Poet, but he deserves it just the same. "Railroad Avenue," "Brass Spitoons," "Prize Fighter," "Elevator Boy," "Porter," "Saturday Night," and the songs from the Georgia Roads, all have their roots deep in the lives of workers. They give voice to the philosophy of men of the people, more rugged, more beautiful, better food for poetry, than the philosophy of the "middle classes."

This is a valuable example for all poets of what can be done with simple technique and "every day" subjects, but it is particularly valuable, I believe, for other Negro poets. Booker T. Washington's adjuration to "educate yourself" has sunk too deep in the Race philosophy. As in all American life, there is a strong urge to escape life's problems by reaching another station. "The life of a professional man must surely be happier than that of a factory worker," America reasons. "A teacher must surely find greater satisfaction than a farmer." Poets, influenced by this group sentiment, want to write about "nicer" emotions than those of the prize fighter who reasons

Only dumb guys fight.
If I wasn't dumb
I wouldn't be fightin'
I could make six dollars a day
On the docks,
And I'd save more than I do now.
Only dumb guys fight.

or the pondering on circumstances of the boy who cleans spittoons

Babies and gin and church
and women and Sunday
All mixed up with dimes and
dollars and clean spittoons
and house rent to pay.
Hey, boy!
A bright bowl of brass is beautiful to the Lord
Bright polished brass like the cymbals
of King David's dancers,
Like the wine cups of Solomon.
Hey, boy!

Yet this, much more than the neurotic fantasies of more sophisticated poets, is the stuff of life.

There is evidence in this book that Langston Hughes is seeking new mediums, and this is a healthy sign. If he were to remain the poet of the ubiquitous "blues" he would be much less interesting. He will find new forms for himself, and I do not believe that he will lose his hold on the simple poignancy that he put into the "blues" as he adds to his poetic stature. The strong, craftsmanlike handling of "Mulatto," one of the best poems in the book, the delicate treatment of "Prayer," the effective rhythm shifts of "Saturday Night" are promises of growing power.

Not all of the poems of *Fine Clothes to the Jew* are of equal merit. Many of them are the product of too great facility. To be able to write easily is a curse, that hangs over many a poet, tempting him to produce good verse from which the fine bead of true poetry is lacking. But even the most demanding critic cannot expect poets to publish perfect volumes. It ought to be enough to find one exquisite lyric like the "New Cabaret Girl" surcharged with an emotion kept in beautiful restraint,

My God, I says,
You can't live that way!
Babe, you can't
Live that way!

and here are many such.

Common Clay and Poetry

Alain Locke*

Fine clothes may not make either the poet or the gentleman, but they certainly help; and it is a rare genius that can strip life to the buff and still poetize it. This, however, Langston Hughes has done, in a volume that is even more starkly realistic and colloquial than his first,—*The Weary Blues*. It is a current ambition in American poetry to take the common clay of life and fashion it to living beauty, but very few have succeeded, even Masters and Sandburg not invariably. They get their effects, but often at the expense of poetry. Here, on the contrary, there is scarcely a prosaic note or a spiritual sag in spite of the fact that never has cruder colloquialism or more sordid life been put into the substance of poetry. The book is, therefore, notable as an achievement in poetic realism in addition to its particular value as a folk study in verse of Negro life.

The success of these poems owes much to the clever and apt device of taking folk-song forms and idioms as the mold into which the life of the plain people is descriptively poured. This gives not only an authentic background and the impression that it is the people themselves speaking, but the sordidness of common life is caught up in the lilt of its own poetry and without any sentimental propping attains something of the necessary elevation of art. Many of the poems are modelled in the exact metrical form of the Negro "Blues," now so suddenly popular, and in thought and style of expression are so close as scarcely to be distinguishable from the popular variety. But these poems are not transcriptions, every now and then one catches sight of the deft poetic touch that unostentatiously transforms them into folk portraits. In the rambling improvised stanzas of folk-song, there is invariably much that is inconsistent with the dominant mood; and seldom any dramatic coherence. Here we have these necessary art ingredients ingenuously added to material of real folk flavor and origin. "Gal's Cry for a Dying Lover" is an excellent example:

Heard de owl a hootin',
Knowed somebody's bout to die.
Heard de Owl a hootin',
Knowed somebody's 'bout to die.
Put ma head un'neath de kiver,
Started in to moan and cry.

Hound dawg's barkin'
Means he's gonna leave dis world.
Hound dawg's barkin'

*Reprinted from the *Saturday Review of Literature* 3 (9 April 1927):712, by permission of the magazine.

Means he's gonna leave dis world.
O, Lawd have mercy
On a po' black girl.

Black an' ugly
But he sho do treat me kind.
I'm black an' ugly
But he sho do treat me kind.
High-in-heaben Jesus,
Please don't take this man o' mine.

After so much dead anatomy of a people's superstition and so much sentimental balladizing on dialect chromatics, such vivid, pulsing, creative portraits of Negro folk foibles and moods are most welcome. The author apparently loves the plain people in every aspect of their lives, their gin-drinking carousals, their street brawls, their tenement publicity, and their slum matings and partings, and reveals this segment of Negro life as it has never been shown before. Its open frankness will be a shock and a snare for the critic and moralist who cannot distinguish clay from mire. The poet has himself said elsewhere,—"The 'low-down' Negroes furnish a wealth of colorful, distinctive material for any artist, because they hold their individuality in the face of American standardizations. And perhaps these common people will give to the world its truly great Negro artist, the one who is not afraid to be himself." And as one watches Langston Hughes's own career, one wonders.

The dominant mood of this volume is the characteristic "Blue's emotion,"—the crying laugh that "eases its misery" in song and self pity. However, there are poems of other than the folk character in the book,—none more notable than "The Mulatto,"—too long to quote, even though it is a lyric condensation of the deepest tragedy of the race problem. One that is just as pregnant with social as well as individual tragedy can serve as a brief sample of this side of younger Negro genius for tragic vision and utterance:

SONG FOR A DARK GIRL

Way Down South in Dixie
(Break the heart of me)
They hung my black young lover
To a cross roads tree.

Way Down South in Dixie
(Bruised body high in air)
I asked the white Lord Jesus
What was the use of prayer.

Way Down South in Dixie
(Break the heart of me)

Love is a naked shadow
On a gnarled and naked tree.

After this there is nothing to be said about the finest tragedy having always to be Greek.

[Review of *Fine Clothes to the Jew*] Lewis Alexander*

Fine Clothes to the Jew, reveals the fact that Mr. Hughes understands completely the lives of the more primitive types of Negro. No one who knows intimately the Negro crap shooters, gamblers, typical gin Mary's, bootblacks, bell boys, cabaret girls, piano plunkers, makers of folk songs, street walkers, and old rounders can deny this. This poet enters into the spirit of the lives of these people and paints them with a sympathy and understanding not matched in contemporary literature. It is true that there is much sordidness and ugliness in the lives of the more primitive types of the Negro, but yet the same is true of the more primitive types of any racial group. The sordidness and ugliness present in the lives of these folks do not constitute a reason why they are not fit subjects for literary treatment. In real life we find ugliness along side of beauty; hence in literature which is true to life we must expect to find the same conditions existing and without a shadow of doubt, Mr. Hughes has not failed to portray the life of which he treats with all its terrible reality.

Nowhere does he attempt to cover up; therefore his work has that fine sincerity which is the essence of all true poetry. We may select from his work at random but at all times we feel that the author knows whereof he speaks. He has actually lived with and knows well the people and conditions of which he writes. No vain pretensions or fanciful imagination here—only reality.

In addition to his sincerity, Mr. Hughes possesses an originality in his writing which is quite refreshing. He goes directly to the source for his material and reports his findings as he sees them. The result is quite delightful.

Mr. Hughes also shows that he understands something of the economic revolution which is taking place in the mind of the Negro. Let us read his poem entitled "The Porter."

I must say
Yes, sir,

*Reprinted from the *Carolina Magazine* 57 (May 1927):41–44.

To you all the time.
Yes, sir!
Yes, sir!
All my days
Climbing up a great big mountain
Of yes, sirs!

Rich old white man
Owns the world.
Gimme yo' shoes
To shine.

Yes, sir!

In this poem the porter realizes the servility of his position. There was a time in Negro history when the porter and other domestic servants of the white folks felt themselves superior to the Negro farm hand or the Negro laborer, or even the Negro mechanic. This condition existed in the minds of the former type of Negro, probably because he wore clean clothes, a tie and collar while the latter wore soiled clothes and greasy overalls. Of course, this is the same fallacy which makes the small white American clerk think himself superior to any and all other workers simply because he has a "white collar" job. There are many poems in this book which might come in for specific mention but as space is limited I cannot consider all of them; but I daresay there is the poem "Mulatto" which is the masterpiece of the book.

I am your son, white man!

Georgia dusk
And the turpentine woods.
One of the pillars of the temple fell.

You are my son!
Like hell!

The moon over the turpentine woods.
The Southern night
Full of stars,
Great big yellow stars.
    Juicy bodies
    Of nigger wenches
    Blue black
    Against black fences.
    O, you little bastard boy,
    What's a body but a toy?
The scent of pine wood stings the soft
night air.
    What's the body of your mother?

Silver moonlight everywhere.
What's the body of your mother?
Sharp pine scent in the evening air.
A nigger night,
A nigger joy,
A little yellow
Bastard boy.

Naw, you ain't my brother.
Niggers ain't my brother.
Not ever.
Bastard boy.

The Southern night is full of stars,
Great big yellow stars.
O, sweet as earth,
Dusk dark bodies
Give sweet birth
To little yellow bastard boys.

Git on back there in the night,
You ain't white.

The bright stars scatter everywhere.
Pine wood scent in the evening air.
A nigger night,
A nigger joy.

I am your son, white man!

A little yellow
Bastard boy.

Nowhere do we find a more powerful picture of a delicate Negro-White situation. Mr. Hughes has said in the space of one short poem all that can be said about the matter. One could write a volume on what he implies in this one short poem. And the poem is excellently done too—vivid, graphic, poignant. Who has written a more piercing lyric on the terrible crime, lynching, than his "Song For A Dark Girl"?

Way Down South in Dixie
(Break the heart of me)
They hung my black young lover
To a cross roads tree.

Way Down South in Dixie
(Bruised body high in air)
I asked the white Lord Jesus
What was the use of prayer.

Way Down South in Dixie
(Break the heart of me)

Love is a naked shadow
    On a gnarled and naked tree.

Mr. Hughes will continue in his good work. He is a real poet and at the rate he is going will develop into a genuine folk poet worthy of being called the spokesman of the black masses of America. He is a real poet despite the fact that he does not adhere strictly to the conventional subject matter and conventional poetic patterns, but those who understand anything about the matter at all will concede that the essence of real poetry certainly does not lie in conventionality.

Limiting Devices

Kenneth Fearing*

The poems in this volume have a certain amount of power, and a great deal of ease. Hughes is colorful, unsentimental, sharp, and at time [*sic*] strange. He uses Negro dialect and jazz rhythm, in this particular volume, with as much success as anyone has achieved using those limiting devices. But with the American language, to which Hughes will have to turn, he is not yet familiar. An indication of what he may do when he learns a way to use "American" may be seen in the following:

SPORTS

Life
For him
Must be
The shivering of
A great drum
Beaten with swift sticks
Then at the closing hour
The lights go out
And there is no music at all
And death becomes
An empty cabaret
And eternity an unblown saxophone
And yesterday
A glass of gin
Drunk long
Ago

In the main, however, Hughes sticks to dialect poetry: he handles this well, is nearly always successful with it, is precise, imaginative, simple.

*Reprinted from *New Masses* 3 (September 1927):29.

De railroad bridge's
A sad song in de air.
De railroad bridge's
A sad song in de air.
Every time de train pass
I wants to go somewhere.

The trouble with these successes is that they are all small; the poems are little better than poignant playthings. Dialect of any kind, it seems, automatically reduces a poem from the adult to a miniature plane, to a state of unreality. Paradoxically, though the language may be straight from life, a work in dialect is always slightly stagey, a tour de force.

But Hughes has done more with his conventional "Negro stuff"—has used its style to better advantage—than, in my opinion, any other dialect writer.

[Review of *Not Without Laughter*]

V. F. Calverton*

Here is the Negro in his most picturesque form—the blues-loving Negro, the spiritual-singing Negro, the exuberant, the impassioned, the irresponsible Negro, the Negro of ancient folk-lore and romantic legend. "Good-natured, guitar-playing Jim Boy"; Angee Rogers loving Jim Boy no matter where he goes or whom he lives with; Aunt Hager, the old mammy of a dead generation, "whirling around in front of the altar at revival meetings . . . her face shining with light, arms outstretched as though all the cares of the world had been cast away"; Harriet, "beautiful as a jungle princess," singing and jazzing her life away, sneering at sin as a white man's body, and burying beneath peals of laughter "a white man's war for democracy"; and Sandy, seeing his people as a "band of black dancers captured in a white world," and resolving to free them from themselves as well as from their white dictators—these are the Negroes of this novel, these the people who make it live with that quick and intimate reality which is seldom seen in American fiction.

Not Without Laughter continues the healthy note begun in Negro fiction by Claude McKay and Rudolph Fisher. Instead of picturing the Negro of the upper classes, the Negro who in too many instances has been converted to white norms, who even apes white manners and white morality and condemns the Negroes found in this novel as "nig-

*Reprinted from the *Nation* 31 (6 August 1930):157–58. Copyright 1930, *Nation Magazine*, Nation Associates, Inc. Reprinted by permission.

gers," McKay, Fisher, and Hughes have depicted the Negro in his more natural and more fascinating form. There can be no doubt that the Negro who has made great contributions to American culture is this type of Negro, the Negro who has brought us his blues, his labor songs, his spirituals, his folk-lore—and his jazz. And yet this very type of Negro is the one that has been the least exploited by contemporary Negro novelists and short-story writers. It has been white writers such as DuBose Heyward, Julia Peterkin, Howard W. Odum, and Paul Green who have turned to this Negro for the rich material of their novels, dramas, and stories. These writers, however, have known this Negro only as an exterior reality, as something they could see, listen to, sympathize with, even love; they could never know him as an inner reality, as something they could live with as with themselves, their brothers, their sweethearts—something as real as flesh, as tense as pain. Langston Hughes does. As a Negro he has grown up with these realities as part of himself, as part of the very air he has breathed. Few blurs are there in these pages, and no fumbling projections, and no anxious searching for what is not. Here is this Negro, or at least one vital aspect of him, as he really is, without ornament, without pretense.

All this praise, however, must not be misconstrued. *Not Without Laughter* is not without defects of style and weaknesses of structure. The first third of the novel, in fact, arrives at its points of interest with a pedestrian slowness; after that it picks up tempo and plunges ahead. Unfortunately, there are no great situations in the novel, no high points of intensity to grip and overpower the reader. Nor is there vigor of style—that kind of vigor which could have made of Sandy's ambition to emancipate his race, for example, a more stirring motif. But *Not Without Laughter* is significant despite these weaknesses. It is significant because even where it fails, it fails beautifully, and where it succeeds—namely, in its intimate characterizations and in its local color and charm—it succeeds where almost all others have failed.

[Review of *Not Without Laughter*]

Sterling Brown*

We have in this book, laconically, tenderly told, the story of a young boy's growing up. Let no one be deceived by the effortless ease of the telling, by the unpretentious simplicity of *Not Without Laughter*. Its simplicity is the simplicity of great art; a wide observation, a long

*Reprinted from *Opportunity* 15 (September 1930):279–280, by permission of the journal.

brooding over humanity, and a feeling for beauty in unexpected, out of the way places, must have gone into its makeup. It is generously what one would expect of the author of *The Weary Blues* and *Fine Clothes to the Jew.*

Not Without Laughter tells of a poor family living in a small town in Kansas. We are shown intimately the work and play, the many sided aspects of Aunt Hager and her brood. Aunt Hager has three daughters: Tempy, Annjee and Harriett. Tempy is doing well; having joined the Episcopalian Church she has put away "niggerish" things; Annjee is married to a likeable scapegrace, Jimboy, guitar plunker and rambling man; Harriett, young, full of life and daring, is her heart's worry. She has a grandchild, Sandy, son of Annjee and Jimboy. And about him the story centers.

Sandy with his wide eyes picking up knowledge of life about the house; Sandy listening to his father's blues and ballads in the purple evenings, watching his Aunt Harriett at her dancing; Sandy at school; Sandy dreaming over his geography book; Sandy at his job in the barbershop and hotel; Sandy at his grandmother's funeral; Sandy learning respectability at Aunt Tempy's,–and learning at the same time something of the ways of women from Pansetta; Sandy in Chicago; Sandy with his books and dreams of education– so run the many neatly etched scenes.

But the story is not Sandy's alone. We see Harriett, first as a firm fleshed beautiful black girl, quick at her lessons; we see her finally a blues singer on State Street. The road she has gone has been rocky enough. She has been maid at a country club where the tired business men made advances; she has been with a carnival troupe, she has been arrested for street walking. We follow Annjee in her trials, and Jimboy, and Tempy. And we get to know the wise, tolerant Aunt Hager, beloved by whites and blacks; even by Harriett who just about breaks her heart. Lesser characters are as clearly individualized and developed. We have Willie Mae, and Jimmy Lane, and Joe Willis, "white folks nigger," and Uncle Dan, and Mingo, and Buster, who could have passed for white. The white side of town, the relationships of employers with laundresses and cooks, all these are adequately done. The book, for all of its apparent slightness, is full-bodied.

One has to respect the author's almost casual filling in of background. The details are perfectly chosen; and they make the reader *see.* How representative are his pictures of the carnival, and the dance at which "Benbow's Famous Kansas City Band" plays, and the gossip over back fences! How recognizable is Sister Johnson's "All these womens dey mammy named Jane an' Mary an' Cora, soon's dey get a little somethin', dey changes dey names to Janette or Mariana or Corina or somethin' mo' flowery than what dey had."

As the title would suggest the book is not without laughter. Jimboy's guitar-playing, Harriett's escapades, the barber shop tall tales, the philosophizing of the old sheep "who know de road," all furnish something of this. Sandy's ingenuousness occasionally is not without laughter. But the dominant note of the book is a quiet pity. It is not sentimental; it is candid, clear eyed instead—but it is still pity. Even the abandon, the fervor of the chapter called *Dance*, closely and accurately rendered (as one would expect of Langston Hughes) does not strike the note of unclouded joy. We see these things as they are: as the pitiful refugees of poor folk against the worries of hard days. It is more the laughter of the blues line—*laughin' just to keep from cryin'*.

The difference between comedy and tragedy of course lies often in the point of view from which the story is told. Mr. Hughes' sympathetic identification with these folk is so complete that even when sly comic bits creep in (such as Madame de Carter and the Dance of the Nations) the laughter is quiet—more of a smile than a Cohen-like guffaw. But even these sly bits are few and far between. More than Sandy's throwing his boot-black box at the drunken cracker, certainly a welcome case of poetic justice, one remembers the disappointments of this lad's life. Sandy went on Children's Day to the Park. "Sorry," the man said. "This party's for white kids." In a classroom where the students are seated alphabetically, Sandy and the three other colored children sit behind Albert Zwick. Sandy, in the white folks' kitchen, hears his hardworking mother reprimanded by her sharp tempered employer. And while his mother wraps several little bundles of food to carry to Jimboy, Sandy cried. These scenes are excellently done, with restraint, with irony, and with compassion.

Sandy knows the meaning of a broken family, of poverty, of seeing those he loves go down wtihout being able to help. Most touching, and strikingly universal, is the incident of the Xmas sled. Sandy, wishful for a Golden Flyer sled with flexible rudders! is surprised on Christmas Day by the gift of his mother and grandmother. It is a sled. They had labored and schemed and sacrificed for it in a hard winter. On the cold Christmas morning they dragged it home. It was a home-made contraption—roughly carpentered, with strips of rusty tin along the wooden runners. "It's fine," Sandy lied, as he tried to lift it.

Of a piece with this are the troubles that Annjee knows—Annjee whose husband is here today and gone tomorrow; Annjee, who grows tired of buffeting and loses ground slowly; and the troubles of Aunt Hager who lives long enough to see her hopes fade out, and not long enough to test her final hope, Sandy. . . . Tempy, prosperous, has cold-shouldered her mother; Annjee is married to a man who frets Hager; Harriett has gone with Maudel to the sinister houses of the bottom.

"One by one they leaves you," Hager said slowly. "One by one yo' chillen goes."

Unforgettable is the little drama of Harriett's rebellion. It is the universal conflict of youth and age. Mr. Hughes records it, without comment. It is the way life goes. Harriett, embittered by life, wanting her share of joy, is forbidden to leave the house. The grandmother is belligerent, authoritative, the girl rebellious. And then the grandmother breaks. . . . "Harriett, honey, I wants you to be good." But the pitiful words do not avail; Harriett, pitiless as only proud youth can be, flings out of doors—with a cry, "You old Christian Fool!" A group of giggling sheiks welcomes her.

Of all of his characters, Mr. Hughes obviously has least sympathy with Tempy. She is the *Arriviste*, the worshipper of white folks' ways, the striver. "They don't 'sociate no mo' with none but de high toned colored folks." The type deserves contempt looked at in one way, certainly; looked at in another it might deserve pity. But the point of the reviewer is this: that Mr. Hughes does not make Tempy quite convincing. It is hard to believe that Tempy would be as blatantly crass as she is to her mother on Christmas Day, when she says of her church "Father Hill is so dignified, and the services are absolutely refined! *There's never anything niggerish about them—so you know, mother, they suit me.*"

But, excepting Tempy, who to the reviewer seems slightly caricatured, all of the characters are completely convincing. There is a universality about them. They have, of course, peculiar problems as Negroes. Harriett, for instance, hates all whites, with reason. But they have even more the problems that are universally human. Our author does not exploit either local color, or race. He has selected an interesting family and has told us candidly, unembitteredly, poetically of their joy lightened and sorrow laden life.

Langston Hughes presents all of this without apology. Tolerant, humane, and wise in the ways of mortals, he has revealed beauty where too many of us, dazzled by false lights, are unable to see it. He has shown us again, in this third book of his—what he has insisted all along, with quiet courage:

> *Beautiful, also, is the sun.*
> *Beautiful, also, are the souls of my people. . . .*

Paying for Old Sins

Sherwood Anderson*

Carl Carmer went to Alabama a bit too anxious to please. He is so sunny and good-natured about everything from grits and collard greens to Scottsboro that it rather makes your bones ache. These Alabamans are so persistently and so confoundedly cute, even in their cruelties, the old aristocracy is so aristocratic and the niggers so niggery. Thank you kindly. Hand me the Bill Faulkner.

Sample, page ninety-three: "We had planned a few days' tour before the visit Mary Louise had planned was to begin. An hour or so after we had started we had seen the red-gold of the dust turn to white. Below that white surface black soil—the Black Belt from whose dark and fertile land rose pillard glories with names that are poems—Rosemont, Bluff Hall, Gainswood, Oakleigh, Farmdale, Snow Hill, Tulip Hill, Windsor, Chantilly, Athol, Longwood, Westwood, Waldwie."

Poems man? Yo do not make words poetic by asserting they are poetic. Where is your poetry?

The book promises well. There is poetry in the title and the foreword excites. And then, too, Farrar and Rinehart have made the book well. Physically it is beautiful and Mr. Cyrus Leroy Baldridge has made some drawings that are charming, but for me the book doesn't come off. I have already seen that some critic has said that it was not made for home consumption and I think he is wrong. I think the Southerners will love it, particularly the professional Southerners of New York and Chicago. Mr. Stribling you are quite safe. This man will never steal your Alabama from you.

Nerts, say I. All this fuss because some Alabama farmer invites you to supper. It always did annoy me, this business, some Yank going South. No one shoots him. A Negro woman brings a cup of coffee to his bed in the morning. He eats hot bread. The hotel rooms are dirty. Now he is off. . . . "Oh this gorgeous land, home of old romance," etc., etc. Not that it isn't all true enough, if you could get below Alabama life, down into it. . . . Indiana Life for that matter . . . what makes people what they are, the real feel of the life around you, get down into you, become a part of you and come out of you.

I don't think Mr. Carmer does it. He skirts it now and then and when he becomes what he really is, a very competent gatherer-up of names of fiddlers' tunes, collector of folk tales told by others, etc., the book begins to have real value. He should have confined himself to that work. The man is not a story teller.

*Reprinted from the *Nation* 139 (11 July 1934):49–50. Copyright 1934, *Nation Magazine*, Nation Associates, Inc. Reprinted by permission. The first book to which Anderson refers is Carl Carmer's *Stars Fell in Alabama.*

And, as I have said, this other business, this damned half apology before Southerners for being born a Northerner, this casualness about Southern cruelty. There is an innocent school teacher taken out to a tree and hanged because he had a relative who was a murderer. "Give me a cigarette. Let's go down to Mary Louise's house. These Alabamans are so cute, don't you think."

There is one favorite Southern tale I didn't find in the book. It is about the white farmer who came down to the cross-road general store. Several other white farmers lounging about. "Well," he says, "I killed me a nigger this morning." Silence. He yawns. "Boys," he says, "I bet you that nigger will go three hundred pounds." To make his book quite perfect, Mr. Carmer should have got that one in. It is so cute.

The Ways of White Folks is something to puzzle you. If Mr. Carmer goes one way, Mr. Langston Hughes goes another. You can't exactly blame him. Mr. Hughes is an infinitely better, more natural, story teller than Mr. Carmer. To my mind he gets the ball over the plate better, has a lot more on the ball but there is something missed. Mr. Carmer is a member of the Northern white race gone South, rather with jaws set, determined to please and be pleased, and Mr. Hughes might be taken as a member of the Southern colored race gone North, evidently not determined about anything but with a deep-seated resentment in him. It is in his blood, so deep-seated that he seems himself unconscious of it. The Negro people in these stories of his are so alive, warm, and real and the whites are all caricatures, life, love, laughter, old wisdom all to the Negroes and silly pretense, fakiness, pretty much all to the whites.

It seems to me a paying for old sins all around, reading these two books. We'll be paying for the World War for hundreds of years yet and if we ever get that out of us we may still be paying interest on slavery.

Mr. Hughes, my hat off to you in relation to your own race but not to mine.

It is difficult. The difficulties faced by Mr. Hughes, as a story teller, are infinitely greater than those faced by Mr. Carmer. Mr. Carmer has but to take the old attitude toward the American Negro. "They are amusing. They are so primitive." If you go modern you go so far as to recognize that Negro men can be manly and Negro women beautiful. It is difficult to do even that without at least appearing to be patronizing. You begin to sound like an Englishman talking about Americans or a Virginian talking about a Texan. Even when you don't mean it you sound like that.

The truth is, I suspect, that there is, back of all this, a thing very little understood by any of us. It is an individualistic world. I may join the Socialist or the Communist Party but that doesn't let me out of my own individual struggle with myself. It may be that I can myself establish something between myself and the American Negro man or woman that is sound. Can I hold it? I am sitting in a room with such a man or woman and we are talking. Others, of my own race, come in. How can I tell what is asleep in these others? Something between the Negro man and myself gets destroyed . . . it is the thing D. H. Lawrence was always speaking of as "the flow." My neighbor, the white man, coming in to me as I sit with my Negro friend, may have qualities I value highly but he may also stink with old prejudice. "What, you have a damn nigger in here?" In the mind of the Negro: "Damn the whites. You can't trust them." That, fed constantly by pretense of understanding where there is no understanding. Myself and Mr. Carmer paying constantly for the prejudices of a whole race. Mr. Hughes paying too. Don't think he doesn't pay.

But story telling is something else, or should be. It too seldom is. There are always too many story tellers using their talents to get even with life. There is a plane to be got on—the impersonal. Mr. Hughes gets on it perfectly with his Negro men and women. He has a fine talent. I do not see how anyone can blame him for his hatreds. I think Red-Headed Baby is a bum story. The figure of Oceola Jones in the story, The Blues I'm Playing, is the most finely drawn in the book. The book is a good book.

[Review of *The Ways of White Folks*]

Alain Locke*

These fourteen short stories of Negro-white contacts told from the unusual angle of the Negro point of view are challenging to all who would understand the later phases of the race question as it takes on the new complications of contemporary social turmoil and class struggle. Their sociological significance is as important as their literary value, perhaps more so, because although written with some personal reaction of disillusionment and bitter despair, they reflect the growing resentment and desperation which is on the increase in the Negro world today. Though harped upon almost to the extent of a formula, there is an important warning in what has been called "the sullen, straight, bitter realism" of this book. It has reportorial courage and presents new angles, but it offers no solutions, doctors no situations and points no morals. Its most illuminating moods are those of tragic irony as in the particularly effective concluding story, Father and Son, the tragedy of

*Reprinted from *Survey Graphic* 23 (November 1934):565.

a planter killed by his own illegitimate son who is lynched for the crime; and of caustic satire as in Cora Unashamed. In most of the stories there is the double motif of the inconsistency of racial discriminations and the injustice of class lines, with frequent hints of the recent radical insistence that the two are below the surface closely related. This is an important book for the present times; greater artistry, deeper sympathy and less resentment would have made it a book for all times.

Forerunner and Ambassador

Richard Wright*

The double role that Langston Hughes has played in the rise of a realistic literature among the Negro people resembles in one phase the role that Theodore Dreiser played in freeing American literary expression from the restrictions of Puritanism. Not that Negro literature was ever Puritanical, but it was timid and vaguely lyrical and folkish. Hughes's early poems, *The Weary Blues* and *Fine Clothes to the Jew*, full of irony and urban imagery, were greeted by a large section of the Negro reading public with suspicion and shock when they first appeared in the middle twenties. Since then the realistic position assumed by Hughes has become the dominant outlook of all those Negro writers who have something to say.

The other phase of Hughes's role has been, for the lack of a better term, that of a cultural ambassador. Performing his task quietly and almost casually, he has represented the Negros' case, in his poems, plays, short stories and novels, at the court of world opinion. On the other hand he has brought the experiences of other nations within the orbit of the Negro writer by his translations from the French, Russian and Spanish.

How Hughes became this forerunner and ambassador can best be understood in the cameo sequences of his own life that he gives us in his sixth and latest book, *The Big Sea*. Out of his experiences as a seaman, cook, laundry worker, farm helper, bus boy, doorman, unemployed worker, have come his writings dealing with black gals who wore red stockings and black men who sang the blues all night and slept like rocks all day.

Unlike the sons and daughters of Negro "society," Hughes was not ashamed of those of his race who had to scuffle for their bread. The jerky transitions of his own life did not admit of his remaining in one place long enough to become a slave of prevailing Negro middle-class prejudices. So beneficial does this ceaseless movement seem to Hughes

*Reprinted from the *New Republic* 103 (July–December 1940):600–601.

that he has made it one of his life principles: six months in one place, he says, is long enough to make one's life complicated. The result has been a range of artistic interest and expression possessed by no other Negro writer of his time.

Born in Joplin, Missouri, in 1902, Hughes lived in half a dozen Midwestern towns until he entered high school in Cleveland, Ohio, where he began to write poetry. His father, succumbing to that fit of disgust which overtakes so many self-willed Negroes in the face of American restrictions, went off to Mexico to make money and proceeded to treat the Mexicans just as the whites in America had treated him. The father yearned to educate Hughes and establish him in business. His favorite phrase was "hurry up," and it irritated Hughes so much that he fled his father's home.

Later he entered Columbia University, only to find it dull. He got a job on a merchant ship, threw his books into the sea and sailed for Africa. But for all his work, he arrived home with only a monkey and a few dollars, much to his mother's bewilderment. Again he sailed, this time for Rotterdam, where he left the ship and made his way to Paris. After an interval of hunger he found a job as a doorman, then as second cook in a night club, which closed later because of bad business. He went to Italy to visit friends and had his passport stolen. Jobless in an alien land, he became a beachcomber until he found a ship on which he could work his way back to New York.

The poems he had written off and on had attracted the attention of some of his relatives in Washington and, at their invitation, he went to live with them. What Hughes has to say about Negro "society" in Washington, relatives and hunger are bitter poems in themselves. While living in Washington, he won his first poetry prize; shortly afterwards Carl Van Vechten submitted a batch of his poems to a publisher.

The rest of *The Big Sea* is literary history, most of it dealing with the Negro renaissance, that astonishing period of prolific productivity among Negro artists that coincided with America's "Golden age" of prosperity. Hughes writes of it with humor, urbanity and objectivity; one has the feeling that never for a moment was his sense of solidarity with those who had known hunger shaken by it. Even when a Park Avenue patron was having him driven about the streets of New York in her town car, he "felt bad because he could not share his new-found comfort with his mother and relatives." When the bubble burst in 1929, Hughes returned to the mood that seems to fit him best. He wrote of the opening of the Waldorf-Astoria: "Now, won't that be charming when the last flophouse/ has turned you down this winter?"

Hughes is tough; he bends but he never breaks, and he has carried on a manly tradition in literary expression when many of his fellow writers have gone to sleep at their posts.

[From "Seven American Poets"]

Alfred Kreymborg*

. . . A new volume by Langston Hughes, with delightful drawings by E. McKnight Kauffer, is a lively event in these troubled times. He calls his *Shakespeare in Harlem* a book of light verse—"Blues, ballads and reels to be read aloud, crooned, shouted, recited, and sung. Some with gestures, some not—as you like. None with a faraway voice." The intimate relation with the old music halls is a happy reminder of such mastersingers of vaudeville as Bert Williams and Eddie Leonard. For here is no highbrow verse, no heavy thinking, and nothing low-born either. The careless reader might easily fall into the error of thinking that these delicate notes and rhythms are funny or gay. It is only the skillful surface that is funny or gay; the heart of the matter is tragic. Rarely in our poetry do we find this subtle blending of tragedy and comedy. It is an exquisite art and a difficult one. The salient character behind the verse of Langston Hughes is social and sociable. And he has the perfect gift of writing quatrains with more than one meaning or overtone. "Wake" is a tiny thing with the broadest connotations.

*Reprinted from the *Saturday Review of Literature* 25 (April 1942):9, by permission of the magazine.

To Be Sung or Shouted

H. R. Hays*

This is a book of light verse and, as such, the only demands that should be made upon it are those of entertainment. It has charm and spontaneity. It expresses temporary nostalgias, passing moods of weariness or gaiety and, occasionally, irony and racial bitterness. Mr. Hughes writes easily without much caring about formal pattern. As he says himself, the poems are to be crooned, shouted or sung. Perhaps the best in the volume are those in which he captures a genuine folk feeling. In the following:

> Levee, levee,
> How high have you got to be
> To keep them cold muddy waters
> From washin' over me.

he achieves what might be an actual work song. In a poem called *Klu Klus*, he strikes hard at white brutality:

*Reprinted from *Poetry* 60 (April–September 1942):223–24. Copyright 1942 by the Modern Poetry Association. Reprinted by permission of the editor of *Poetry*.

They hit me in the head
And knock me down
And then they kicked me
On the ground.
A cracker said "Nigger,
Look me in the face
And tell me you believe in
The great white race."

It is interesting to compare the work of Hughes with the Cuban, Nicolás Guillén, or the Puerto Rican, Palés Matos, who are creating a new Negro art in Spanish. The Latin-Americans are much closer to their African origins, they employ primitive folklore and write with great sensual abandon and gusto. The American Negro poet expresses, especially in the Harlem poems, a certain feeling of rootlessness, a sense of isolation in the crowd of not belonging. Says Hughes:

Say! you know I believe I'll change my name
Change my color, change my ways
And be a white man the rest of my days!
I wonder if white folks ever feel bad
Getting up in the morning lonesome and sad.

In countries like Cuba or Puerto Rico where there is a mulatto majority, the artist feels sure of himself and his work breathes a certain optimism even though it is full of protest. But the American Negro can never rid himself of the realization that he is on a racial island surrounded by a dominant people which does not understand him. He is already urbanized and frustrated. Hence the blues mood is characteristic, a restless searching for small pleasures and small compensations.

Much of *Shakespeare in Harlem* is in popular song style and really calls for music. Mr. Hughes would be an excellent lyricist for a singer such as Ethel Waters. Having already explored the medium, he is the logical poet to write a blues opera. One hopes he will some day try his hand at a libretto.

[Review of *Shakespeare in Harlem*]

Owen Dodson*

This Shakespeare still rolls dice in Harlem, grabs a wishbone, makes a wish for his sweet mama, long gone, long lost; still lies in bed

*Reprinted from *Phylon* 11 (Fall 1942):337–38. Copyright 1942. Reprinted with permission by *Phylon: Atlanta University Review of Race and Culture.*

in the noon of the day. This Shakespeare is lazy, unpoetic, common and vulgar. In short Mr. Langston Shakespeare Hughes is still holding his mirror up to a gold-toothed, flashy nature. It is the same mirror he has held up before but somehow the glass is cracked and his deep insight and discipline has dimmed. There is no getting away from the fact that this book, superior in format, is a careless surface job and unworthy of the author Mr. Van Vechten calls the "Negro Poet Laureate," who loves his race and reports and interprets it feelingly and understandingly to itself and other races. His verse resounds with the exultant throb of Negro pain and gladness.

Once Mr. Hughes wrote

Because my mouth
Is wide with laughter
You do not hear
My inner cry;
Because my feet
Are gay with dancing
You do not know
I die.

In this volume we merely hear the laughter; loud, lewd, unwholesome and degenerate. We see and hear a cartoon doing a black-face, white-lip number, trying terribly to please the populace. None of the inner struggle is revealed, no bitter cries, no protests, no gentleness, no ladders of hope being climbed. These things are hard to say about a poet I very much admire. But they must be said.

Mr. Hughes states at the beginning of the book that this is "light verse. Afro-Americana in the blues mood. Poems syncopated and variegated in the colors of Harlem, Beal Street, West Dallas, and Chicago's South Side. Blues, ballads and reels to be read aloud, crooned, shouted, recited and sung. Some with gestures, some not—as you like. None with a far-away voice." This statement screens a thousand sins. Because verse is "light" it doesn't therefore follow that anything goes. The technique of light verse is as exacting as that of serious verse, almost more so.

If this were Mr. Hughes' first book we would say, here is some promise but in a few years he will deepen this stream, he will broaden this stream. But as this is his fourth volume of verse all I can say is that he is "backing into the future looking at the past" to say nothing of the present.

Eight sections make up the book: "Seven Moments of Love," "Declarations," "Blues for Men," "Death in Harlem," "Mammy Songs," "Ballads," "Blues for Ladies," "Lenox Avenue."

The section called "Death in Harlem" has, perhaps, some of his better work

They done took Cordelia
Out to stony lonesome ground.
Done took Cordelia
To stony lonesome,
Laid her down.

Another poem in this section that has a haunting and poetic shine is "Crossing."

The real "nitty gritty" is a poem in the "Lenox Avenue" section called "Shakespeare in Harlem"

Hey ninny neigh!
And a hey nonny no!
Where, oh, where
Did my sweet mama go?
Hey ninny neigh!
With a tra-la-la-la!
They say your sweet mama
Went home to her ma.

But the "cup" is poems like "Hey-Hey Blues," and "Little Lyric." Whoever drinks will choke on these.

After hearing some of these poems read aloud a fellow who hadn't heard of Mr. Hughes said: "that Langston Hughes must be a cracker." Lord have mercy!

Poems by Langston Hughes

Hubert Creekmore*

This fifth book of poems by Langston Hughes is notable for the brevity and leanness of its lyrics. Many are only four to six lines long, and others would be, if the regular lines were not broken up. For instance, the last stanza of "Snail":

Weather and rose
Is all you see,
Drinking
The dewdrop's
Mystery.

However, the physical appearance of a poem has little to do with its effect or its value. In most cases, the effect here is of a sudden, sensitive gasp of feeling. Often the poems project a sketchiness of

*Reprinted from the *New York Times Book Review*, 4 May 1947, 10. Copyright 1947 by the New York Times Company. Reprinted by permission.

image, a questionable logic (as in the lines quoted above), or a suspicion in the reader that the emotional climate has not been rendered fully.

Since the poems are so stripped, so direct, except in the abundance of repetition and abstract or general terms, their brevity allows for little expansion within the reader. Among the successful ones, "Snake," "Songs" and "Personal" have the hardness of Greek epigrams. But others—poems of nature, longing, love or "Dreamdust," as one is called—are frugally romantic in treatment. Little in the book is regionally or racially inspired, and much of the latter seems strained and lacking in the easy power of Mr. Hughes' earlier poems. However, after a trite beginning, "Trumpet Player: 52nd Street" shows fine penetration in its last page.

For all its variety of subject matter, the collection seems monotonous in treatment. In spite of a certain individuality in Mr. Hughes' approach, there are such strong echoes of other poets that the names of Emily Dickinson, Stephen Crane, and a whisper of E. A. Robinson and Ernest Dowson (there are even two Pierrots and a Pierrette) keep coming to mind. "Montmartre" is pure Imagism:

Pigalle:
A neon rose
In a champagne bottle.
At dawn
The petals
Fall.

This matter of influences or resemblances is, of course, unavoidable and no censure of Mr. Hughes' work. His poems have their own qualities of delicate lyricism and honesty of vision, and undoubtedly many of them will appeal to the great audience now crying for verse that appeals to their emotions wtihout being stereotypes of the Victorian models.

Old Form, Old Rhythms, New Words

Saunders Redding*

It is a tribute to Langston Hughes's earlier accomplishments that his reputation continues undimmed by verse which of late is often jejune and iterative. Intellectual recognition of the thinning out of his creativeness is inescapable, but emotional acceptance of the fact comes hard. An old loving admiration simply will not die. It is not easy to say that a favorite poet's latest book is a sorry falling off. It is not easy to declare that *One-Way Ticket* is stale, flat, and spiritless.

*Reprinted from the *Saturday Review of Literature* 32 (22 January 1949):24, by permission of the magazine.

The reason for this dull level of lifelessness has a simple explanation: Hughes harks back to a youthfulness that is no longer green. He has long since matured beyond the limited expressive capacity of the idiom he uses in *One-Way Ticket.* It is many a year since he was the naive and elemental lyrist of *The Weary Blues* and the folklike storyteller of *The Ways of White Folks.* In mind, emotion, and spirit (and in time, space, and event as well) he has traveled a "far piece," and he has not traveled in circles. The old forms, the old rhythms, the old moods cannot encompass the things he sees and understands and loves and hates now.

While Hughes's rejection of his own growth shows an admirable loyalty to his self-commitment as the poet of the "simple, Negro commonfolk"—the peasant, the laborer, the city slum-dweller—, it does a disservice to his art. And of course the fact is that Langston Hughes is not now, nor every truly was one of the simple, common people. Back in the Twenties and Thirties, his sympathy for them had the blunt, passionate forthrightness of all youthful outpourings of emotion, but lately that sympathy seems a bit disingenuous and a bit strained, like a conversation between old acquaintances who have had no mutual points of reference in a dozen years.

As an example of the artful use of folk idiom and folk rhythm, *One-Way Ticket* will interest those who know only this volume of the author's work, but it will disappoint those who remember the beauty and brilliance of *The Dream Keeper* and *Fields of Wonder.*

Dialogues but Barbed

Carl Van Vechten*

On frequent occasions the late James Weldon Johnson, Negro author, was heard to observe: "There is no doubt in my mind that the solution of the 'race problem' depends on a sense of humor." Then he would say that persons who would permit Negroes to prepare their food, to lave their garments, to suckle their children, and then refuse to allow these same Negroes to sit next to them in street cars or buses (although they often sat next to them in their carriages and motor cars) must be a trifle cracked. "The only way to make these benighted souls see the light," he would continue, "is to convince them that their conduct is a huge joke."

*Reprinted from the *New York Times Book Review*, 7 May 1950, 10.

Langston Hughes, the poet, may be performing that very service in a book which is perhaps not new in form (Mr. Dooley comes to mind as a similar creative effort), but which presents the Negro in a new way. Jesse Simple is wise, witty, as mad as the Madwoman of Chaillot and invariably race conscious. He is the naive propagandist, through a series of dialogues.

Since these papers were originally written for a Negro newspaper and, consequently, an exclusive Negro audience, there is no attempt at obfuscation. The papers probably exhibit the Negro in bedroom slippers and pajamas—that is, as nearly himself as it would be possible to show him. Simple is completely frank in his opinions about white people: he dislikes them intensely. The race problem is never absent, but the flow of the book is light-hearted and easy.

This is the sane approach to real insanity and I wouldn't be surprised if this book reaches more people and has wider influence than any volume on a similar subject since *Uncle Tom's Cabin. Simple Speaks His Mind* will start a lot of people thinking hard. For those who have to swallow bitter pills it provides a sugar-coating of humor. Only a Negro could have written this book, and only a Negro as wise as Langston Hughes.

What It Means to Be Colored

Saunders Redding*

The tradition is an old one, for it goes back to the "horse sense humorists" of the final quarter of the last century. It goes back to Charles Heber Clark and his "Cooley"; to Josh Billings and Artemus Ward and Finley Peter Dunne, who created "Mr. Dooley." The tradition demands a rich awareness, an unclouded eye, an unstopped ear. It demands the salt of sincerity. It demands a sense of humor delicately balanced between gross, playful burlesque and acute satire.

In *Simple Speaks His Mind* Langston Hughes has completely fulfilled the tradition and perhaps gone a step beyond, for whereas Clark's "Cooley" and Dunne's "Mr. Dooley" give voice to the contemporary mind at work with merely current problems, Hughes's Jess B. Semple (Simple) ranges the universe. It is true that "Simple" has equipment insufficient to cope with the universal, but this merely enlarges one's sympathetic understanding of him. It is also true that he relates world-wide

*Reprinted from the *New York Times Book Review*, 11 June 1950, 13. Copyright 1950 by the New York Times Company. Reprinted by permission.

problems to his own and reduces them all to a personal level, but this only evidences his humanity and arouses one's smiles and tears with equal facility and point.

"Simple" speaks his unlearned mind on every conceivable subject and, though his accents are those of Harlem, he utters a great many of the world's hopes and fears. "Lord, kindly please, take the blood off my hands and off my brother's hands, and make us shake hands clean and not be afraid.... Too many mens and womens are dead. The fault is mine and theirs, too. So teach us all to do right, Lord, please, and to get along together with that atom bomb on this earth...."

Instances are numerous, but "Simple's" spoken mind is a revelation in another way, too. What he says opens windows on a corner of life much publicized but little known. For though "Simple" is first a man, he is one qualified by the color of his skin. As he himself states, he knows more about being colored than "n'ar almost" any other one of God's "mens." What he knows, he says. That he was originally created to speak only to people of his own kind makes the revelation more complete. Thus one is made acquainted with the complexities of Negro life and Harlem life—the real complexities which cannot be resolved by the social and moral equivalents of sticks of red peppermint candy.

One should space the reading of *Simple Speaks His Mind* as if the pieces were each a weekly column (as indeed they were). Otherwise "Simple's" speech may grow monotonous—and this in spite of its flashes of sheer brilliance, its wisdom and its humor.

Langston Hughes in an Old Vein with New Rhythms

Saunders Redding*

In *Montage of a Dream Deferred*, Langston Hughes again proves himself the provocative folk singer who enchanted and sometimes distressed readers of *The Weary Blues, Fine Clothes to the Jew* and *Fields of Wonder*. In the interval between the publication of *One-Way Ticket* (1949) and this new book, he seems to have made a spiritually rewarding return to the heritage that was distinctly his in the days of the Negro renaissance. His images are again quick, vibrant and probing, but they no longer educate. They probe into old emotions and experiences with fine sensitiveness—

*Reprinted from the *New York Times Book Review*, 11 March 1951, 5. Copyright 1951 by the New York Times Company. Reprinted by permission.

Into the laps
of black celebrities
white girls fall
like pale plums from a tree
beyond a high tension wall
wired for killing
which makes it
more thrilling–

but they reveal nothing new. He still views his function as being useful to social reform and (though it is no fault in itself) such a view tends to date him in the same way that a poet like Byron is dated.

The Roosevelt, Renaissance,
    Gem, Alhambra:
Harlem laughing in all the
    wrong places
  at the crocodile tears
  of crocodile art
  that you know
  in your heart
  is crocodile:
    (Hollywood
      laughs at me,
      black–
      so I laugh
      back.)

The idiom, like the heritage to which he returns, is also distinctly Hughes'. In earlier work, however, it was adapted to the smooth and relatively simple rhythm of jazz. In *Montage of a Dream Deferred* it is fitted to the jarring dissonances and broken rhythms of be-bop. The result is a bold and frequently shocking distortion of tempo and tone, and this will fret and repel some readers. But Hughes has always required of his readers a sophisticated ear. It is the price of admission into the meanings of his experiences, and when he is at his best, it is not too high a price. In some of the pieces in *Montage*, he is at his best, in "Island," for instance, and "Freedom Train" and "Tell Me."

Yet it seems to me that Hughes does have a too great concern for perpetuating his reputation as an "experimenter." That he was this cannot be denied. Few present-day poets have been so impatient of tradition and so zealous in seeking new and more flexible forms. But experimentation is for something: it leads to or produces a result. One would think that after twenty-five years of writing (*The Weary Blues* appeared in 1926), Hughes has long since found his form, his idiom and his proper, particular tone. If he has, let him be content with the apparatus he has fashioned, and let him go on now to say the things which many readers believe he, alone of American poets, was born to say.

Waste Land of Harlem

Babette Deutsch*

The title of this little book of verse tells a good deal about it. The language is that of the work-a-day urban world whose pleasures are sometimes drearier than its pains. The scene is the particular part of the Waste Land that belongs to Harlem. The singer is steeped in the bitter knowledge that fills the blues. Sometimes his verse invites approval, but again it lapses into a facile sentimentality that stifles real feeling as with cheap scent. As he bandies about the word "dream," he introduces a whiff of the nineteenth century that casts a slight mustiness on the liveliest context.

Langston Hughes can write pages that throb with the abrupt rhythms of popular music. He can draw thumbnail sketches of Harlem lives and deaths that etch themselves harshly in the memory. Yet the book as a whole leaves one less responsive to the poet's achievement than conscious of the limitations of folk art. These limitations are particularly plain in the work of a man who is a popular singer because he has elected to remain one. His verse suffers from a kind of contrived naiveté, or from a will to shock the reader, who is apt to respond coldly to such obvious devices.

It is a pity that a poet of undeniable gifts has not been more rigorous in his use of them. There are several contemporaries, especially among the French, whose subject matter and whose method are not too different from his, but who, being more sensitive artists, are also more powerful. Mr. Hughes would do well to emulate them.

*Reprinted from the *New York Times Book Review*, 6 May 1951, 23.

For Your Recreation and Reflection

G. Lewis Chandler*

Langston Hughes cannot shed his skin—no more than any author who has found his gait. This is normal and is not meant to be a criticism. For established authors have always stamped their personalities on their themes and techniques—hence adjectives like Shakespearean, Chaucerian, Wordsworthian, Emersonian, Miltonic, Byronic. Why not Hughesian? Everything Langston Hughes writes—poetry or prose; lyrics or narratives—bears his stamp: a predilection for common life and everyday situations treated with a paradoxical mixture of genial humor and uncomfortable satire. For thirty years he has done this in "Thirteen books and many stories, articles, plays, poems, opera librettos, and songs." In all of them, he injects a special type of worldliness, humor, pathos, tragedy, racism, eroticism, proletarianism, optimism. Hughes cannot shed his skin. And *Simple Speaks His Mind* again illustrates this fact. It is another *Shakespeare in Harlem*, or "Madam to You" (*One-Way Ticket*), or *Freedom's Plow* done narratively in a series of prose vignettes.

Divided into four parts ("Summer Time"; "Winter Time"; "Hard Times"; "Any Time"), *Simple Speaks His Mind*—beginning as a weekly series in the Chicago *Defender*—is a book of short-stories photographing the mind and chronicling the droll experiences of a semiliterate Harlemite, Simple, who confides in or talks back to his creator (Hughes) in much the same way as does Charlie McCarthy to Edgar Bergen. But Charlie is white and is an aristocrat. Simple is colored and is proletariat. This makes the vast difference between the two in what they see, feel, and say. Simple is completely race conscious, sex conscious, and bread conscious. Suffering from the impact of such consciousness, he makes articulate what the average Negro experiences, mentally and physically, in a segregated society struggling for integration. The capacity to feel as a Negro and to think and talk as a man makes Simple more than a marionette. He is a live character who, though not a capital debater, takes a definite stand on many issues within the areas of sex, security, and race relations. In the matter of sex, he stands firm for male supremacy; he is genuinely indifferent to his wife (Isabel), completely loves Joyce (his girl friend), thoroughly disrespects Zarita, with whom he drinks away his money and time. Again, he has not had much economic security, though he has drudged hard to earn so little. He says rather metaphorically: "These feet have supported everything from a cotton bale to a hongry [*sic*] woman. These feet have walked ten thousand miles working for white folks.... These feet have stood at

*Reprinted from *Phylon* 12 (Spring 1951):94–95. Copyright 1951. Reprinted with permission by *Phylon: Atlanta University Review of Race and Culture.*

altars, crap tables, free lunches, bars, graves, kitchen doors . . . hospital clinics, W.P.A. desks, social security railings, and in all kind of lines from soup lines to the draft." However, if Simple is anything, he is a thoroughgoing race man. He hates prejudice; he hates segregation; he hates the white man. But he loves Mrs. Roosevelt, and the Brooklyn Dodgers—because Jackie Robinson plays for them. He would have Negro officers pin medals on white soldiers. He would have Congress do less resolving and more solving. He stands squarely for F.E.P.C. and urges that Adam Powell should out filibuster Southern filibusters. Simple is indeed a character—a Hughesian character: ignorant and wise; selfish and magnanimous—a roustabout and angel; a coward and hero; an hypochondriac and idealist.

But the significance of this book does not lie wholly in the character and reflections of Simple. It lies also in Hughes' characteristic skill in treating the serious humorously, in deftly handling dialogue (he matches Hemingway here), in selecting and compressing material germane to mood, character, and action—in achieving unity out of diversity. In short, if you read *Simple Speaks His Mind* for sheer entertainment, you will not be disappointed. If you read it, however, for esthetic and civic implications, you will be challenged. This is just like Langston Hughes—in both verse and prose. He can simultaneously turn the corners of your mouth up or down. He cannot help it. That's his skin.

Black and Bubbling

Arna Bontemps*

Few people have enjoyed being Negro as much as Langston Hughes. Despite the bitterness with which he has occasionally indicted those who mistreat him because of his color (and in this collection of sketches and stories he certainly does not let up), there has never been any question in this reader's mind about his basic attitude. He would not have missed the experience of being what he is for the world.

The story "Why, You Reckon?," which appeared originally in *The New Yorker*, is really a veiled expression of his own feeling. Disguised as a young Park Avenue bachelor who comes with a group of wealthy friends for a night of colorful, if not primitive, entertainment in a Harlem night club, the Langston Hughes of a couple of decades ago can be clearly detected. He too had come exploring and looking for fun in the unfamiliar territory north of 125th Street. The kidnapping and

*Reprinted from the *Saturday Review of Literature* 35 (5 April 1952):17, by permission of the magazine.

robbing of the visitor in the story is of course contrived, but the young man's reluctance to rejoin his friends or to go back to the safety of his home downtown reflects the author's own commentary. "This is the first exciting thing that's ever happened to me," he has the white victim say to the amazement of his abductors as he stands in a coal bin stripped of his overcoat and shoes, his wallet and studs. "This was real."

Over this tale, as over most of the others in "Laughing to Keep from Crying," the depression of the Thirties hangs ominously, and it serves as more than just an indication of the dates of their writing. It provides a kind of continuity. After a while it begins to suggest the nameless dread which darkens human lives without reference to bread-lines and relief agencies.

A sailor, for example, makes a fast pick-up on the West Coast in jive talk ("Well, all reet! That's down my street! Name it!" "White Horse. Send it trotting!" "Set her up, and gimme a gin. What's your name, Miss Fine Brown Frame?") only to learn that the hard times and the general hopelessness of their lives frustrate pleasure even on that level.

A dark mother, in another story, consoles herself by attributing the prohibition-time ruin of her good-looking mulatto son to his Spanish blood. In another a rounder laughs at his misfortunes: "The next thing I knew I was in the hospital, shot everywhere but in my big toe. He fired on me point-blank—and barefooted. I was nothing but a target." And elsewhere a pushcart man becomes a sort of taperecorder for grim, depression-shaded, Saturday night talk on Eighth Avenue; a blossoming girl painter is denied through prejudice a prize she had won; and in the occasionally anthologized Christmas story "On the Road" an unemployed black man, given a quick brush-off by a high-toned preacher, breaks into a church and sees a vision of Christ before the police arrest him and start breaking his knuckles with their sticks.

Langston Hughes has practised the craft of the short story no more than he has practised the forms of poetry. His is a spontaneous art which stands or falls by the sureness of his intuition, his mother wit. His stories, like his poems, are for readers who will judge them with their hearts as well as their heads. By that standard he has always measured well. He still does.

In the Heart of Harlem

Carl Van Vechten*

It is not as generally known as it should be that Langston Hughes laughs with, cries with, and speaks for the Negro (in all classes) more understandingly, perhaps, than any other writer. Harlem is his own habitat, his workshop and his playground, his forte and his dish of tea. He is so completely at home when he writes about Harlem that he can afford to be both careless and sloppy. In his Simple books he is seldom either, and *Simple Takes a Wife* is a superior achievement to the first of the series, *Simple Speaks His Mind.* The new book is more of a piece, the material is more carefully and competently arranged, more unexpectedly presented, it is more brilliant, more skillfully written, funnier, and perhaps just a shade more tragic than its predecessor.

The genre has been employed extensively by other writers: by Finley Peter Dunne in "Mr. Dooley," by A. Neil Lyons in "Arthurs" and by Joel Chandler Harris in "Uncle Remus"; it is not too far, indeed, from the scheme of Gorky's *The Lower Depths.* The locale, however, is original, the taste truly Harlem, the matters discussed pertinent to the inhabitants, and the effect prevailingly evocative. The question and answer formula is used throughout the book, but frequently Simple's replies are somewhat protracted. The views expressed for the most part have a sane basis, and it is probable that at least a modicum of these are the beliefs of Mr. Hughes himself, although they find expression on Simple's tongue.

It would be easy to refer to the author as the Molière of Harlem who has just got around to writing his "School for Wives" (or is it his "School for Husbands"?). At any rate, Mr. Hughes (himself a bachelor) seems to be as cynical in his viewpoint as Colette, when he deals with the war between the sexes. Here and there he suggests that he is writing the Harlem version of Colette's "Cheri."

There are several women in this book. The first is Mabel, "the woman like water." "Do you want me to tell you what that woman was like? Boy, I don't know. She was like some kind of ocean, I guess, some kind of great big old sea, like the water at Coney Island on a real hot day, cool and warm all at once—and company like a big crowd of people—also like some woman you like to be alone with, if you dig my meaning. Yet and still, I wasn't in love with that woman." Simple passes on to other conquests and to discussions of other ideas. For instance, in chapter seven there is a long and cheerful lesson in English grammar and usage. Chapter two is an addition to the folklore of Harlem, in

*Reprinted from the *New York Times,* 31 May 1953, 5. Copyright 1953 by the New York Times Company. Reprinted by permission.

which Simple describes the custom under which each roomer in a house is allotted a different ring.

> "Joyce's landlady objects to my ringing her bell late. Seven rings is a lot for ten or eleven o'clock at night. So I go at six-thirty or seven. Then, I have only to ring once, which is seven times. If I go later and nobody hears me, I have to ring twice, which is fourteen times. And, if I ring three times, which is three times seven, twenty-one times is too much for the landlady's nerves."
>
> "Colored rooming houses certainly have a lot of different bell signals," I commented.
>
> "You told that right," said Simple. "I lived in a house once that had up to twenty-one rings, it were so full of roomers. Mine was twelve. I often used to miss count when somebody would ring. One time I let in another boy's best girl friend—she were ringing eleven. He had his second best girl friend in the room."

Somewhat further on, there is a learned discussion of Bebop, which Simple declares has its origin in the police habit of beating up Negroes' heads. "Every time a cop hits a Negro with his billy club that old club says Bop! Bop! . . . BE-BOP! . . . MOP! . . . BOP!"

In chapter sixteen, Simple and Joyce, his lady friend, warmly discuss the disturbing subject of miscegenation. There is a touch of Mr. Hughes' special kind of poetry in his description of night: "Night, you walk easy, sit on a stoop and talk, stand on a corner, shoot the bull, lean on a bar, ring a bell and say 'Baby, here I am.'" In chapter fifty-seven, Simple dilates on the unpleasant connotations of the word black. "'What I want to know,' asks Simple, 'is where white folks gets off calling everything bad black? If it is a dark night, they say it's black as hell. If you are mean and evil, they say you got a BLACK heart. I would like to change all that around and say that the people who Jim Crow me have a WHITE heart. People who sell dope to children have got a WHITE mark against them. And all the gamblers who were behind the basketball fix are the WHITE sheep of the sports world.'"

This is true humor with a bite to it, spoken in the authentic language of the 135th Street and set down good-naturedly in a book which tells us more about the common Negro than a dozen solemn treatises on the "race question."

[Review of *Simple Stakes A Claim*]

Luther Jackson*

In a foreword to this book of sketches on the life and times of Harlem's Jesse B. Semple, better known as Simple, the author suggests that a humorous Negro monthly magazine would be a welcome addition to American life. Expanding this idea, Hughes lists 16 potential contributors—including cartoonists, journalists, novelists and comedians, ranging from Jackie Mabley to George S. Schuyler.

This reviewer would never sell a Hughes' idea short, for his literary brainchildren have enjoyed some 30 years of artistic success. But with Simple, Hughes has struck commercial gold. He has exploited the vein to the extent of three books and a Broadway theatrical production, all adapted from newspaper columns from the *Chicago Defender.*

Hughes' and Simple's successes are well deserved, for in Jesse B. the author has created a tribute to the dignity of a common man who happens to be a Negro. This is no mean trick. In hands less skilled than Hughes', portrayals of some Negroes—"colleged" as well as "uncolleged"—are apt to wind up in racial embarrassment.

Of the 16 named by Hughes for his magazine, Harlem's Nipsey Russell is one comedian who can tell a racial joke in an integrated audience without any loss of dignity. Perhaps America's best literal interpreter of life among poor, urban Negroes is the cartoonist, Ollie Harrington. His "Mr. Bootsie" is a constant delight to his fellow Negroes, but he is hardly the type they would want to introduce to a new white neighbor.

Although Hughes' awareness of racial sensitivities is clearly shown in the Broadway production of *Simply Heavenly*, which he obviously tidied up for white consumption, *Simple Stakes a Claim* is pure, unadulterated Grade-A Simple. In this new book, Simple reaches new glorious heights of racial indignation and disgust. Everybody goes when Simple's wagon comes.

During "White History Week," for example, Simple would have President Eisenhower appear on television "knocking a golf ball all the way from Augusta, Georgia, to Alabama . . . right into Reverend King's Montgomery backyard."

"Just as Negro History Week honors a few good white folks," Simple continues, "so White History Week should honor a few good black folks." During whites' week, Simple says he would pay Louis Armstrong "to blow his horn whilst the bombs is blowing up the dance hall."

"Then I would hire Nat King Cole," Simple adds, "to sing again in Birmingham and act out how he was knocked down by white folks on the stage but did not even get mad about it."

*Reprinted from *Crisis* 64 (May 1957):576–77, by permission of the journal.

Both North and South share Simple's outrage. Simple says he told his alcoholic cousin Minnie from Virginia that "the rainbow with the pot of gold at its end arches right on over New York City. It must terminate somewhere out in the Atlantic Ocean, because it sure do not end in Harlem."

Yet, Simple continues; "None of them jim-crow states is worth the left hand corner of 125th St. and Lenox Ave. All of them states put together, from Virginia to Florida and Florida to Texas, I would not trade for one barstool in New York."

But Mississippi is the state which Simple singles out for special attention. In an hilarious stroke of double entendre, Simple tells what Mississippi ain't from and what he would do when he got to heaven, attached his wings, and flew over the state. ("As I fly, I hope none of them Dixiecrats has time to get his umbrella up.").

Simple comments on everything from the atomic age to chicken necks, but no matter what he starts talking about, he always winds up on the racial problem. But, alas, Simple is almost forced to admit that he doesn't know the answers. In this exchange between himself and the author:

> "Inscrutable are the ways of
> nature," says Hughes.
> "Screwed up and unscrew-
> able," Simple replies.

Sermons and Blues

James Baldwin*

Every time I read Langston Hughes I am amazed all over again by his genuine gifts—and depressed that he has done so little with them. A real discussion of his work demands more space than I have here, but this book contains a great deal which a more disciplined poet would have thrown into the waste-basket (almost all of the last section, for example).

There are the poems which almost succeed but which do not succeed, poems which take refuge, finally, in a fake simplicity in order to avoid the very difficult simplicity of the experience! And one sometimes has the impression, as in a poem like "Third Degree"—which is about the beating up of a Negro boy in a police station—that Hughes has had to hold the experience outside him in order to be able to write at all.

*Reprinted from the *New York Times*, 29 March 1959, 6. Copyright 1959 by the New York Times Company. Reprinted by permission.

And certainly this is understandable. Nevertheless, the poetic trick, so to speak, is to be within the experience and outside it at the same time—and the poem fails.

Mr. Hughes is at his best in brief, sardonic asides, or in lyrics like "Mother to Son," and "The Negro Speaks of Rivers." Or "Dream Variations":

To fling my arms wide
In some place of the sun,
To whirl and to dance
Till the white day is done.
Then rest at cool evening
Beneath a tall tree
While night comes on gently,
    Dark like me—
That is my dream!

To fling my arms wide
in the face of the sun.
Dance! Whirl! Whirl!
Till the quick day is done.
Rest at pale evening . . .
A tall, slim tree . . .
Night coming tenderly
    Black like me.

I do not like all of "The Weary Blues," which copies, rather than exploits, the cadence of the blues, but it comes to a remarkable end. And I am also very fond of "Island," which begins "Wave of sorrow / Do not drown me now."

Hughes, in his sermons, blues and prayers, has working for him the power and the beat of Negro speech and Negro music. Negro speech is vivid largely because it is private. It is a kind of emotional shorthand—or sleight-of-hand—by means of which Negroes express, not only their relationship to each other, but their judgment of the white world. And, as the white world takes over this vocabulary—without the faintest notion of what it really means—the vocabulary is forced to change. The same thing is true of Negro music, which has had to become more and more complex in order to continue to express any of the private or collective experience.

Hughes knows the bitter truth behind these hieroglyphics: what they are designed to protect, what they are designed to convey. But he has not forced them into the realm of art where their meaning would become clear and overwhelming. "Hey, pop! / Re-bop! / Mop!" conveys much more on Lenox Avenue than it does in this book, which is not the way it ought to be.

Hughes is an American Negro poet and has no choice but to be acutely aware of it. He is not the first American Negro to find the war between his social and artistic responsibilities all but irreconcilable.

Laura and Essie Belle

Gilbert Millstein*

About the most convenient capsule description of this short novel by Langston Hughes is to call it a sort of Negro *Elmer Gantry*, mildly sardonic where Sinclair Lewis' gaudy assault on evangelism was savage, and gently funny where the other was undeviatingly and harshly satirical. As a literary work, *Tambourines to Glory*, is skillful and engaging. The consistently high quality of Hughes' production over the years is, considering its great quantity, a remarkable phenomenon and the mark of an exuberant professionalism. Yet in the end, the book is a minor effort, a side glance at a major phenomenon, with an industriously contrived climax.

The phenomenon Hughes has chosen to examine here is the rise (over the last couple of decades) of a vagrant type of church in Harlem—the sidewalk, storefront, basement, apartment, abandoned-theatre church. It is fervently Christian, of course, in its origins; it is carefully non-denominational. Sometimes it is used, with equal fervor, by hustlers out for an easy buck. In his two protagonists—the stolid Essie Belle Johnson, and the free-and-easy Laura Wright Reed—Hughes offers the reader an example, respectively, of the honest Christian and the cynical operator in search of a Cadillac.

Essie Belle and Laura team up with nothing much more between them than a tambourine; an $18.50 installment-plan Bible and a street corner. From there, they progress to an apartment and from there to an aged theatre. Along the way, Essie Belle piles up riches in Heaven and enough money to bring her pretty teen-age daughter, Marietta, up North to live with her. Sister Laura acquires her Cadillac and her fancy man. This character, Big-Eyed Buddy Lomax, has a connection downtown with the numbers people. He first persuades Laura to bottle tap-water and sell it as consecrated essence of Jordan. Later, she gives out "lucky texts" from the Bible at prayer meetings to increase his numbers take.

The odd partnership between Essie Belle and Laura is ended violently when Buddy tries to move in on Marietta and is stabbed to death

*Reprinted from the *New York Times Book Review*, 23 November 1959, 51.

by Laura. Laura tries to pin the killing on Essie Belle but is first turned in by another member of the congregation who witnessed it. She repents behind bars. Essie Belle praises the Lord and goes on to greater glory.

What has happened here, in the reviewer's opinion, is that the author elected to avoid the serious implications of his thesis. He has done it gracefully, it is true, but he *has* avoided it. The technique of using humor to make a point in deadly earnest is as old as mankind—Hughes has done it innumerable times and with great success in his "Simple" stories. In *Tambourines to Glory*, it has fogged up the things he clearly meant to say.

A Trio of Singers in Varied Keys

Dudley Fitts*

. . . Langston Hughes' twelve jazz pieces cannot be evaluated by any canon dealing with literary right or wrong. They are non-literary—oral, vocal, compositions to be spoken, or shouted, to the accompaniment of drum and flute and bass. For that matter, they speak from the page, the verses being set in capitals throughout; and there is a running gloss of dynamic signs and indications for the proper instrument to use at the moment. (One of these signs, used repeatedly, is "TACIT," which I find as obscure as Mr. Ciardi's "dust like darks howling," unless indeed it stands for the orchestral indication *tacet.*)

In this respect, *Ask Your Mama* goes back to Vachel Lindsay and his *Congo*; and I suppose it is fair to say that this is stunt poetry, a night-club turn. The fury of indignation and the wild comedy, however, are very far from Lindsay. The voice is comparable to that of Nicolás Guillén, the Cuban poet, or of the Puerto Rican Luis Palés Matos—comparable, not imitative; insistent and strong in what is clearly a parallel development.

*Reprinted from the *New York Times Book Review*, 29 October 1961, 16. © 1961 by the New York Times Company. Reprinted by permission.

Jazz as a Marching Jubilee

Rudi Blesh*

Jazz and the blues have been with us all the years of this century; Langston Hughes not quite that long—"jazz poetry" began in 1926 with his well-remembered volume, *The Weary Blues*. Now, with *Ask Your*

*Reprinted from the *New York Herald Tribune Books*, 26 November 1961, 4.

Mama, it begins to appear that perhaps we have as little understood the poet as the music. For, though jazz is "good time" music, within it has always been something else, something dark yet shining, harsh yet gentle, bitter yet jubilant—a Freedom Song sung in our midst unrecognized all these years. Just so, opening the covers of this gaily-designed book is to find poetry whose jazz rhythms hide the same fire and steel.

Langston Hughes is no mere observer of Africa's stormy, shuddering rise and the awakening of dark-skinned peoples all over the world. They are his people; he sings their marching Jubilees. But Langston Hughes is also an American: he sings to all of us, of the freedom that must go to all before it can be freedom for any.

"Go Ask Your Mama" is the retort—half-derisive, half-angry—to the smug, the stupid, the bigoted, the selfish, the cruel, and the blind among us, all those to whom these truths that America was built upon, are, even today, not yet self-evident.

With this great theme, a talented poet finds a universal voice. Like Satchmo's golden trumpet and Yardbird's blues-haunted alto, the poetry of Langston Hughes sings for—and to—all of us.

[Review of *The Panther and the Lash*]

W. Edward Farrison*

This collection of poems was prepared for publication by the author himself and was in press when he died. Its title was derived from two recent outgrowths of matters racial in America—the Black Panthers and the white backlash. The work is dedicated to Mrs. Rosa Parks of Montgomery, Alabama, who refused to move to the back of a bus, "thus setting off in 1955 the boycotts, the sit-ins, the Freedom Rides, the petitions, the marches, the voter registration drives, and *I Shall Not Be Moved*."[1] Twenty-six of the seventy poems in the collection were selected from Hughes's previously published volumes of verse. The other forty-four are herein published in one volume, seventeen of them having formerly appeared in periodicals, and twenty-seven now appearing in print for the first time. All of them are indeed poems of our times, for all of them pertain directly or indirectly to the Negro's continuing struggle to achieve first-class citizenship in America. The poems are written in short-line verse or in occasional rhymes, by both of which Hughes's poetic work has long been distinguished.

*Reprinted from the *CLA Journal* 3 (March 1968):259–61, by permission of the journal.

The selections are grouped under seven headings, the first of these being "Words on Fire." In this group is "The Backlash Blues," one of the two title poems in the collection. Not only is this one of the new poems but also it has been said to have been the last poem that Hughes submitted for publication before he died. It is an emphatic expression of determined aggressiveness against the opponents of civil rights for Negroes. Also in the first group and new is "Black Panther," the other title poem. Avowedly militant, like Claude McKay's "If We Must Die," this poem has for its theme the determination of black men to give no further ground to oppressors but to stand and fight back desperately, like a panther when cornered.

More ironical than militant is the group called "American Heartbreak," in whose initial poem with the same title a Negro declares generically that "I am the American heartbreak— / The rock on which Freedom / Stumped its toe—" Still more ironical as a whole is the group called "The Bible Belt"—a group in which life principally in Alabama and Mississippi is portrayed at its non-Biblical worst. Singularly memorable as well as new is the poem in this group entitled "Birmingham Sunday," which consists of reflections on the deaths of four little Negro Sunday-school girls who were victims of the bombing of a church in Birmingham on September 15, 1963.

Especially noteworthy at present because of prevailing international affairs is the small group entitled "The Face of War." Two provocative poems in this group are "Mother in Wartime" and "Without Benefit of Declaration," both of which deal with the common failure to understand the wherefores and the futility of war. The mother, "Believing everything she read / In the daily news," was quite unaware that both sides "Might lose." Meanwhile the draftee must go "Out there where / The rain is lead," but is told "Don't ask me why. / Just go ahead and die." What simple, convincing explanation is there to give him? Alas one is reminded of John Dewey's all but forgotten observations that "The more horrible a depersonalized scientific mass war becomes, the more necessary it is to find universal ideal motives to justify it"; and "The more prosaic the actual causes, the more necessary is it to find glowingly sublime motives."

The group puckishly entitled "Dinner Guest: Me" satirizes a variety of things. Its title poem, which is based on a personal experience,[2] ridicules white quasi-liberalism. "Un-American Investigators" coarsely twits a Congressional committee for its arbitrary methods of dealing with persons summoned before it. "Cultural Exchange," the longest poem in the volume, envisions a radical change in Southern culture in the sociological sense—an inversion of the positions of Negroes and white people in the South with Negroes living "In white pillared mansions," white sharecroppers working on black plantations, and Negro children attended by "white mammies." The bouleversement imagined in this poem, which was published in *Ask Your Mama* in 1961, is more ingeniously recounted in "Rude Awakening" in *Simple's Uncle Sam*, which was published in 1965.

Finally there is the group called "Daybreak in Alabama"—a title in which there is a ray of hope for the optimistic, among whom Hughes belonged. As should now be evident, two of the poems in this group rang with prophetic tones when they were published in *One-Way Ticket* in 1949. Observing that first-class citizenship would never come "Through compromise and fear," "Democracy," now entitled "Freedom," left no doubt that other means of achieving it must be employed. And admonishing America to "Beware the day" when Negroes, "Meek, humble, and kind," changed their minds, "Roland Hayes Beaten," now entitled "Warning," foreshadowed at least implicitly the various freedom movements mentioned in the dedication of *The Panther and the Lash.* From the beginning of his career as an author, Hughes was articulate in the Negro's struggle for first-class citizenship. It is indeed fitting that this volume with which his career ended is a vital contribution to that struggle as well as to American poetry.

Notes

1. *The Crisis: A Record of the Darker Races*, 74 (June, 1967):251.
2. Langston Hughes, *The Big Sea: An Autobiography* (New York: 1940), pp. 312–326.

Poetry and Chronicle

Laurence Lieberman

Langston Hughes's new poems, written shortly before his death last summer, catch fire from the Negro American's changing face. To a degree I would never have expected from his earlier work, his sensibility has kept pace with the times, and the intensity of his new concerns—helping him to shake loose old crippling mannerisms, the trade marks of his art—comes to fruition in many of the best poems of his career: "Northern Liberal," "Dinner Guest: Me," "Crowns and Garlands," to name a few.

Regrettably, in different poems, he is fatally prone to sympathize with starkly antithetical politics of race. A reader can appreciate his

*Reprinted from *Poetry* 112 (August 1968):339. © 1968 by the Modern Poetry Association. Reprinted by permission of the editor of *Poetry*. This is excerpted from a review essay which begins on 337.

catholicity, his tolerance of all the rival—and mutually hostile—views of his outspoken compatriots, from Martin Luther King to Stokely Carmichael, but we are tempted to ask, what are Hughes's politics? And if he has none, why not? The age demands intellectual commitment from its spokesmen. A poetry whose chief claim on our attention is moral, rather than aesthetic, must take sides politically. His impartiality is supportable in "Black Panther," a central thematic poem of "The Panther and the Lash." The panther, a symbol of the new Negro militancy, dramatizes the shift in politics from non-violence to Black Power, from a defensive to an offensive stance: Hughes stresses the essential underlying will to survival—against brutal odds—of either position. He is less concerned with approving or disapproving of Black Power than with demonstrating the necessity and inevitability of the shift, in today's racial crisis.

"Justice," an early poem that teaches the aesthetic value of rage, exhibits Hughes's knack for investing metaphor with a fierce potency that is as satisfying poetically as it is politically tumultuous:

That justice is a blind goddess
Is a thing to which we black are wise:
Her bandage hides two festering sores
That once perhaps were eyes.

But this skill is all but asphyxiated in many of the new poems by an ungovernable weakness for essayistic polemicizing that distracts the poet from the more serious demands of his art, and frequently undermines his poetics. Another technique that Hughes often employs successfully in the new poems is the chanting of names of key figures in the Negro Revolution. This primitive device has often been employed as a staple ingredient in good political poetry, as in Yeats's "Easter 1916." But when the poem relies too exclusively on this heroic cataloguing—whether of persons or events—for its structural mainstay, as in "Final Call," it sinks under the freight of self-conscious historicity.

ARTICLES AND ESSAYS

General

Three Negro Poets

Nancy Cunard*

It was the anti-Fascist German writer, Ludwig Renn, a commander in the People's Army in Spain, who said, speaking at the Second International Writers' Congress in Madrid, that the role of the militant writer was no longer to "make stories but to make history." It was another German, Gustav Regler, who went to the attack of Brunete pencil in hand. Both have been fighting against the Fascists for a year; how many other writers have been, are in, and will go to Spain? For now, to all those who have a true sense of life, writing perforce rhymes with fighting.

It was Vaillant-Couturier, speaking at the end of this same congress in Paris, who said: "The period of the *phrase* is over." And Vishnevski, young Soviet author who is also the producer of *The Sailors of Kronstadt*, who was the first there to crystallise an expression for this need of the artist to link himself in the most material way possible with the struggle, "the mobilisation of the writers."

And it was the militia-men, those of the Spanish soil, who used to say to me in Spain, at the very start of the war: "After this, no more hatreds between men, no more frontiers. You, writers and intellectuals, it is impossible for you *not* to be with us." Are not these words true?

From over thirty countries came writers to the Paris Congress, testifying their hatred of Fascism, their most active sympathy and concern for the people of Republican Spain. And from the Western World came as delegates three young militants, three poets of colour. *Of Colour.* Which means that, to them, Fascism has been a familiar enemy since birth—for what else are imperialism, race prejudice, the myriad brutalities and injustices of the dominant white? All three spoke at the Congress, and, as each said, it is unthinkable for the Negro to be else than anti-Fascist. For the Fascist ideology heaps every insult and indignity

*Reprinted from *Left Review* 3 (October 1937):529–31. This is excerpted from the complete article which runs to p. 536.

on the coloured races; it is an attempt to reinstitute, to prolong, slavery. If the names of these posts are not yet widely known in England, they are greatly honoured—and feared—in their own countries: Langston Hughes, of America; Nicolas Guillen, of Cuba; Jacques Roumain, of Haiti.

All three are in their thirties. Guillen and Roumain have been imprisoned by the dictatorships of their respective islands: "for subversive activities" (i.e. defending the working class in their writings, "thinking dangerously," coming out with the facts). Roumain was arrested on the preposterous charge of sending a bomb by post, but actually because he possessed certain books which are on sale in all other countries, and for speaking on behalf of the innocent Scottsboro boys and of the black workers in his native land. He was held incommunicado a long time, did twenty months in jail. A companion imprisoned with him died of the terrible conditions there; they hoped he would die, too. At length he was released, he had been in prison before, at that, for similar political reasons. He left Haiti and came to Europe.

Guillen, who is now recognised even by his enemies as the greatest poet in Cuba and the Spanish Caribbean, has worked many years in journalism and printing. At one time he was editor of *Mediodia*, an important Left weekly. He, too, has spent some time in prison, for political reasons, in the Castillo del Principe, Havana's sinister, and famous jail.

Langston Hughes has had an adventurous round-the-world life. He has worked his way repeatedly in the U.S. and in France; studied and travelled throughout the Soviet Union, and been arrested (for that fact) while passing through Japan; spoken, lectured and read his poems and those of other militant poets in hundreds of meetings, and colleges throughout America and the West Indies. Much breaking down of race prejudice in America, in precisely such milieus and for this reason, is due to him. He has battled from the start for the liberation of the Scottsboro martyrs, and has been the link beween Latin-American and American culture, besides being an excellent translator, and one ever ready to help other young poets. Yes, Langston Hughes is the travelling star of coloured America, the leader of the younger intellectuals. The American reactionary authorities and the Fascists of the U.S. have tried incessantly to browbeat and silence him, but the resilient determination of this fighter for Equal Rights (of class as well as colour) has always come through winning. Nor can any white (I say this mainly, but not only, to America) ever hope to impress this mulatto poet with any sort of "race complex."

One of the main characteristics of Langston Hughes is ease—both of manner and of mind. The impression of one who skates over the difficulties with grace and with tact. But this charm of manner does not signify that Langston is not very much *all there.* And doubtless the particular problems which face the coloured intellectual in that strange mixture of ferocity, ignorance and, more recently, appreciation of talent, which is the U.S.A., have engendered this manner—an excellent "professionalism" in the handling of life. Add to this a lovely sense of humour and a heart that forgets never friend—nor foe.

To the credit of this very active life are the following works: *Weary Blues, Fine Clothes of the Jew* (poems); *Not Without Laughter,* his first novel; *The Ways of White Folks,* inter-racial stories of the Afro-American and the American, written in a magnificent and objective manner; amongst these, *Red-Headed Baby,* a perfect modern classic on colour. Another of these stories, *Mulatto,* on lynching, has run as a play for months in the States—banned, of course, in the South. Lastly, Hughes came from Hollywood, where he wrote the libretto for the opera that is being composed there by a coloured musician, William Grant Still. Five short volumes of poetry are coming out simultaneously in California; in one of these, *A New Song,* the poet addresses himself to Revolution and to the workers of the world. And there is also *Scottsboro Limited,* a one-act drama on that long heartache. Many of these are translated in Russia, a few in France.

"He never forgets his comrades," said Roumain as we listened together to Langston's words at the Congress. And it is true that this speech of America's delegate spans the universe in its allusion to the fighters and oppressed of all lands.

Hughes's Black Esthetic

Onwuchekwa Jemie*

Perhaps the most remarkable fact about Langston Hughes's career in his singlemindedness. It would appear that relatively early in life he discovered what he wanted to do and how he wanted to do it, and he spent most of his life doing it. What he wanted to do was to record and interpret the lives of the common black folk, their thoughts and habits and dreams, their struggle for political freedom and economic well-being. He wanted to do this using their own forms of expression: their language, humor, music, and folk verse. And consistently, through a career of four decades and in the face of opposition not only from much of the white world which constituted the majority of his audience,

*Reprinted from Onwuchekwa Jemie, *Langston Hughes: An Introduction to the Poetry* (New York: Columbia University Press, 1976), 1–32, by permission of the author and the publisher.

but from an important portion of his black audience who objected to his matter and manner, Hughes did what he set out to do, and did it well. Unlike Countee Cullen, for instance, who wore his color like a shroud,[1] Hughes wore his "Like a banner for the proud / . . . Like a song soaring high."[2]

To say that Hughes matured early, or that he was singleminded, is not to say that he did not grow and change. In his first book he demonstrated mastery of his craft and spoke in his own authentic voice, but still his technique improved over the years, and his angle of attack shifted with the times. What is unique, however, is that for a career that lasted so long, Hughes's subject matter and his commitment to black folk expression remained stubbornly undiluted. And literary history has vindicated him, for the "temples for tomorrow" which he and his fellow believers in a distinctive black art insisted on building, regardless of the pleasure or displeasure of their contemporaries, are the temples in which pan-African artists of the *negritude* school worshipped in the 1930s and 40s, and in which Afro-American artists of the 1960s and 70s still worship.[3]

Hughes's argument in favor of a distinctive black art was hammered out in the heat of controversy. Even before the abolition of slavery, what might be called the Great Black Controversy had already made its appearance, for instance, in the heated debates over "colonization": should blacks be integrated into the body politic (could they?), or should they (could they?) be repatriated en masse to West Africa? First of all, are they Americans, or are they Africans? Or are they some separate new mutation, neither one nor the other? Or are they (could they be) all three? The question of Afro-American identity is at the heart of the Great Black Controversy. The terms of the dispute have shifted from generation to generation, but its core is perennial, its essence unchanging. As W. E. B. DuBois so accurately stated it, the black man in America is burdened with a double identity, a "double-consciousness. . . . two souls, two thoughts, two unreconciled strivings; two warring ideals in one dark body."[4] The controversy involves an effort to bring this double consciousness to an end; an effort to achieve a harmonious, healthy self by excising one or other of the two selves, or by welding them together into a single and undivided whole.

The terms of the dispute involve the means by which a healthy self is to be achieved. Through the years, a portion of the Afro-American people have urged and attempted total effacement of the African self and total assimilation into white American culture and identity. But the very conditions (racism) which created that option also made it impossible to fulfill. So that in the final analysis, the most enduring voices in Afro-American life and history have been those who have insisted that the African identity is fundamental and definitive, that it is a positive structure onto which additions borrowed from white American culture and elsewhere are to be built, not a structure to be razed and replaced.

Without reducing the pan-African dimensions of his vision, Marcus Garvey could be said to have been the purveyor, during the 1920s, of this latter, "nationalist" position, a position of which Langston Hughes was to become the most eloquent articulator in the field of arts and letters. Although rarely acknowledged by the black writers of his day, and frequently maligned by his fellow-Jamaican Claude McKay, Garvey's magnetic presence, and the sweeping power of his philosophy, nevertheless left a firm imprint on the art and thought of the period, including Claude McKay's. Indeed, it was Garvey's rhetoric, his pride of ancestry, his dreams of a rebuilt and once again powerful African homeland, that provided the infrastructure of the nationalist revival that was the Harlem Renaissance.

As in other eras, black nationalism did not flourish unchallenged in the 1920s, whether in politics and public life, or in the arts. In 1925 Garvey was thrown into the penitentiary, a political prisoner on trumped-up charges, and his Universal Negro Improvement Association fell into disarray. Garvey had a program and was therefore "politically dangerous"; the artists and intellectuals had none and could carry on their debates "harmlessly."

In June 1926, in the pages of a prestigious journal, two young black writers, Langston Hughes and George S. Schuyler, joined issue on the esthetic aspects of the Great Black Controversy. Schuyler's lofty contempt for the idea of a distinctive black art and esthetic, so highly touted especially in the pages of Alain Locke's anthology, *The New Negro* (1925), is unmistakable even from the title of his essay, "The Negro-Art Hokum."[5] Black art, he declares, exists in Africa, but to suggest that it also exists in America is "self-evident foolishness." Spirituals, blues, ragtime, jazz and the Charleston, usually regarded as examples of a distinct black art, are, he argues, not so much the products of an ethnic group as of a peasant class or caste, and as such have less in common with the soul and sense of Afro-Americans as a people than with peasant music and dance the world over. "Any group under similar circumstances would have produced something similar," and it is sheer coincidence that this peasant group happens to be black. Furthermore, he argues, this peasant music is not universal to blacks: it is "foreign" to blacks in the North, in the West Indies and in Africa, and therefore could no more be regarded as "expressive or characteristic of the Negro race than the music and dancing of the Appalachian highlanders or the Dalmatian peasantry are expressive or characteristic of the Caucasian race."

As with folk art, so with the self-conscious productions of the middle classes: these are, he argues, "identical in kind with the literature, painting, and sculpture of white Americans: that is, [they show] more or less evidence of European influence." Black artists are trained in the same schools as white artists, and their work could not therefore be said to be "expressive of the Negro soul."

Schuyler founds his argument on the faulty premises that "education and environment [have been] about the same for blacks and whites," and that the Afro-American is "merely a lampblacked Anglo-Saxon," a white man in everything but skin color. He assumes that blacks have already been assimilated into white culture; that America is a melting pot and blacks have not only melted but have melted as totally and irretrievably as the various waves of European immigrants were presumed to have melted. And if the latter could not (or did not choose to) claim for themselves an ethnic culture and art distinct from the "mainstream," how could (or why should) blacks?

Schuyler paints a picture of harmonious assimilation so replete with half-truths and inaccuracies that it deserves to be quoted at length:

> Again, the Aframerican is subject to the same economic and social forces that mold the actions and thoughts of the white Americans. He is not living in a different world as some whites and a few Negroes would have us believe. When the jangling of his Connecticut alarm clock gets him out of his Grand Rapids bed to a breakfast similar to that eaten by his white brother across the street; when he toils at the same or similar work in mills, mines, factories, and commerce alongside the descendants of Spartacus, Robin Hood, and Erik the Red; when he wears similar clothing and speaks the same language with the same degree of perfection; when he reads the same Bible and belongs to the Baptist, Methodist, Episcopal, or Catholic church; when his fraternal affiliations also include the Elks, Masons, and Knights of Pythias; when he gets the same or similar schooling, lives in the same kind of houses, owns the same makes of cars (or rides in them), and nightly sees the same Hollywood version of life on the screen; when he smokes the same brands of tobacco and avidly peruses the same puerile periodicals; in short, when he responds to the same political, social, moral, and economic stimuli in precisely the same manner as his white neighbor, it is sheer nonsense to talk about "racial differences" as between American black man and the American white man.[6]

Schuyler ignores profound differences, qualitative and quantitative, in favor of superficial resemblances. And when he carries his argument to Europe, he is equally obtuse: overlooking the very crucial differences between the black experience in Europe and in America, he argues that if European blacks such as Pushkin, Latino, and the elder and younger Dumas could produce work that "shows the impress of nationality rather than race," why not blacks in America? "Why should Negro artists of America vary from the national artistic norm when Negro artists of other countries have not done so?"

Schuyler's perspective, compounded from inaccurate observation and wishful thinking, was not uncommon in that era, nor, for that matter, in earlier and later eras. Nor was his perspective unique to blacks. Many white liberals were just as anxious to forget the shameful history of slavery and inequality, and to usher in a new era largely by proclaiming that such an era was already there. Or they subscribed, sometimes unconsciously, to some variant of the myths of the "white man's burden," "manifest destiny" and "civilizing mission"—except that they were convinced that the mission had already been accomplished, and that blacks had been (or should be or were about to be) duly inducted to full membership in white civilization. In the face of such high purpose and good will it seemed almost impertinent to insist on racial differences. Such a high-minded believer, for instance, was Melville Herskovits, a white liberal scholar whose reputation today rests superbly on his contention, supported with a mass of data painstakingly gathered from all over the pan-African world, that blacks in the Americas did not lose nearly as much of their African culture and life style as was popularly supposed, but in fact retained so much of it as to distinguish them radically from the white "mainstream."[7] But that was in 1941. Back in 1925, young Herskovits was blithely asserting, as Schuyler does, that the black community of Harlem was "just like any other American community. The same pattern, only a different shade": "What there is today in Harlem distinct from the white culture which surrounds it, is, as far as I am able to see, merely a remnant from the peasant days in the South. Of the African culture, not a trace. . . . Black America represents a case of complete acculturation."[8]

Seconding Schuyler but with none of his vitriol were such leading black writers of the period as Countee Cullen and William Stanley Braithwaite. Cullen was notorious for his repeated insistence that he saw himself and wished that others would see him as "a poet, not a Negro poet."[9] In so saying he was of course, as he explained, defending himself against the condescension and double standard of some white critics. But at the same time there is the implication, much as Schuyler would have it, that there were or should be no discernible differences between black artists and white artists, or between black art and white art. And if, as Schuyler claims, education and environment have been about the same for black artists and white artists, and if, as would have to be the case, their education and environment were controlled by the mainstream, then it follows that the art they produce would be faithful replicas of the mainstream sensibility and tradition. In other words, their art would be white. Thus, there would be no discernible differences in the artistic productions of blacks and whites only when the mainstream sensibility and tradition are exclusive or dominant in those productions; when, in other words, the black artist has erased from his work all traces of his African heritage. Only then (if then) would he be, in the given time and place that is racist America, just another artist instead of a Negro or black artist. For over and beyond the fact of color, it is his concern with the black situation and, above all, the black sensibility which suffuses his work, that defines the black artist.

Countee Cullen swam against the current of his natural inclinations only to find, to his dismay, that the racial theme would not leave him alone, and that his strongest poems tended to be those rooted in his experience as a black man, those that defined him as a distinctly black poet. "A number of times I have said I wanted to be a poet and known as such and not as a Negro poet. . . . In spite of myself, however, I find that I am activated by a strong sense of race consciousness. This grows upon me, I find, as I grow older, and although I struggle against it, it colors my writing. . . . Somehow or other I find my poetry treating of the Negro, of his joys and sorrows, mostly of the latter and of the heights and depths of emotion which I feel as a Negro."[10]

But no writer of the period went further out of his way to avoid identifiably racial themes and styles than William Stanley Braithwaite. His poetry, almost uniformly colorless and lifeless, is a study in assiduous racial self-effacement. In addition, Braithwaite was an editor and critic with a national reputation, but few of his readers were aware that he was black. And it seems he was anxious to keep it that way; and if Claude McKay is to be believed, he even advised younger black writers to do the same: "He [Braithwaite] said that my poems were good, but that, barring two, any reader could tell that the author was a Negro. And because of the almost insurmountable prejudice against all things Negro, he said, he would advise me to write and send to magazines only such poems as did not betray my racial identity."[11] The willful McKay rejected this advice, arguing that his [McKay's] poetic expression was "too subjective, personal, and tell-tale"—not unlike those of the poets he admired most—to be thus suppressed and whitewashed: "I felt more confident in my own way because, of all the poets I admire, major and minor, Byron, Shelley, Keats, Blake, Burns, Whitman, Heine, Baudelaire, Verlaine and Rimbaud and the rest—it seemed to me that when I read them—in their poetry I could feel their race, their class, their roots in the soil, growing into plants, spreading and forming the backgrounds against which they were silhouetted. I could not feel their reality without that. So likewise I could not realize myself writing without conviction."[12]

Langston Hughes, too, was of a quite different persuasion from Schuyler, Cullen, and Braithwaite. He would have agreed with McKay that the writers usually held up as examples of raceless universality were indeed as time-and-place-bound as anyone, as expressive of their particular *race, moment, milieu,* to borrow Taine's classic formulation,[13] as the most consciously racial artist could ever be. If their works carry universal appeal, it is not because they avoid the local and particular, but, if anything, at least partly because they so intimately and profoundly embrace the local and particular as particles of general human experience. But more on universality later.

In his seminal essay "The Negro Artist and the Racial Mountain," written as a rebuttal to Schuyler and appearing in *The Nation* the following week,[14] Hughes contends that far from being totally assimilated into American life, blacks had in fact retained their ethnic distinctness. Hughes does not go into the historical reasons for this, but he welcomes it, regards it as an asset for black people and a boon to the black artist. For he sees it as one of the writer's challenges to translate into literature this ethnic distinctness, with its "heritage of rhythm and warmth, [and] incongruous humor that so often, as in the Blues, becomes ironic laughter mixed with tears." Whatever his medium, the work of the black artist who uses material from his own rich culture cannot but be identifiably racial. Therefore for him to wish to be regarded as an artist but not as a black artist—as though the two things were mutually exclusive—is, in Hughes's view, in effect to turn his back on his identity, to cast aspersions on his heritage, to wish to be other, to wish he were white. It is to accept the white world's definition of his people as ugly and inferior, unworthy of serious exploration in art.

Longstanding white prejudice against things black (Braithwaite's argument) is, in Hughes's view, no excuse for such abandonment of self. Prejudice has bred self-hate—"this urge within the race toward whiteness," this reaching for "Nordic manners, Nordic faces, Nordic art . . . and an Episcopal heaven" so common among the Negro middle and upper classes. But the artist's mission is to counter self-hate, not to pander to it. "To my mind, it is the duty of the younger Negro artist, if he accepts any duties at all from outsiders, to change through the force of his art that old whispering 'I want to be white,' hidden in the aspirations of his people, to 'Why should I want to be white? I am a Negro—and beautiful!' "

The writer who accepts this mission will find a sturdy ally and positive example in the black masses, the "low-down folks," with their confident humanity, their indifference to white opinion, their *joie de vivre* amidst depressing circumstances. Unlike the middle and upper classes, the common folk "accept what beauty is their own without question." They are the uncontaminated reservoir of the strength of the race, the body and vehicle of its traditions. In their lives, and in black-white relations "with their innumerable overtones and undertones," the writer will find "a great field of unused material ready for his art. . . . an inexhaustible supply of themes." The writer will also find two temptations, two monsters conspiring to swallow him: he must steer a straight course between the scylla of stereotyped portraits of blacks so beloved by much of the white public who comprise the majority of his audience, and the charybdis of idealized and compensatory portraits sometimes demanded by vigorous defenders of the race. The transforming energy of his art would have to radiate from accurate representations of black people in all their human splendor—and human deformity. "We know we are beautiful. And ugly too." Like other races of mankind, the black race is neither uniformly admirable nor uniformly despicable. There is therefore no need either to apologize for it or to exaggerate its virtues. The artist's currency is reality and truth, and he should offer these "without fear or shame." He should create with an inner freedom, refusing to give in to pressure from any camp. "If white people are pleased we are glad. If they are not, it doesn't matter. . . . If colored people are pleased we are glad. If they are not, their displeasure doesn't matter either." Succumbing to pressure from the racist majority is unthinkable. But it is equally important to avoid, on the one hand, artistic propaganda of the "best foot forward" type, and, on the other, the romanticism of the "primitivists" and bohemians for whom all things black or non-Western are beautiful and pure. Hughes calls instead for *critical realism*—a balanced presentation as free from chauvinism as from apology, a view in which blacks are neither monsters nor saints but richly and complexly human.

Hughes's essay amounts to a manifesto, an apologia not only for his work but for the black art of his generation and the generations before and after him. It is an admonition to his fellow writers to "cast down your bucket where you are" (if I might quote Booker T. Washington in such an alien context). The creators of great black music and dance, including the blues and jazz artists of the day, invariably rooted themselves in black tradition. Naturally and without urging, they have utilized the vast cultural wealth into which they were born. This is what gives their music its depth and power. Their music is black folk music elaborated and extended. Of the black masses, Hughes says: "Jazz is their child." What black musicians have done with black folk music, he argues, black writers, sculptors, painters, and dramatists can and should do with black folklore and folk life. Moreover, writers like Dunbar and Chesnutt, and in Hughes's own day, Jean Toomer, had already shown that it could be done in literature. "Now I await the rise of the Negro theater. . . . And within the next decade I expect to see the work of a growing school of colored artists who paint and model the beauty of dark faces and create with new technique the expressions of their own soul-world."

In his own work, Hughes attempted to follow the example of Dunbar and Chesnutt and the musicians: "Most of my own poems are racial in theme and treatment, derived from the life I know. In many of them I try to grasp and hold some of the meanings and rhythms of jazz." His "theme" (matter) is black people and their concerns; and for his "treatment" (manner, style, technique, point of view) he adopts the technical resources of the culture: black idiom and dialect; black folk humor, including the tragicomic irony of the blues; the form and spirit of jazz. The "meaning" of black life in America, Hughes implies, is to be found in black music: in the *blues*, a philosophy of endurance of the apparently unendurable ("pain swallowed in a smile"); in *jazz*, subversion of the status quo ("revolt against weariness in a white world, a world of subway trains, and work, work, work"). *Black music, in short, is a paradigm of the black experience in America.* It is not only black America's most profound cultural expression and "product," but, in its most complex, representative contemporary forms of blues and jazz, it encompasses the polar extremes of that experience, namely: *resignation*, or the impulse towards assimilation; and *revolt*, or the impulse towards nationalism.

Implicit in Hughes's essay is a call for the reeducation not only of the black artist but of the black middle class public as well; a call for the emergence of a black audience that would take the initiative in recognizing and patronizing black talent, instead of waiting for white public approval first. To do this, of course, implies a proper valuation of black culture, the communal recognition, in other words, of a black esthetic. A critically alert black audience, Hughes seems to imply, might have been able to prevent the works of important artists, such as Dunbar and Chesnutt, from going out of print, or Jean Toomer's *Cane* from suffering so total a commercial failure. But of course what is involved here, among other things, is the ancillary issue of black control of black publishing, an issue which Hughes does not explore.

Hughes's insistence on a distinct black art utilizing black themes and styles is an affirmation of black existence, a recognition of the fact that Afro-Americans are a distinct people within the American nation, and an insistence on their continued ethnic distinctness. Hughes, in other words, could accurately be described as a nationalist although he did not articulate his position in those terms. The revolutionary potential which he perceives in black art will be redefined and given ideological direction in the following decade.

The 1930s was a Marxist decade for Hughes as it was for some other American writers. Communism promised an alternative to the capitalist order which feeds on racism and the exploitation of the working classes. It emphasized the identity of interests of all oppressed peoples, regardless of race or nationality, and called upon them to unite and overthrow their oppressors. Unlike Richard Wright, Hughes never specifically joined the Communist Party; but he found in its ideology a fresh perspective, an effective tool of social analysis, a broader conception of the black struggle as part of a world-wide struggle against oppression.

Hughes dates his involvement with communism as commencing with the Scottsboro case in 1931 and ending with the Nazi-Soviet Pact of 1939.[15] Under Marxist influence he reworked his esthetic somewhat, giving it a consciously political and ideological thrust. The central document of this period is his essay "To Negro Writers,"[16] a militant blueprint for an expository and hortatory literature serving the cause of the proletarian revolution. It should be pointed out right away that except for its vocabulary and tone of urgency, this essay says little that was not already said in "Racial Mountain." Hughes calls on black writers to address their work to the masses, both black and white, and seek to unify them, and to use their work to lay bare the true nature of America: the hypocrisy of philanthropy and of organized religion; the betrayal of workers by white labor leaders, and of the black masses by false Negro leaders who were controlled by the ruling class; the manipulation of patriotic sentiment in support of wars which destroy the citizenry and profit the ruling class. The black writer should use his art to expose "all the economic roots of race hatred and race fear."

In short, Hughes calls for a functional literature, or what Jean-Paul Sartre was to call a *littérature engagée*, a literature committed to revolution. As he sees it, the black writer has a clear and unequivocal role in the struggle for revolution, for that struggle is being waged for him and his. Writers who place themselves aloof from the struggle at best condemn themselves to social irrelevance; at worst, they are aiders and abetters of the status quo, partners in oppression, whether they are of it or not.[17] In the literature struggle there is no place for the romanticisms of the Harlem Renaissance which celebrated the gaiety and rhythm of black life; and the tragicomic laughter of the blues is to be transformed into laughter that "chokes the proletarian throat and makes the blood run to fists that must be increasingly, militantly clenched to fight the brazen terror" of capitalism. Black laughter has to become menacing, as in Burck's cartoons, foreshadowing "the marching power of the proletarian future," a future which the oppressor cannot laugh off so easily.[18]

Such a literature cannot have at its center celebrations of nature, of moonlight and roses:

> Or would you rather write about the moon?
>
> Sure, the moon still shines over Harlem. Shines over Scottsboro. Shines over Birmingham, too, I reckon. Shines over Cordie Cheek's grave down South.

Write about the moon if you want to. Go ahead. This is a free country.[19]

Hughes's radical concerns during the 1930s are reflected in *Scottsboro Limited* (1932) and *A New Song* (1938), and in numerous uncollected magazine pieces written to Marxist specifications. Years later, he was to describe these works as "outdated," unrepresentative of his ideals: "I was strongly attracted by some of the promises of Communism, but always with the reservations, among others, of a creative writer wishing to preserve my own freedom of action and expression—and as an American Negro desiring full integration into our body politic."[20]

The fact that this plea was entered on the occasion of a Congressional witchhunt against communists and "fellow travelers" should automatically render it suspect. Hughes's immersion in communist dogma may not have been total, but neither the shock of the Nazi-Soviet Pact of 1939 nor the punitive terror of Senator McCarthy's committee in the early 1950s was enough to annul his communist sympathies. On the contrary, he held on to his Marxist vision and terms of rhetoric—with this concession, that, no doubt for reasons of expediency, he routed them underground, as it were: he continued to publish Marxist proletarian poetry and prose in various periodicals, but, with the significant exception of "Good Morning Stalingrad," which was included in *Jim Crow's Last Stand* (1943), he excluded them from his collected works.[21]

Hughes abandoned Marxist terms of rhetoric in his collected works, but not the principle of literature as an instrument of social change. On the contrary, as we have seen, he had enunciated this principle as early as "The Negro Artist and the Racial Mountain," and only elaborated and extended it in his more specifically Marxist declarations. Indeed it would be fair to say that "The Negro Artist and the Racial Mountain" is the basic document of his esthetic, and future pronouncements are restatements and elaboration, footnotes and glosses. In subsequent statements he downplays the hortatory functions of literature and expands on the expository. He continues to stress the social responsibility of the black artist, and no doubt saw his own career as fulfilling that socially responsible role. In "My Adventures As A Social Poet,"[22] his most important restatement of the 1940s, Hughes defines himself as a primarily social as distinct from a primarily lyric poet, thus giving formal recognition to a bias which became visible quite early in his career. "The major aims of my work have been to interpret and comment upon Negro life, and its relations to the problems of Democracy."[23] Taking the American Dream as his cue, Hughes had developed his poetic metaphor of the dream, a concept which was to become a strategic theme, a major artery running through the body of his work. The dream is transmitted along two channels: first, as an assortment of romantic fantasies and desires, including the desire for a life rich in love and adventure; secondly, as the dream of political freedom and economic well-being. The latter is an extension of the former, and it is this latter that is the "dream deferred" of the black man and black race. Although he did not coin the phrase itself until *Montage of a Dream Deferred* (1951), which came in mid-career, his dual vision of the dream is introduced in his first book, *The Weary Blues.*

As might be expected, the theme of the "dream deferred" finds its fullest expression in his social poetry, whereas his lyric poetry is the particular vehicle of the dream as romantic fantasy ("love, roses and moonlight").[24] *The Weary Blues* (1926) was evenly divided between social and lyric poetry; but his second volume, *Fine Clothes to the Jew* (1927) showed an unmistakable swing toward social themes, so much so that one contemporary critic heralded it as a "final frank turning to the folk life of the Negro."[25] Hughes preferred his second book for precisely the reason that it was less conventionally lyrical, "more impersonal, more about other people than myself . . . about work and the problems of finding work, that are always so pressing with the Negro people."[26]

Hughes did not then cease writing lyric poetry, but the balance had tipped heavily in the direction of social poetry. In "My Adventures as a Social Poet" he explains why: much as he had stated in his Marxist essay, beauty and lyricism, or poems about love, moonlight, and roses, are "really related to another world, to ivory towers, to your head in the clouds, feet floating off the earth," rather than to the everyday world of poverty and Jim Crow in which he was born and bred and still lived. In his world, the sentiment of romantic love, for example, is all too often twisted and blasted by the economic imperative as the ghetto wasteland of *Montage of a Dream Deferred* was to demonstrate. Roses are fine, but "almost all the prettiest roses I have seen have been in rich white people's yards—not in mine." And as for moonlight, "sometimes in the moonlight my brothers see a fiery cross and a circle of Klansmen's hoods. Sometimes in the moonlight a dark body swings from a lynching tree."[27]

Roses and moonlight, yes, but their thorny dark sides. To Hughes's thinking, the social realities of black life in America are so overwhelming that the concerned black artist could not but make these realities the central matter of his art. Hughes is not attempting to legislate subject matter for the black artist; but he is insisting, stubbornly, that given the Afro-American situation, beauty and lyricism, love and moonlight and roses, are insufficient matter. Whether they are sufficient for the rich, middle class, comfortable and white, is something else.

Because he deals with sensitive public issues, the social poet invariably runs into censorship and confrontations with authority, with the upholders of the status quo. Hughes was no exception, and "My Adventures as a Social Poet" is, among other things, a humorous inventory of the unpleasantness he had been subjected to because of his poetry.

It was during this same period (1940s) that to the question, "Is Hollywood Fair to Negroes?" Hughes answered an unequivocal "No."[28] Hollywood, he argues, presents a one-sided picture of blacks: the same age-old stereotypes dating back to minstrelsy. The motion picture industry had in effect replaced the minstrel stage, and had become perhaps the most powerful propaganda and educational medium yet invented. "Millions of people take what they see on the screen to be an approximate representation of contemporary life in America," and accordingly find in the fantasies, caricatures, distortions, and lopsided portrayals of blacks a confirmation of their inherited prejudices and further reason to continue supporting (or ignoring) the oppression of blacks.

Hollywood propaganda is even more effective in that black actors lend their talents to this racial betrayal. The economic argument, says Hughes, "explains, but can never excuse" black complicity. The artist's social responsibility overrides all others; and he calls on black actors to cease and desist: "it is time now, actors, for you-all to stop."

If Hollywood were fair to blacks, he argues, it would present a rounded, realistic picture of black life in which "educated, well-groomed, self-respecting" blacks appear at least as regularly as loose women and comic servants.

The need for realistic portraiture of black life is a theme that Hughes returns to again and again. From his earliest days his own work had been repeatedly denounced by "respectable" Negroes for focussing on lower-class life and for daring to portray prostitutes, pimps, and other disreputable characters. But Hughes had always resisted the "best foot forward" argument. His theory and practice was to portray the ugliness as readily as the beauty of black life, the unsavory as readily as the admirable. Critical realism demanded both. However, toward the end of his career we find what on the surface might appear like a shift toward the position of his critics. Dismayed by the alienation and despair, foul language, and explicit sexuality with which so much of the literature of the early 1960s by and about blacks was replete, Hughes urged black artists "not necessarily to put our *best* foot forward, but to try at least to put a balanced foot forward, so that we do not all appear to be living in a *Cool World* in *Another Country* in the *Crazy House of the Negro* in which the majority of *The Blacks* seem prone to little except the graffiti of *The Toilet* or the deathly behavior of a *Slow Dance on the Killing Ground*."[29] If there is a shift, it is more semantic than substantive, for the demand for a "balanced foot" is a demand for proportion, for an exacting fidelity to fact which would preclude biassed and exaggerated concern with either the unsavory aspects of black life, or the admirable. The politics of the civil rights era would, in his view, make such balance even more urgent: "The Negro image deserves objective, well-rounded (rather than one-sided) treatment, particularly in the decade of a tremendous freedom movement in which all of us can take pride."[30]

I said before that Hughes recognized music as the quintessential Afro-American art. Into music more than any other art form, black people from earliest times have poured their daily concerns. Music accompanied the African, newly arrived in the Americas, at work in the slavemaster's house and in his fields, and at work or play in the slave quarters. From slavery to freedom, music has provided a slave for the cut and hurt soul and body. It has served as an ecstasy-inducer, an escape, a manifestation and affirmation of the transcendent beauty of life.

Hughes's experience with black music began in early youth: "It was fifty years ago the first time I heard the Blues on Independence Avenue in Kansas City. Then State Street in Chicago. Then Harlem in the twenties with J. P. and J. C. Johnson and Fats and Willie the Lion and Nappy playing piano—with the Blues running all up and down the keyboard through the ragtime and the jazz. House rent party cards. I wrote *The Weary Blues*. . . ."[31] He came to maturity in the 1920s, a decade of overwhelming importance for the development and diffusion of black music, and the classic age of both jazz and blues. From their homes in the lower Mississippi River region (for jazz, New Orleans in particular), jazz and blues had traveled north with the Great Migration and established themselves in various regional centers, especially Kansas City, Chicago, and New York. And through the 1920s each of these regions developed its own styles and orientations (Kansas City jazz, for instance, was noted for its strong blues orientation), but not in isolation: all the while a process of cross-fertilization, of fusion and diffusion, was taking place. This cross-fertilization, and the spread of black music on the national and international scene, was greatly facilitated by the introduction of commercial phonograph recordings of black music in 1923. In fact the so-called jazz age may be said to have properly begun in 1923 when black music first became readily available on phonograph records.

It was during that same decade that Fletcher Henderson, based in New York, developed precision in jazz instrumentation, introduced orchestral arrangements, and organized the jazz orchestra into what was to become the Big Band. Many of the best known names in jazz, including Coleman Hawkins, J. C. Higginbotham, Russell Procope, Benny Carter, Ben Webster, Don Redman, Cootie Williams, Dicky Wells, and Eddie Barefield played in Henderson's band at one time or another. Even Louis Armstrong, the first great jazz virtuoso, played briefly with Henderson before returning to Chicago to found his famous Hot Five and Hot Seven groups. And it was in the 20s that Armstrong established what came to be regarded as the standard jazz structure, including solo and improvisation, and introduced the trumpet as the prime solo instrument (a preeminence which the trumpet was to enjoy until the 1940s when Charlie Parker supplanted it with the saxophone). And while these developments were taking place, Duke Ellington, a young man, was learning his craft and was to emerge in the following decade as one of the great jazz leaders.

It was also in the 1920s that the classic blues structure was established: three lines of lyric, the second line a repetition in whole or part of the first line, the third line rhyming with the first two. The era was dominated by women singers, worthy successors to Ma Rainey, with Bessie Smith as "Empress" and Ida Cox, Victoria Spivey, and the other Smiths—Mamie, Laura, Clara and Trixie—in attendance. These singers were frequently accompanied by jazz orchestras. Toward the end of the 20s, however, commercial interest in classic blues declined, and by 1929 the blues women had been forced out of the spotlight and out of the recording studios. The recording industry had discovered fresh sources: male blues singers who had recently migrated north to Chicago. And the depression ushered in the era of Blind Lemon Jefferson, Bill Broonzy, Tampa Red, and Georgia Tom (Thomas A. Dorsey, "Father of Gospel Music") and their Chicago city blues.[32]

In 1921 Hughes persuaded his father to send him to college in New York rather than in Europe, out of "an overwhelming desire to see Harlem. . . . the greatest Negro city in the world."[33] And he more than saw Harlem: he attended shows, followed the progress of black musicians, singers, and actors, and sat up in the gallery night after night watching Noble Sissle and Eubie Blake's "Shuffle Along"—the black musical which became the prototype of the Broadway musical comedy.[34]

Hughes, in short, was from his early youth a sensitive and involved witness to the growth and maturation of what in the mid-1920s emerged as classic black music; and even in that early era black music was universally acknowledged as the greatest indigenous American music (as against the musics inherited from Europe), and was enjoyed and imitated the world over. In tune as he was with the currents of life around him, it is not surprising that he came to regard this music as a paradigm of the black experience and a metaphor for human life in general. "The rhythm of life / Is a jazz rhythm," he declared in 1926.[35] Conversely, a poem in jazz rhythm has the rhythm of life; to capture the rhythm of jazz is to capture (as an aspect of, a slice of) life. And the rhythm of life: long, incantative, endless like the jazz, with its riffs and breaks and repetitions, with love and joy and pain interchanging, alternating in "Overtones, / Undertones, / To the rumble of street cars, / To the swish of rain"[36]—the hard fierce beat of street cars and rain an appropriate urban metaphor for the movements and vibrations and cycles of which human life is composed.

Jazz is everyone's life, everyone's heartbeat: "Jazz is a heartbeat—its heartbeat is yours"[37]—whoever you may happen to be and even if you cannot comprehend or define it. Recalling Louis Armstrong's rebuke—"Lady, if you have to ask what it is, you'll never know"—Hughes says: "Well, I wouldn't be so positive. The lady just might know—without being able to let loose the cry—to follow through—to light up before the fuse blows out."[38] The lady may feel and know in her marrows "the meanings and rhythms of jazz" even if she is unable to articulate them.

Again, jazz is "a montage of a dream deferred. A great big dream—yet to come—and always *yet*—to become ultimately and finally true."[39] And that same or other lady, "dressed so fine," who has not bop but Bach on her mind, if she was to listen she would surely hear, "way up in the treble" of the Bach, that same music of a dream deferred, that same "tingle of a tear," of mixed sorrow and hope that is jazz.[40] Jazz is process-music, a dynamic force whose thrust is forwards towards the future. It is anti-static, developing, moving. Its impulse is recalcitrant, rebellious, revolutionary. With its free and easy, open-ended improvisational construction, its invitation to joy and the uninhibited movements of the body, jazz constitutes rebellion in a puritan society. It goes against the grain of the accepted and expected in music (Western music) and in life (Puritan Christian life). It challenges the established: Western industrial society and its weary materialism, its demand of "work, work, work," its destruction of human beings with inhuman machineries. Jazz carries within it the vision of an alternative mode of life; and just as continued black existence in circumstances of deprivation is a reproach to American democracy, so is jazz (and by extension, all black music and culture) a rival and subverter of the mainstream culture.

It should of course be pointed out that this view of jazz as a music of revolt is not entirely original with Hughes. It is adapted from J. A. Rogers's essay of the year before.[41] Also, the bohemian rebellion in the America of the 1920s, of which the Harlem Renaissance was a manifestation, generally viewed black music and culture in this light. And this view is in keeping with the history of European thought of the last half millenium which, surveying the world through the elaborate manichean binoculars of Judeo-Christianity, saw in the non-Western world, its manners and morals, an exotic "other" antithetical to the West, a magnetic pole whose powerful attraction is fatal to "civilization" and "reason," whose embrace would mean drastic change or revolution. What Hughes did was to convert this idea into an operative principle of black art.

When Hughes speaks of jazz in these terms he is to be understood to mean black music in general. Jazz in this broad sense stands for the

Afro-American Spirit out of which the total musical culture flows. Jazz, he says, is a big sea "that washes up all kinds of fish and shells and spume and waves with a steady old beat, or off-beat."[42] That Spirit, that sea, is the source of blues, gospel, and rock and roll, as it was of spirituals, work songs, field hollers, shouts, and ragtime. These varied emanations of the Spirit come and go: "A few more years and Rock and Roll will no doubt be washed back half forgotten into the sea of jazz."[43] And other forms will emerge and take its place.

Life, too, is such a sea: "Life is a big sea / full of many fish. / I let down my nets / and pull."[44] And literature: "Literature is a big sea full of many fish. I let down my nets and pulled. I'm still pulling."[45] Jazz and literature are the same sea of life out of which all things of human significance and meaning emerge, and to which they return. Jazz, literature, and life share the same heart-beat and constitute a unity. Each is a metaphor for the others; in their structures and significances they parallel and illuminate and reinforce one another.

Hughes therefore proposes to pour life as he knows it into the molds so magnificently provided by black music. He proposes to do in literature what others were doing in music, to create, in effect, a literary equivalent of black music. He wants to create literature that is as *rooted* in the life of the folk and as *deep* and *accessible* to them as black music is. Literature in which the masses of black people would find their life experiences reflected and illuminated; in which the community would find itself expressed. Accordingly, he devoted the opening section of his first book to "poems mostly about jazz in which I tried to capture the rhythms of jazz and the blues,"[46] and named the volume *The Weary Blues*. His subsequent works are similarly suffused with the spirit of black music. *Fine Clothes to the Jew* opens and closes with a section of blues poems, with a section of gospel shouts, moans, and prayers in the center, and a multitude of ballads, blues, and jazz poems in between. Of the eight sections of *Shakespeare in Harlem* (1942), three are entirely in the blues mode, the rest mixtures of jazz, blues, ballads, and free verse. *One-Way Ticket* (1949) and *The Panther and the Lash* (1967) include poems in the blues and jazz modes. But it is in *Montage of a Dream Deferred* (1951) and *Ask Your Mama* (1961) that Hughes attains the highest peaks of complexity in his life-long effort to integrate his poetry with music. *Montage* is written in the powerful be-bop mode of the mid-40s and the 50s, and *Ask Your Mama* is a straight jazz-poem sequence set to the accompaniment of jazz and blues. Hughes's major poetry lives and breathes, to use his own phrase, in the "shadow of the blues."[47]

The characteristic quality of Hughes's poetry is simplicity, and one of its strategic ingredients is humor. His poems are stark, unadorned, crystal-clear surfaces through which may be glimpsed tremendous depths and significant human drama. In "The Negro Artist and the Racial Mountain" he spoke of his efforts to capture and express the ironic humor of the blues. (In his Marxist pronouncement he seemed to consider humor out of place—unless it was the laughter of a triumphant proletariat—and the two Marxist-influenced works are uncharacteristically humorless.) Hughes never seemed to take himself too seriously, was rarely in too deadly earnest to be able to laugh. However tragic or serious his subject matter, he usually manages to see the humorous and ironic side—which is precisely what the blues artist does. Commenting on black life and its relations to the problems of democracy is a serious matter; but still, Jim Crow is so "desperately and grotesquely funny"[48] that the comedy often outweighs the tragedy. He criticizes the "serious colored magazines" like *The Crisis* and *Phylon* which "evidently think the race problem is too deep for comic relief." But most black people do not think so; it is the ability of the black masses to see the funny side that has helped them survive oppression. "Colored people are always laughing at some wry Jim Crow incident or absurd nuance of the color line. If Negroes took all the white world's daily boorishness to heart and wept over it as profoundly as our serious writers do, we would have been dead long ago."[49] But of course Jim Crow is not always funny. "The race problem in America is serious business, I admit. But must it *always* be written about seriously?"[50] To Hughes, lack of humor is unnatural, something akin to lack of humanity. And he speculates that there might be a connection between humorlessness and rabid racism and brutality.

> Personally, I know that not all white Americans practice Jim Crow at home and preach democracy abroad. But what puzzles me about those who do is their utter lack of humor concerning their own absurdities.
>
> I have read that Hitler had no sense of humor either. Certainly, among Hitler's hunting trophies today are thousands of human heads, scattered across the world in the bloody mud of battle. I suppose the greatest killers cannot afford to laugh. Those most determined to Jim Crow me are grimly killing America.[51]

Afro-American humor represents a profound criticism of America, a sane antidote to an insane circumstance. And if Jim Crow humor is sometimes macabre, it is a quality inherent in the situation, certainly not the fault of the victims. Following the example of the black masses and of the blues, Hughes seeks to capture, in all its density and complexity, that humor that is "too deep for fun."[52]

Hughes's people are the lower classes, the urban folk: porters, bell boys, elevator boys, shoe shine boys, cooks, waiters, nurse maids, rounders, gamblers, drunks, piano players, cabaret singers, chorus girls, prostitutes, pimps, and ordinary, decent, hard-working men and women. These are the "low-down folks, the so-called common element,"[53] the ones who crowd the street corners, stoops, bars, beauty shops and barber shops and churches, hot rented rooms and stuffy apartments all over the black sections of cities. They are the dwellers on Beale Street, State Street and Seventh Avenue, Central Avenue and Lenox Avenue. They are the ones who made Chicago's South Side and New York's Harlem both famous and infamous. Hughes has himself listed them in "Laughers."[54] His treatment of them is stark and unsentimental, capturing at once the wretchedness and beauty of their lives. As Charles S. Johnson has pointed out, there is in Hughes's depiction of them "no pleading for sympathy, or moralizing; there is a moment's blinding perception of a life being lived fiercely beneath the drunken blare of trombones, or in blank weariness of the Georgia roads."[55]

Hughes's particular world is the inner city and, specifically, Harlem. The "colored middle class" or "black bourgeoisie" rarely appear, and when they do they are " 'buked and scorned." The disrespect was mutual: the "black bourgeoisie" and their spokesmen denounced his work vehemently. Critic Allison Davis called Hughes's poems "vulgar," "sordid" and "sensational."[56] Benjamin Brawley, whom Hughes has described as "our most respectable critic," wrote of *Fine Clothes to the Jew* that "it would have been just as well, perhaps better, if the book had never been published. No other ever issued reflects more fully the abandon and vulgarity of its age."[57] To them and the many who thought like them, Hughes's answer is a shrug of the shoulders: "I have never pretended to be keeping a literary grazing pasture with food to suit all breeds of cattle."[58] The "respectable" people hated his preference for blues and jazz and the cabaret and its habitués over the middle class (white) arts and places and people. Hughes's supreme creation, Jesse B. Semple, and his exemplary urban domain, for instance, were to the "black bourgeoisie" no more than reminders of a heritage they were struggling to leave behind in their "progress forward and upward." To Hughes, however, it is the Simples that are the soul of the race and that most deserve to be expressed in black art. It is the *simple* folk, their life styles, their dreams, their stupidities, and their deep wisdom that Hughes immortalizes in his work.

Hughes's speech on accepting the Spingarn Medal in 1960[59] is an homage to these simple folk, an expression of profound gratitude for the things they gave him. They are, he says, the source and substance of his poems and stories, plays and songs. It was their singing in the little churches of his childhood that opened his ears to "the lyric beauty of living poetry not of books." It was a blind guitar player on a Kansas City street corner singing, "Going down to the railroad, lay my head on the track—but if I see the train a-coming, I'll jerk it back," that opened his eyes to the laughter and sadness of the blues which was to become a part of his own poetry. It was the old folks recounting their memories of slavery that made possible his great heritage poems such as "The Negro Speaks of Rivers," "Aunt Sue's Stories," "Mother to Son," and "The Negro Mother." And it was the endless stories, tall tales, jokes, comments, and complaints, which he assiduously listened to in black communities across the nation, that enabled him to create the irrepressible, lifelike figure of Jesse B. Semple and the cycle of Simple tales. Hughes's relentless mining of his literary black gold is in keeping with his prescription in "Racial Mountain" and a lesson for all black writers.

Hughes entertained no doubts as to the sufficiency and greatness of the molds provided by black music, nor of black life as subject matter. On the question of whether such black matter and manner could attain "universality," Hughes in his Spingarn Speech issued a definitive answer:

> There is so much richness in Negro humor, so much beauty in black dreams, so much dignity in our struggle, and so much universality in our problems, in us—in each living human being of color—that I do not understand the tendency today that some American Negro artists have of seeking to run away from themselves, of running away from us, of being afraid to sing our own songs, paint our own pictures, write about ourselves—when it is our music that has given America its greatest music, our humor that has enriched its entertainment media, our rhythm that has guided its dancing feet from plantation days to the Charleston, the Lindy Hop, and currently the Madison. . . .
>
> Could you possibly be afraid that the rest of the world will not accept it? Our spirituals are sung and loved in the great concert halls of the whole world. Our blues are played from Topeka to Tokyo. Harlem's jive talk delights Hong Kong. Those of our writers who have concerned themselves with our very special problems are translated and read around the world. The local, the regional can—and does—become universal. Sean O'Casey's Irishmen are an example. So I would say to young Negro writers, do not be afraid of yourselves. You are the world.[60]

Hughes's confidence in blackness is a major part of his legacy, for the questions he had to answer have had to be answered over again by subsequent generations of black artists. Black culture is still embattled; and Hughes provides a model for answering the questions and making the choices. Whether they say so or not, those who, like Cullen and Braithwaite, plead the need to be "universal" as an excuse for avoiding racial material, or for treating such material from perspectives rooted in alien sensibilities, invariably equate "white" or "Western" with "universal," and "black" or "non-Western" with its opposite, forgetting that the truly universal—that is, the foundation elements of human experience, the circumstances attending birth, growth, decline, and death, the emotions of joy and grief, love and hate, fear and guilt, anger and pain—are common to all humanity. The multiplicity of nations and cultures in the world makes it inevitable that the details and particulars of human experience will vary according to time, place, and circumstance, and it follows that the majority of writers will dramatize and interpret human life according to the usages of their particular nation and epoch. Indeed, the question whether a writer's work is universal or not rarely arises when that writer is European or white American. It arises so frequently in discussions of black writers for no other reason than that the long-standing myth of white superiority and black inferiority has led so many to believe that in literature, and in other areas of life as well, the black particular of universal human experience is less appropriate than the white particular.

The question of universality, in the terms in which it has invariably been raised, usually by hostile critics of black literature, is a false issue. The real issue is whether the drama is lively, whether the portrait is vivid and memorable, whether the interpretation is perceptive and accurate; in short, whether the work is well done. But of course, to be able to judge whether the work is well done, one must have standards of judgement derived from the nation, epoch, and milieu from which the work itself derives. One cannot judge a European sonnet and a Japanese haiku by exactly the same criteria; nor a German lieder and an Afro blues; nor a Beethoven symphony and a Coltrane set; nor Wordsworth's "Intimations of Immortality" and Hughes's "Mother to Son." The cultures are that distinct, each autonomous, governed by its own laws. Which brings us to the central issue involved in the idea of a black esthetic, namely, the extrapolation of standards for judging black art from within the culture-sensibility.

Whatever the technical excellences of a work of imaginative literature by a black writer, if it is rooted in an alien sensibility it cannot be central or important to blacks. On the other hand, mere fidelity to the culture-sensibility is not enough: what is required is a happy marriage of technical excellence and sensibility. Langston Hughes is a great poet because, among other things, he combines *to an unusual degree* such poetic virtues as economy, lucidity, evocativeness of imagery, and mellifluousness of movement, with a deep-rooted fidelity to the Afro-American sensibility. He is therefore a proper source for extracting some of the governing principles of black art, some of the standards by which black literature, and in particular black poetry, is to be judged. These principles are implicit in his work, as follows:

(1) His central concern is the central concern of the Afro-American people, namely, their struggle for freedom. His is, from first to last, a socially committed literature, utilizing, for a brief period of time at least, a Marxist ideological frame. Whether he says it in these terms or

not, one of the aims and ultimate effects of his work is the raising of our consciousness, the strengthening of black people in their struggle in America and elsewhere. Starting with black America, he expands into the pan-African world in his later years, especially in *Ask Your Mama* and *The Panther and the Lash.*

(2) Hughes has anchored his work in Afro-American oral tradition, thereby serving the vital function of cultural transmission. His utilization of black musical forms—jazz, blues, spirituals, gospel, sermons—is the most comprehensive and profound in the history of Afro-American literature. Blues appears in various guises: in the strict, classic, three-line verse form; in a variety of modified verse forms paralleling the infinite variety of folk blues which do not conform to the classic verse pattern; and in the blues spirit and world view incorporated into non-blues poems and into his prose fiction and drama. His jazz poems are appropriately cast in free verse and often in black idiom, and they approximate the bouncy rhythms and light-hearted exuberance of the music. Much of his poetry is in Afro-American idiom, usually Northern urban, sometimes unalloyed, sometimes modified with standard English usage. In addition, he employs the forms and techniques of contemporary "street poetry"—rapping, signifying, toasting, and playing the dozens (ranking, screaming, sounding, louding, woofing). The effect of his choice of forms, and his ease and smoothness in handling them is to situate his works brilliantly and unequivocally in the black world.

(3) Finally, Hughes's black characters are authentic and memorable, the greatest of them being Jesse B. Semple, Madam Alberta K. Johnson of "Madam to You," and the Black Madonnas of "Mother to Son" and "The Negro Mother." Hughes is essentially *a dramatic poet.* He speaks in a multiplicity of voices, through a multitude of personas, each of them the purveyor of authentic black attitudes—attitudes, views, and lifestyles that are as heterogeneous as the Afro-American population.

The matter of greatness in art extends beyond the narrow limits of formal esthetics into the realm of politics. However well written, it is unlikely that a pro-Nazi novel would be well received at this time in Western Europe or America, or in Israel. If blacks had greater power in America, it would have been impossible, for instance, for William Styron to receive a national award for his novel, *The Confessions of Nat Turner* (1968), which turns history upside down, slanders the Afro-American people and their heroes, and mocks black suffering. In short, the question of an autonomous black esthetic is centrally involved with politics, as all questions of esthetics, which is itself a branch of ethics, ultimately are. When therefore I speak of the qualities that make for greatness in Hughes's work, I speak with awareness of the political existence of black people in America as a suppressed nation within a nation. If it were not for oppression, the matter of commitment to liberation and raising of consciousness might not arise. But it is from the standpoint of the distinctive character and needs of a long oppressed people that the conservation and transmission of the folk heritage, of which Hughes is so smooth a vehicle, becomes not merely and indifferently "desirable," but *essential* to cultural coherence and group survival.

Charles S. Johnson, a perceptive contemporary observer and interpreter of the arts of the Harlem Renaissance, wrote of the new racial poetry of which Hughes's was a leading example:

> The new racial poetry of the Negro is the expression of something more than experimentation in a new technique. It marks the birth of a new racial consciousness and self conception. It is a first frank acceptance of race, and the recognition of difference without the usual implications of disparity. It lacks apology, the wearying appeals to pity, and the conscious philosophy of defense. In being itself it reveals its greatest charm. In accepting this life it invests it with a new meaning. . . . Who would know something of the core and limitations of this life should go the Blues. In them is the curious story of disillusionment without a saving philosophy and yet without defeat.[61]

Hughes had forecast that perhaps the common people, the folk whose lives formed the axis on which the new poetry revolved, "will give to the world its truly great Negro artist, the one who is not afraid to be himself." Hughes is himself the fulfillment of that dream. His work stands as a Great Pyramid against which all other monuments in the Valley of Afro-American Poetry will have to be measured.

Notes:

1. Cullen, "The Shroud of Color," *Color* (New York, Harper, 1925), pp. 26–35.

2. Hughes, "Color," *Jim Crow's Last Stand* (Atlanta, Negro Publication Society, 1943), p. 7.

3. See Hughes, "The Negro Artist and the Racial Mountain," *The Nation*, June 23, 1926, pp. 692–94. For an account of the influence of Langston Hughes and other writers of the Harlem Renaissance on Leopold Senghor, Aimé Césaire, and Leon Damas, the founders of the *negritude* movement, see Lilyan Kesteloot, *Black Writers in French: A Literary History of Negritude*, tr. Ellen Conroy Kennedy (Philadelphia, Temple University Press, 1974), pp. 55–74.

4. W. E. B. DuBois, *The Souls of Black Folk* [1903] (New York, New American Library, 1969), p. 45.

5. George S. Schuyler, "The Negro-Art Hokum," *The Nation*, June 16, 1926, pp. 662–63.

6. Ibid.

7. See Melville J. Herskovits, *The Myth of the Negro Past* [1941] (Boston, Beacon, 1958).

8. Herskovits, "The Negro's Americanism," in Alain Locke, ed., *The New Negro* [1925] (New York, Atheneum, 1968), pp. 353–60.

9. Countee Cullen, interview with Lester Walton, *The World*, May 15, 1927, p. 16M. See also Nathan Huggins, *Harlem Renaissance* (New York, Oxford Univ. Press, 1971), p. 209.

10. "Countee Cullen," *Chicago Bee*, December 24, 1927.

11. Claude McKay, *A Long Way From Home* [1937] (New York, Harcourt, Brace, 1970), p. 27.

12. Ibid., p. 28.

13. See Hippolyte-Adolphe Taine, Introduction to his *History of English Literature* (1863).

14. *The Nation*, June 23, 1926, pp. 692–94. Reprinted in Addison Gayle, *The Black Aesthetic*, pp. 167–72.

15. "Langston Hughes Speaks," *Negro Digest*, May 1953, p. 279. A selection of Hughes's proletarian pieces was recently published under the title *Good Morning Revolution: Uncollected Writings of Social Protest*, ed. Faith Berry (New York, Lawrence Hill, 1973). "Langston Hughes Speaks" is reprinted on pp. 143–45.

16. Hughes, "To Negro Writers," in Henry Hart, ed., *American Writers' Congress* (New York, International Publishers, 1935), pp. 139–41. Reprinted in *Good Morning Revolution*, pp. 125–26.

17. Hughes, "Letter to the Academy," *International Literature*, July 1933, p. 112. Reprinted in *Good Morning Revolution*, p. 3.

18. Hughes, "The Negro," in Jacob Burck, *Hunger and Revolt: Cartoons by Burck* (New York, The Daily Worker, 1935), pp. 141–42.

19. "To Negro Writers."

20. "Langston Hughes Speaks."

21. See *Good Morning Revolution.*

22. Hughes, "My Adventures as a Social Poet," *Phylon*, 8, No. 3 (1947), pp. 205–12. Reprinted in *Good Morning Revolution*, pp. 135–43.

23. "Some Practical Observations: A Colloquy," *Phylon*, 11, No. 4 (Winter 1950), p. 307.

24. The terms "social poetry" and "lyric poetry" are misleading in that "social poetry" may be lyrical and "lyric poetry" may deal with matters of social and political weight. Certainly such is the case in Hughes's poetry, as, for instance in his "Dream Variation" and "Our Land" (*The Weary Blues* [New York, Knopf, 1926], pp. 43, 99), or in "Sweet Words on Race," "Dream Dust," and "Slum Dreams" (*The Panther and the Lash* [New York, Knopf, 1967], pp. 75, 93, 95). But these are Hughes's own terms, and I find them useful in distinguishing two broad categories of his poetry: "social poetry" for those poems which are preeminently social and / or "racial," i.e., those with immediate and socio-political import as well as those modeled on black folk song forms such as jazz, blues, ballads, and gospel; and "lyric poetry" for poems that are not modeled on black folk forms and that are more private and personal than public and political. Thus, blues poems, though lyrical and private, would be classifiable as "social poetry" because of their black folk song form, whereas poems like "Sport" (*Fine Clothes to the Jew* [New York, Knopf, 1927], p. 40) and "Drum" (*Dear Lovely Death* [Amenia, New York, Troutbeck Press, 1931], n.p.), though drawing their images from black music, are primarily private and therefore "lyric." By the same token, "When Sue Wears Red" (*Weary Blues*, p. 66), whose form and spirit derive from gospel, is primarily a love poem and therefore "lyric."

25. Charles S. Johnson, "The Negro Enters Literature," *The Carolina Magazine*, May 1927, pp. 3–9, 44–48.

26. Hughes, *The Big Sea* [1940] (New York, Hill and Wang, 1963), p. 263.

27. "My Adventures as a Social Poet."

28. "Is Hollywood Fair to Negroes?," *Negro Digest*, April 1943, pp. 19–21.

29. "The Task of the Negro Writer as an Artist," *Negro Digest*, April 1965, pp. 65, 75. Italics in original.

30. Ibid.

31. Hughes, "Jazz as Communication," *The Langston Hughes Reader* (New York, George Braziller, 1958), pp. 492–94.

32. See Alain Locke, *The Negro and His Music* [1936] (New York, Arno, 1969); Marshall Stearns, *The Story of Jazz* (Oxford Univ. Press, 1956); Andre Hodeir, *Jazz: Its Evolution and Essence* (New York, Grove, 1956); Gunther Schuller, *Early Jazz* (Oxford Univ. Press, 1967); Maude Cuney-Hare, *Negro Musicians and Their Music* (New York, Associated Publishers, 1936).

33. *Big Sea*, p. 62.

34. Ibid., p. 85.

35. "Lenox Avenue: Midnight," *Weary Blues*, p. 39.

36. Ibid.

37. "Jazz as Communication."

38. Ibid. This rebuke, sometimes attributed to Fats Waller, is part of jazz lore.

39. Ibid.

40. "Lady's Boogie," *Montage of a Dream Deferred* (New York, Henry Holt, 1951), p. 44.

41. J. A. Rogers, "Jazz at Home," in Locke, *The New Negro*, pp. 216–24.

42. "Jazz as Communication."

43. Ibid.

44. Epigraph, *Big Sea*.

45. Ibid., p. 335.

46. Quoted in Nat Hentoff, "Langston Hughes: He Found Poetry in the Blues," *Mayfair*, August 1958, pp. 27 ff.

47. Hughes's phrase, used as a section title in his *Selected Poems* (New York, Knopf, 1959), p. 31.

48. Hughes, "White Folks Do the Funniest Things," *Negro Digest*, February 1944, p. 34.

49. Hughes, "Humor and the Negro Press," address at the Windy City Press Club Banquet, Chicago, Illinois, January 10, 1957. Hughes Archive, Schomburg Collection, New York Public Library.

50. Ibid.

51. Hughes, "Laughing at White Folks," *Chicago Defender*, National Edition, September 8, 1945, p. 12.

52. Hughes's Spingarn Medal Acceptance Speech, NAACP Convention, St. Paul, Minnesota, June 26, 1960. Hughes Archive, Schomburg Collection.

53. "The Negro Artist and the Racial Mountain."

54. "Laughers," *Fine Clothes*, pp. 77–78.

55. Charles S. Johnson, "Jazz Poetry and Blues," *The Carolina Magazine*, May 1928, pp. 16–20.

56. Allison Davis, "Our Negro 'Intellectuals,'" *The Crisis*, 35, No. 8 (August 1928), pp. 268–69 ff.

57. Benjamin Brawley, *The Negro Genius* (New York, Dodd, Mead, 1937), p. 248; Hughes, *Big Sea*, p. 266.

58. Hughes, Letter to the Editor, *The Crisis*, 35, No. 9 (September 1928), p. 302.

59. See n. 52.

60. Ibid.

61. Charles S. Johnson, "Jazz Poetry and Blues."

[Langston Hughes]

Melvin Tolson*

HIS LIFE

I am Dark Youth
Seeking the truth
Of a free life beneath our great sky.[1]

Countee Cullen and Langston Hughes represent the antipodes of the Harlem Renaissance. The former is a classicist and conservative; the latter, an experimentalist and radical. However, they are staunch friends and mutual admirers. With a biography that reads like a page from the *Arabian Nights*, Langston Hughes, the idealistic wanderer and defender of the proletariat, is the most glamorous figure in Negro literature.[2]

Langston Hughes comes from an old aristocratic family. He was born in Joplin, Missouri, on February 1, 1902. His father was a prominent lawyer and his mother a school teacher. His grandparents on his mother's side belonged to that fortunate group known as Free Negroes before the Emancipation Proclamation was issued. They were a heroic pair, engaged in the dangerous activities of the Under Ground [*sic*] Railroad. The greater part of Langston's childhood was spent with his maternal grandmother, Mary Sampson Patterson Leary Langston, whose husband, Lewis Sheridan Leary, was one of the five Negroes with old John Brown at Harper's Ferry. The aged woman's husband was killed during the raid, and this maternal grandmother was later honored by President Theodore Roosevelt as the last surviving widow of John Brown's quixotic thrust at the slave system in the United States.[3]

*Reprinted from Melvin Tolson, "The Harlem Group of Negro Writers" (M.A. thesis, Columbia University, 1940). Reprinted by permission of Melvin B. Tolson, Jr. This essay appears for the first time in print in this collection.

During the Reconstruction Period there were two Negro senators and many black congressmen, and from Virginia came one by the name of John M. Langston, Hughes' granduncle. His grandmother married Charles Langston, a brother of this congressman, and they migrated to Kansas where the mother of the poet was born.[4]

Hughes spent his early boyhood in Lawrence, Kansas, the same town in which the grandmother of Wallace Thurman, the Harlem playwright and novelist, lived for many years before going to Salt Lake City. As a small boy, Langston visited Old Mexico where his father had "mountain property near the city of Toluca."[5] During his stay there an earthquake occurred. The awe-inspiring scene of thousands of kneeling figures crying and praying to a God who answered not still clings to his memory.

On the death of his grandmother, Langston went to live with his mother at Lincoln, Illinois. A few months later they moved to Cleveland, Ohio, where he attended the high school from which he was graduated in 1920. During this period he had written poems about factories, workers, and poverty, which were inspired by his reading of Max Eastman, Floyd Dell, Claude McKay in the *Liberator*, and the poems of Carl Sandburg; these produced "the unconventionality of his work and style,"[6] which critics have observed.

This was followed by fifteen months spent with his father in Old Mexico. While there he learned Spanish, taught English in a business academy, and attended bullfights.[7] He also witnessed a revolution and saw three bandits hanged. He exercised his young body by furious riding through the open country and climbing the perilous sides of volcanoes. Here, too, he wrote "The Negro Sings of Rivers," his first poem to be published in a national magazine.[8]

In 1921 he came to New York City and entered Columbia University, which James Weldon Johnson had attended before him. Then came the break with his father, and he was compelled to earn his own living. For a while he worked on a Staten Island truck farm, and this was followed by his becoming a delivery boy for a New York florist.

But the wanderlust was in his blood, and for the next three years he entered a period of extensive travel. He became a member of a crew voyaging on a freight steamer to the Canary Islands and the Azores; then as a cabin boy he went to the West Coast of Africa, journeyed to the great Dakar Desert, drank palm wine with the natives of the Gold Coast, bought a monkey up the historic Niger, and almost ended his hectic career by falling into the Congo.[9] A few months later, feeling himself a real sailor, he returned to New York with his companionable monkey and six parrots.

In 1923 he made several voyages to Northern Europe and spent Christmas in Rotterdam, but February of 1924 found him stranded in

Paris. He became doorman at a Montmartre night club on the Rue Fontaine, receiving for his work the tips and one meal a day. Since few Americans visited the place, the tips were conspicuously absent. The Grand Duc, where Florence Mills, the internationally famous black songster held forth nightly, needed a second cook.[10] Langston secured the job, but after he had seen the Olympic games he began, during the summer, his pilgrimage to Italy. The lure of the Italian lakes and the historic ruins held him in thrall until his money slipped away. Venice was the city of his misfortune. He tried to get back to Paris, where he would find American Negroes who might help him, but his passport was stolen in Milan.

Genoa is famous for its beach combers: derelicts of all nations are to be discovered among them. Langston Hughes joined these outcasts, eating their figs and black bread. In his quest for beauty, unlike his friend Countee Cullen, Hughes found it among the flotsam and jetsam of life, whether he pilgrimaged in Europe or roamed a "nigger street" in Harlem.

Finally he secured a job as an ordinary seaman on a tramp steamer sailing for New York City; and for six weeks he painted bulk heads and scrubbed decks, while the schooner meandered in and out among the islands of the Mediterranean, thence past Sicily and Spain, before she crept through tossing seas back to the Statue of Liberty. From these experiences Hughes made many vivid and appealing poems, which are contained in *Fine Clothes to the Jew*[11] and *The Weary Blues.*[12]

The turning point in Langston Hughes' career came when he went to Washington, D.C., in 1924. First, he worked in the offices of Dr. Carter G. Woodson, the learned Negro historian and editor of the *Journal of Negro History*. Contact with this scholar from Harvard and the Sorbonne, who possessed a sublime faith in the future of the race in America, enriched the poet's ethnic experience.

But Langston Hughes never remains in one situation for any length of time. Later he became busboy at the Wardman Hotel in the capital. Mr. Lindsay, the poet who had done a fine piece of Negro characterization in "The Congo,"[13] was a guest at the Wardman. One evening Langston gave him three of his poems. Lindsay took them to his room with him and the very next day read them to an audience in the little theatre of the hotel.[14] If one has heard Lindsay read and is aware of the fine dramatic materials of some of Hughes' poems, one can appreciate the wonderful impression that was made for the busboy poet by the itinerant minstrel from Springfield, Illinois.

From that moment of destiny, Langston Hughes became the object of public attention and Lindsay's words of encouragement set his goal before him. In 1925 he won the first prize for poetry in the *Oppor-*

tunity contest; and, in 1926, while a student at Lincoln University, Pennsylvania, he won the national Witter Bynner undergraduate prize in poetry for his poem "A House in Taos."[15]

The wide-spread interest in his poems is attested by the fact that many of them have been translated into German, Spanish, Russian, and Czechoslovakian, and some have been set to music. Hughes was also connected with the younger members of the Harlem group in the publication of *Fire* and *Harlem*, and his novel *Not Without Laughter* won the Harmon Gold Award in creative literature. In 1932 he went with a group of Negro actors to Russia to make a Negro picture under a Soviet director, and while there he wrote the poem "Goodbye Christ," which made the headlines in most of the Negro papers for three or four weeks. The controversy was very violent.[16]

In April of 1934 Langston Hughes published a short story in *Esquire*; the story was called "A Good Job Gone," and it caused the magazine to gain in circulation while at the same time it lost some subscribers and advertisers, because of the brutal realism with which Hughes described the tragic love affair of Mr. Lloyd, a white broker on Wall Street, and brown-complexioned Pauline, a Harlem dancer in the Cabin Club.[17] A variety of comments appeared in *Esquire*'s "The Sound and the Fury," in regard to this Rabelaisian narrative told in the first person by a Negro student in dentistry, who was in attendance at Columbia.

Mr. Irwin S. Johnson wrote to the editors concerning the story as follows: "You were rank traitors to your readers in leading them to expect something remarkable, something extraordinary. Your well-planned scheme of publicizing overshot its mark. 'A Good Job Gone' is perfectly harmless, even insipid."[18]

Mr. John Grimball Wilkins of Charleston, South Carolina, expressed his convictions with the holy passion of a zealot: "This negro must have been born somewhere around the black belt of upper New York, or in the slums of Chicago in walking distance of the 'Loop.' He does not write like a genuine darky, he must have seen the south in the eyes of the regular off-shade 'Yankee.' Not one line of his story showed a clean thought, just gutter stuff."[19]

Mr. Joseph E. Idzal thought the controversy was much ado about nothing and that his suspicions concerning the pre-publication ballyhoo were justified when the story was published. Mr. Idzal thought the story was just another story, but he considered Langston Hughes a very good stylist.[20] On the other hand, Mr. Patrick Tyre at Tyler, Texas, was impressed with the plot and asked the editor to confess that the story had been written by Gertrude Stein.[21] Mr. R. A. Briggs was very much amused by the fury and he was glad that the editor published the story, for it was the direct cause of his beautiful friendship with a girl that he encountered on a Fifth Avenue bus.[22] Miss Doris Stead of New York said: "He knows people and beauty and feeling. . . . I hope you will print Mr. Hughes whenever he sends anything in."[23]

In 1934 Hughes published a volume of short stories called *The Ways of White Folks.*[24] These stories had appeared previously in *Scribner's* and *Esquire.* The narratives were named "Cora Unashamed," "Slave on the Block," "The Folks at Home," "Passing," "A Good Job Gone," "Rejuvenation Through Joy," "The Blues I'm Playing," "Red-Headed Baby," "Poor Little Black Fellow," "Little Dog," "Beery," "Father and Son," "Mother and Child," and "One Christmas Eve." These stories depict the racial attitudes of whites and blacks when their lives touch each other.

Sherwood Anderson thought that Hughes possessed a fine talent, although the young Negro showed at times a seething indignation in some of the portrayals. Hughes, the rebel, is a bold enemy of economic and racial injustice and often his pen is dipped in the acid of satire. However, Sherwood Anderson observes further: "I do not see how anyone can blame him for his hatreds."[25] Hughes writes with a masculine vigor and each of the portraits is done with simplicity and integrity.

The poetic quality which obtains in Hughes' short stories is also revealed in his novel *Not Without Laughter,*[26] "which pictures the life of a poor family in Kansas and the cleavage between the hard-working, religious, conservative elder generation, and the young people coming to maturity in the jazz age, leaving the church and the submissions of the race for a freer life."[27] Harlan Hatcher, in his evaluation of contemporary fiction, does not hesitate to place the book "among the better novels."[28]

THE POETRY OF HUGHES

Alfred Kreymborg says of Langston Hughes: "He is the poet laureate of Upper Seventh Avenue."[29] Of course Mr. Kreymborg, not being a native of Harlem, got his streets confused. Seventh Avenue is the promenade of the upper classes and the strivers.[30] However, we know what Mr. Kreymborg means. Langston Hughes is the chief ballad-singer of proletarian Upper Lenox Avenue, the street of "the unperfumed drifters and workers." There is as evidence the prize poem "The Weary Blues," which pictures the Lenox Avenue locale, the poem that established Hughes as a poet.[32]

In this poem Hughes shows several of his notable attributes; he catches the undercurrent of philosophy that pulses through the soul of the Blues singer and brings the Blues rhythms into American versification. In this ethnic pattern he portrays in a few bold, impressionistic strokes the setting, the theme, the atmosphere, the pathos, the climactic suspense, the Negro character, and the odd denouement of the Blues;

for the Blues, when racially authentic, have all the devices of an O. Henry short story with its surprising crack at the end.[33]

If an example of the original Blues-ballad is placed in juxtaposition with a Blues poem by the poet of Lenox Avenue, two things will be observed: the mastery of this racial form by Hughes and the accumulating repetition that brings the O. Henry surprise at the end. There is little doubt that his concentrated repetition reaches its highest degree of intensity in the Blues form, but it may be observed in other types of versification.

For example, Lafcadio Hearn traces it to the Norse in his discussion of repetition in the verse of Edgar Allan Poe, a lecture delivered at the University of Tokio.[34] The "St. Louis Blues" is the most celebrated ballad of this type:

> I hate to see de evenin' sun go down,
> Hate to see de evenin' sun go down,
> 'Cause my baby, he done lef dis town.
>
> Feelin' tomorrow lak I feel today,
> Feelin' tomorrow lak I feel today,
> I'll pack my trunk, make my get-away.[35]

Of course the full effect of this ballad can not be realized without the sad, sad rhythm of the melody. Here is an example from Hughes' "Po' Boy Blues":[36]

> Weary, weary,
> Weary early in de morn.
> Weary, weary,
> Early, early in de morn.
> I's so weary
> I wish I'd never been born.

If one has that sympathetic imagination which Mr. Mencken likes to talk about, one can, through identification of feeling, experience the utter physical and mental fatigue of that Negro after the cruel sleeplessness of the night-hours, facing the desolate flatness of another day. Langston Hughes understands the tragedy of the dark masses whose laughter is a dark laughter.[37]

Hughes has received much adverse criticism from the colored bourgeoisie, whom Dr. Melville J. Herskovits delights in calling "the most bourgeois of the bourgeoisie." They say his poems are "just like the nigger Blues," unmindful that this is the highest tribute they can pay to these artistic creations. Critics like Dorothy Scarborough and James Weldon Johnson consider the Blues as authentic a form of folk expression as the Spirituals are admitted to be, and Hughes has been able to catch the spontaneity and rhythm and philosophy of this ethnic expression. The Spirituals had a religious origin and the Blues a secular one.

No less an authority than Alfred Kreymborg asserts that there are instances in which Langston Hughes can give in a few lines "the implications of a full-length novel or play"[38] as he did in the poem "Cross":

My old man's a white old man
And my old mother's black.
If ever I cursed my white old man
I take my curses back.

If ever I cursed by black old mother
And wished she were in hell,
I'm sorry for that evil wish
And now I wish her well.

My old man died in a fine big house,
My ma died in a shack.
I wonder where I'm gonna die,
Being neither white nor black.[39]

Has any other poet sung so poignantly about this tragic phase of American life? And to give point to Mr. Kreymborg's statement, Broadway has seen recently the dramatization of this theme in Langston Hughes' *Mulatto*. Professor Alain Locke, one of the best-informed scholars on the Harlem Renaissance, made this observation concerning the poet laureate of Upper Lenox Avenue: "This work of Hughes in the folk-forms has started up an entire school of younger Negro poetry: principally in the blues form and in the folk-ballad vein. It is the latter that seems to be the most promising, in spite of the undeniable interest of the former in bringing into poetry some of the song and dance rhythms of the Negro."[40]

Professor Russell Blankenship sees in Hughes the jazz singer crooning in modern parlance the old, old woes of the black man,[41] while Mrs. Elizabeth Green, the wife of that talented interpreter of Negro life, Paul Green, discovers in Hughes "humor, abandon, and recklessness without self-consciousness."[42] Professor James Weldon Johnson admits that Hughes' work is motivated by race, but he hastens to add that "race means little to Hughes."[43]

Now, the poet of Upper Lenox Avenue, who was not allowed to remain in Japan because of the red complexion of his economic philosophy and who was listed by the government of the United States as a dangerous political radical, would doubtless agree with Mr. Johnson on this matter.

Meanwhile, Charles A. Beard considers Langston Hughes one of the twenty-five most brilliant and social-minded personalities in America.[44]

Notes:

1. Langston Hughes, *Dramatic Recitations*, New York, Golden Stair Publishers, 1932, p. 19.

2. Stanley J. Kunitz, "Langston Hughes," *Living Authors*, p. 184.

3. James Weldon Johnson, "Langston Hughes," *The Book of American Negro Poetry*, p. 233.

4. Countee Cullen, "Langston Hughes," *Caroling Dusk*, New York, Harper, 1927, p. 144.

5. Stanley J. Kunitz, *op. cit.*, p. 184.

6. Robert B. Eleazer, *Singers in the Dawn*, Atlanta, Education and Race Relations, 703 Standard Building, 1933, p. 17.

7. Countee Cullen, *op. cit.*, p. 144.

8. James Weldon Johnson, *op. cit.*, p. 232.

9. Stanley J. Kunitz, *op. cit.*, p. 184.

10. James Weldon Johnson, *op. cit.*, pp. 232–233.

11. Langston Hughes, *Fine Clothes to the Jew*, New York, Knopf, 1927.

12. Langston Hughes, *The Weary Blues*, New York, Knopf, 1926.

13. Roy L. French, "Vachel Lindsay," *Recent Poetry*, New York, Heath, 1926, p. 101.

14. Harriet Monroe, "Langston Hughes," *The New Poetry*, New York, Macmillan, 1932, p. 719.

15. Stanley J. Kunitz, *op. cit.*, p. 185.

16. Melvin B. Tolson, "Goodbye Christ," *Pittsburgh Courier*, Vol. XXIII, pp. 10–11 (January 26, 1933).

17. Langston Hughes, "A Good Job Gone," Esquire, Vol. 1, p. 46 (April, 1934).

18. Irvin S. Johnson, "The Sound and the Fury," *Esquire*, Vol. 1, p. 15 (April, 1934).

19. John Grimball Wilkins, *Ibid.*, p. 15.

20. Joseph E. Idzal, *Ibid.*, p. 16.

21. Patrick Tyre, *Ibid.*, p. 16.

22. R. A. Briggs, "The Sound and the Fury," *Esquire*, Vol. 1, p. 17 (May, 1934).

23. Doris Stead, "The Sound and the Fury," *Esquire*, Vol. 2, p. 166 (June, 1934).

24. Langston Hughes, *The Ways of White Folks*, New York, Knopf, 1934.

25. Sherwood Anderson, *Nation*, Vol. 139, p. 49 (July 11, 1934).

26. Langston Hughes, *Not Without Laughter*, New York, Knopf, 1930.

27. Harlan Hatcher, *Creating the Modern American Novel*, New York, Farrar & Rinehart, 1935, p. 151.

28. Harlan Hatcher, *Ibid.*, p. 151.

29. Alfred Kreymborg, *Our Singing Strength*, p. 576.

30. Rudolph Fisher, "Blades of Steel," *Readings from Negro Authors*, edited by Crowell, Turner, and Dykes, New York, Harcourt, Brace, and Company, 1931, p. 90.

31. *Ibid.*, p. 91.

32. Langston Hughes, *The Weary Blues*, New York, Knopf, 1926.

33. Dorothy Scarborough, *On the Trail of Negro Folksong*, Cambridge, Harvard Press, 1925.

34. Lafcadio Hearn, "Poe's Verse," *Interpretations of Literature*, New York, Dodd, Mead, 1926, pp. 150–166.

35. W. C. Handy, "St. Louis Blues," *Anthology of American Negro Literature*, p. 223.

36. Russell Blankenship, "Negro Poetry," *American Literature*, p. 642.

37. Harlan Hatcher, "Sherwood Anderson," *Creating the Modern American Novel*, p. 169.

38. Alfred Kreymborg, *Our Singing Strength*, p. 578.

39. Langston Hughes, "Cross," *The Book of American Negro Poetry*, edited by James Weldon Johnson, p. 236.

40. Alain Locke, "The Negro in American Culture," *Anthology of American Negro Literature*, edited by V. F. Calverton, New York, Modern Library, 1929, p. 256.

41. Russell Blankenship, *op. cit.*, p. 642.

42. Elizabeth Lay Green, *op. cit.*, p. 15.

43. James Weldon Johnson, *op. cit.*, p. 165.

44. *California News*, Los Angeles, Vol. X, p. 4, (June 21, 1935).

Poetry

Langston Hughes versus the Black Preachers in the *Pittsburgh Courier* in the 1930s

Walter C. Daniel*

During the first half of the twentieth century—a period during which the United States operated largely as two racially separate societies—the black national weekly newspaper reached the zenith of its influence. Its ancestry had begun in the previous century, alongside the pulpit. It exercised a freedom that was also a characteristic of the black church. It communicated among its people and it was read by the majority culture, especially in times of extreme national peril. It is not well known today that fifty years ago the *Pittsburgh Courier, Chicago Defender, New York Age, Amsterdam News, Philadelphia Tribune, California Eagle, Norfolk Journal and Guide, St. Louis Argus, Kansas City Call, Cleveland Call and Post, Baltimore Afro-American*, and *Atlanta World* spoke to the black American communities.

Between the world wars, the *Defender* and the *Courier*, in particular, pretty well covered the nation. Pullman porters and dining car waiters delivered them on the runs of the great coast-to-coast railroad trains. Local newsboys, barbers, and shopkeepers in hundreds of large and small towns and cities made this periodical press available to black America. The news was eclectic. It concerned politics, society, sports, entertainment, religion, education, and the arts. It was the arbiter of what was important in black America. National editions competed with one another as keenly as did the large daily newspapers that were stable items in the nation.

Not surprisingly, then, the *Courier* delighted in carrying for several weeks in 1933 a scintillating argument, among some of the intellectual "heavies," that was precipitated by publication of young Langston Hughes's "Good-Bye Christ." Hughes, now thirty years old, was un-

*This essay was written for this volume and appears here by permission of the author.

doubtedly the most popular rising black literary figure by virtue of his torrent of poetry in *Crisis* and *Opportunity*, his *Not Without Laughter*, his popular collections of poetry of the low life of black Americans, and his readings before youth and American literary societies. He had come out of the Harlem Renaissance the best-known of all the writers. The text of the famous poem, in part, reads:

Listen, Christ,
You did alright in your day, I reckon—
But that day's gone now.
They ghosted you up a swell story, too,
Call it Bible—
But it's dead now.
The popes and the preachers've
Made too much money from it.
They've sold you to too many.
Kings, generals, robbers, and killers—
Even to the Tzar and the Cossacks,
Even to Rockefeller's Church,
Even to the Saturday Evening Post.
You ain't no good no more.
They've pawned you
'Till you've done wore out.
Good-bye
Christ Jesus Lord God Jehovah,
Beat it on away from here now.

Jean Wagner reports that according to a telegram from the American Communist Press Agency that is now in the Schomberg Collection, Hughes stated on 18 June 1932, on the eve of his departure for Russia via Germany, that Communism was the only force leading an active fight against the poverty and wretchedness of the Negro.[1] "Good-Bye Christ," a ritual drama titled "Scottsboro Limited," and "Always the Same" were all published before Hughes visited the Soviet Union. "Good-Bye Christ" appeared first in the November–December 1932 issue of the *Negro Worker*, a German publication that was the organ of the International Trade Union Committee of Negro Workers. It was reprinted in Nancy Cunard's *Negro Anthology* and in Benjamin E. Mays' *The Negro's God as Reflected in His Literature*.

These three works proved troublesome for Hughes when he returned home from Russia because each of them praised communism's fight against racism in America. Richard K. Barksdale, in *Langston Hughes: The Poet and His Critics*, discusses the poet's purpose in writing "Good-Bye Christ." Barksdale calls it a "frank and direct attack on the Christian Church and organized religion in the United States."[2] He goes on to explain that when, in 1931, Hughes made his first tour of the American South, he was appalled by what he saw and experienced there.

He returned with the impression that, "through its apparent actions toward my people," the nation was saying good-bye to Christ and His principles of tolerance, love, and spiritual friendship.[3] Barksdale then explodes the myth that "Good-Bye Christ" results from Hughes's revulsion at going to church as a child. However, Barksdale, in his succinct volume, chose not to comment on the protracted *Pittsburgh Courier* coverage of the intraracial controversy over the poem.

Langston Hughes's problems with the black clergy began early in his career. In his essay "My Adventures as a Social Poet," Hughes reports the following incident:

> My adventures as a social poet began in a colored church in Atlantic City shortly after my first book, *The Weary Blues*, was published in 1926. I had been invited to come down to the shore from Lincoln University where I was a student, to give a program of my poems in the church. During the course of my program I read several of my poems in the form of the Negro folk songs, including some blues poems about hard luck and hard work. As I read I noticed a deacon approach the pulpit with a note which he placed on the rostrum beside me, but I did not stop to open the note until I had finished and had acknowledged the applause of a cordial audience. The note read, "Do not read any more blues in my pulpit." It was signed by the minister. That was my first experience with censorship.[4]

A unique characteristic of the basic institutions of Afro-American society comes to the surface in relation to this subject. For that racially separate society forged a sui generis black church. It was not, and is not, simply the black Baptist church or the black United Methodist church or the black United Presbyterian church on the other side of town from its white denominational counterpart. The black church sanctuary was the concert hall, the meeting house for mass activities, the benevolent society, and the place of worship all in one. Accordingly, Hughes read poetry from the pulpits of black churches. And the more prominent the church the more likely it would be the setting for the poetry readings. How else would he come to be reading blues poetry from the staid pulpit of the pastor of fashionable Wheat Street Baptist Church?

Through this same image of the peculiar nature of the black church and its clergy, one can find that the Reverend J. Raymond Henderson would be the first black minister to fire a salvo against Hughes and his impertinent "Good-Bye Christ." And, quite appropriately, the *Pittsburgh Courier* would be the periodical organ through which Mr. Henderson would make his attack.

Thus, in the 14 January 1933 issue of the *Courier*, one finds the long article about the poem that begins: "We are informed that Langston Hughes, Negro poet, now in Russia, has written a poem which appeared in a German publication in which he with a careless wave of the hand, yet stern voice, dismisses Christ. The title of the poem is 'Good-Bye Christ.' I have read the poem which is not really poetry. Mr. Hughes simply conceived an idea which he thought would shock the public and remind it that he is still alive and in Russia."[5]

Warming up to his subject, the brilliant and caustic Mr. Henderson complained particularly that Hughes ranks Christ with the Pope, Gandhi, Aimee McPherson, and George W. Becton. He exclaims, "What a combination!" For "any man who has no more judgment and discrimination than to like these names is surely to be pitied." He wrote, in fact, "he is either ignorant or stupid and I don't suppose one could call Mr. Hughes ignorant, although it is quite evident that in his wish to dismiss Christ he really shows that he does not know what Christ means to the world."[6]

In orderly fashion the writer then takes exception to the three ideas he says are in the poem: (1) that Christ has had his day; (2) that the Bible is a fictitious story of Christ; and (3) that Christ is "getting in the way of things." And in homiletic fashion—as if he were preaching one of his eloquent sermons to a Christian congregation—Henderson refutes each of these ideas to his own satisfaction.

Two issues later, the *Courier* carried a response to Henderson written by Melvin B. Tolson, a poet and member of the English faculty at Wiley College in Marshall, Texas. His principal point is that "Good-Bye Christ" is "both a challenge and a warning to the churches of America and Afro-America—yes to the churches of the world."[7] The poem cannot, then, be "ignored by the proud; laughed at by the scorners; turned aside by the sophist; nor scandalized by the religionist"[8]—especially since it had gained wide circulation in Negro America and had precipitated wide discussion. Using his own research on Hughes that he had pursued in his study of the Harlem Renaissance at Columbia University, Tolson wrote that Hughes was a Catholic, a rebel, and a proletarian in his personal life and in his poetry and criticism. Surely, then, the poem was not an idea intended to shock readers and to remind Americans that Hughes was still alive. Hughes's life as a black American made him a radical, Tolson declared. In his earliest writing, his treatment of low-life among Negroes had brought the young poet condemnation from most of the black intelligentsia, save for Alain Locke.

For his most stinging and parting shot in his response, Tolson wrote: "Certain gentlemen of the cloth have a way of becoming self-styled judges on everything. Christ had so much to do that He didn't have time to set himself up as a critic of poetry. The Rev. Mr. Henderson seems to think that a knowledge of Pastoral Theology and homiletics warrants his becoming a critic of literature."[9]

Henderson shot back next fortnight: "Let me at the outset make a few things clear. I am not arguing personalities."[10] Nor was he interested in being informed by the writer that he had been to Columbia University. And he reiterated his argument with three points Hughes had made—those I have referred to earlier.

By mid-March Henderson again took to the columns of the *Courier*, this time to complain about troubles within the Christian church. He lamented that many ministers were avoiding preaching "conscientious convictions lest church moguls force him to resign his pastorate."[11] It is impossible to establish any direct relationship between this article and Henderson's troubles with his fashionable Wheat Street Baptist Church, but it is known that he resigned his pastorate soon afterward.

The Methodists became involved about the same time. James Oliver Slade, a member of the Social Sciences Department at Atlanta's Morris Brown College, wrote for the *Courier* to give a new direction to the "Good-Bye Christ" affair. Rather than take Hughes to task for the poem that he admitted had been offensive to large parts of the American black population, Slade wrote that Hughes's poem brought to mind the shocking intelligence that if the church in the United States is Christ, then, indeed, Christ's time is out. The poem should be taken, then, to "awaken us so-called Christians who have abused His institution, the church, to a sense of our lurking and faltering duty to it." Religion has not failed, the writer concluded. Nor had Christ failed in his two-word philosophy—"brotherly love."[12] D. Ormonde Walker, pastor of the St. James A.M.E. Church of Cleveland, and later president of Wilberforce University, defended Hughes's contention. He wrote that Hughes was really saying that "the present order of society buttressed by the sanctity of religion and the church, in the name of Jehovah God and Christ, is an order that has proven insufficient to curb man's prejudices and passions, his vices and his sins." And he said he felt exactly the same.[13]

D. DeWitt Turpeau, Jr., pastor of the Centenary Methodist Episcopal Church of Akron, Ohio, contributed a poem titled "Father Forgive" that the *Courier* published alongside Walker's article. That poem ended with the supplication, in its final stanza:

> Forgive, O Christ, the poet of unlimited promise,
> For his blasphemous words like the thief on the cross.
> Open his eyes to the inevitable ending
> Crowned with disappointment, regret and remorse.
> And for this misinformed and erring young pilgrim
> May I offer a prayer, not as a priest or a preacher,
> That soon he may have a prodigal's awakening,
> And know Thee, O Lord, as his personal redeemer.[14]

During the first six months of 1933, the religion page of the *Courier* was laden with ramifications of the Henderson article about the Hughes poem. Some praised the poet; many condemned him. George C. Schuyler, premier black social critic, attacked the black and white churches for their emphasis on materialism.

Perhaps the particular matter of "Good-Bye Christ" came to rest, so far as the pages of the *Courier* were concerned, with the final remonstrance to Hughes from Reverdy C. Ransom, formerly editor of the prestigious *A.M.E. Church Review*, and at the time presiding bishop of the Fourth Episcopal District of his denomination. The text of his poem reads in part:

ALL HAIL TO CHRIST

Listen Hughes,
You are not sacrilegious—
Just silly.
You are no more profane
Than the flight of a bat
In the twilight,
Or the screech of an owl,
In the Gothic towers of a temple.
This futility great Shakespeare saw,
In the dog that bays the moon.
Step on the brimstone, Hughes.
Go away from that mike,
And get the hell off the air.
Stop your kidding.
"Don't be so slow about moving;
Move."
Not a religion, but a life
Of Peace and Goodwill,
Would the Nazarene give to the Ages,
While your Saints, Lenin and Stalin,
Spread violence, terror and blood. . . .[15]

The point of this brief essay has been that the newspaper is, indeed, a significant source of history—particularly Afro-American history, largely because the black newspaper played so important a role in black society in the first half of the twentieth century. The incident that I have chosen illustrates clearly how one black newspaper—and the same is true of all the others—served as a sounding board for the history of ideas for the race.

Most of the same periodicals exist today. However, with the broadened scope of mass media their influence has been diminished. Still, microforms of these newspapers provide some of the seldom used but vital tools for the study of Afro-American culture. What I have discussed here is merely one example of a fusion of religion and literary art.

Notes:

1. Jean Wagner, *Black Poets of the United States* (Urbana: University of Illinois Press, 1973), 434.

2. Richard K. Barksdale, *Langston Hughes: The Poet and His Critics* (Chicago: American Library Association, 1979), 65.

3. Ibid., 66.

4. "My Adventures as a Social Poet," *Phylon* 8 (Fall 1947):206.

5. *Courier*, 14 January 1933, sec. 2, p. 10.

6. Ibid.

7. Melvin Tolson, "Goodbye Christ," *Courier*, 26 January 1933, 10–11.

8. Ibid., 10.

9. Ibid., 11.

10. *Courier*, 19 March 1933, sec. 2, p. 10.

11. Ibid.

12. *Courier*, 25 February 1933, sec. 2, p. 10.

13. *Courier*, 18 April 1933, sec. 2, p. 10.

14. Ibid.

15. *Courier*, 25 March 1933, sec. 2, p. 12.

The Harlem of Langston Hughes' Poetry

Arthur P. Davis*

In a very real sense, Langston Hughes is the poet-laureate of Harlem. From his first publication down to his latest, Mr. Hughes has been concerned with the black metropolis. Returning to the theme again and again, he has written about Harlem oftener and more fully than any other poet. As Hughes has written about himself: "I live in the heart of Harlem. I have also lived in the heart of Paris, Madrid, Shanghai, and Mexico City. The people of Harlem seem not very different from others, except in language. I love the color of their language: and, being a Harlemite myself, their problems and interests are my problems and interests."

Knowing how deeply Langston Hughes loves Harlem and how intimately he understands the citizens of that community, I have long felt that a study of the Harlem theme in Hughes' poetry would serve a twofold purpose: it would give us insight into the growth and maturing of Mr. Hughes as a social poet; it would also serve as an index to the changing attitude of the Negro during the last quarter of a century.

*Reprinted from *Phylon* 13 (1952):276–83, by permission of *Phylon: The Atlanta University Review of Race and Culture.* Copyright 1952.

When Mr. Hughes' first publication, *The Weary Blues* (1926), appeared, the New Negro Movement was in full swing; and Harlem, as the intellectual center of the movement, had become the Mecca of all aspiring young Negro writers and artists. This so-called Renaissance not only encouraged and inspired the black creative artist, but it served also to focus as never before the attention of America upon the Negro artist and scholar. As a result of this new interest, Harlem became a gathering place for downtown intellectuals and Bohemians—many of them honestly seeking a knowledge of Negro art and culture, others merely looking for exotic thrills in the black community. Naturally, the latter group was much the larger of the two; and Harlem, capitalizing on this new demand for "primitive" thrills, opened a series of spectacular cabarets. For a period of about ten years, the most obvious and the most sensational aspect of the New Negro Movement for downtown New York was the night life of Harlem. The 1925 Renaissance, of course, was not just a cabaret boom, and it would be decidedly unfair to give that impression. But the Harlem cabaret life of the period was definitely an important by-product of the new interest in the Negro created by the movement, and this life strongly influenced the early poetry of Langston Hughes.

Coming to Harlem, as he did, a twenty-two-year-old adventurer who had knocked around the world as sailor and beachcomber, it was only natural that Hughes should be attracted to the most exotic part of that city—its night life. The Harlem of *The Weary Blues* became therefore for him "Jazzonia," a new world of escape and release, an exciting never-never land in which "sleek black boys" blew their hearts out on silver trumpets in a "whirling cabaret." It was a place where the bold eyes of white girls called to black men, and "dark brown girls" were found "in blond men's arms." It was a city where "shameless gals" strutted and wiggled, and the "night dark girl of the swaying hips" danced beneath a papier-maché jungle moon. The most important inhabitants of this magic city are a "Nude Young Dancer," "Midnight Nan at Leroy's" a "Young Singer of *chansons vulgaires*," and a "Black Dancer in the Little Savoy."

This cabaret Harlem, this Jazzonia is a joyous city but this joyousness is not unmixed; it has a certain strident and hectic quality, and there are overtones of weariness and despair. "The long-headed jazzers" and whirling dancing girls are desperately trying to find some new delight, and some new escape. They seem obsessed with the idea of seizing the present moment as though afraid of the future: "Tomorrow . . . is darkness / Joy today!" "The rhythm of life / Is a jazz rhythm" for them, but it brings only "The broken heart of love / The weary, weary heart of pain." It is this weariness and this intensity that one hears above the laughter and even about the blare of the jazz bands.

There is no daytime in Jazzonia, no getting up and going to work. It is wholly a sundown city, illuminated by soft lights, spotlights, jewel-eyed sparklers, and synthetic stars in the scenery. Daylight is the one great enemy here, and when "the new dawn / Wan and pale / Descends like a white mist," it brings only an "aching emptiness," and out of this emptiness there often comes in the clear cool light of morning the disturbing thought that the jazz band may not be an escape, it may not be gay after all:

Does a jazz-band ever sob?
They say a jazz-band's gay . . .
One said she heard the jazz-band sob
When the little dawn was gray.

In this respect, the figure of the black piano player in the title poem is highly symbolic. Trying beneath "the pale dull pallor of an old gas light" to rid his soul of the blues that bedeviled it, he played all night, but when the dawn approached:

The singer stopped playing and went to bed
While the Weary Blues echoed through his head.
He slept like a rock or a man that's dead.

It is hard to fool oneself in the honest light of dawn, but sleep, like dancing and singing and wild hilarity, is another means of escape. Unfortunately, it too is only a temporary evasion. One has to wake up sometime and face the harsh reality of daylight and everyday living.

And in the final pages of *The Weary Blues*, the poet begins to sense this fact; he realizes that a "jazz-tuned" way of life is not the answer to the Negro's search for escape. The last poem on the Harlem theme in this work has the suggestive title "Disillusionment" and the even more suggestive lines:

I would be simple again,
Simple and clean . . .
Nor ever know,
Dark Harlem,
The wild laughter
Of your mirth . . .
Be kind to me,
Oh, great dark city.
Let me forget.
I will not come
To you again.

Evidently Hughes did want to forget, at least temporarily, the dark city, for there is no mention of Harlem in his next work, *Fine Clothes to the Jew*, published the following year. Although several of the other themes treated in the first volume are continued in this the second, it is the only major production[1] in which the name Harlem does not appear.

But returning to *The Weary Blues*—it is the eternal emptiness of the Harlem depicted in this work which depresses. In this volume, the poet has been influenced too strongly by certain superficial elements of the New Negro Movement. Like too many of his contemporaries, he followed the current vogue, and looking at Harlem through the "arty" spectacles of New Negro exoticism, he failed to see the everyday life about him. As charming and as fascinating as many of these poems undoubtedly are, they give a picture which is essentially false because it is one-dimensional and incomplete. In the works to follow, we shall see Mr. Hughes filling out that picture, giving it three-dimensional life and being.

The picture of Harlem presented in *Shakespeare in Harlem* (1942) has very little in common with that found in *The Weary Blues.* By 1942 the black metropolis was a disillusioned city. The Depression of 1929, having struck the ghetto harder than any other section of New York, showed Harlem just how basically "marginal" and precarious its economic foundations were. Embittered by this knowledge, the black community had struck back blindly at things in general in the 1935 riot. The riot brought an end to the New Negro era; the Cotton Club, the most lavish of the uptown cabarets, closed its doors and moved to Broadway; and the black city settled down to the drab existence of WPA and relief living.

In the two groups of poems labeled "Death in Harlem" and "Lenox Avenue," Hughes has given us a few glimpses of this new Harlem. There are no bright colors in the scene, only the sombre and realistic shades appropriate to the depiction of a community that has somehow lost its grip on things. The inhabitants of this new Harlem impress one as a beaten people. A man loses his job because, "awake all night with loving," he cannot get to work on time. When he is discharged, his only comment is "So I went on back to bed . . ." and to the "sweetest dreams" ("Fired"). In another poem, a man and his wife wrangle over the family's last dime which he had thrown away gambling ("Early Evening Quarrel"). Harlem love has lost its former joyous abandon, and the playboy of the cabaret era has become a calculating pimp who wants to "share your bed / And your money too" ("50–50"). In fact all of the lovers in this section—men and women alike—are an aggrieved lot, whining perpetually about being "done wrong." Even the night spots have lost their jungle magic, and like Dixie's joint have become earthy and sordid places: "Dixie makes his money on two-bit gin"; he also "rents rooms at a buck a break." White folks still come to Dixie's seeking a thrill, but they find it unexpectedly in the cold-blooded shooting of Bessie by Arabella Johnson, in a fight over Texas

Kid. As Arabella goes to jail and Bessie is taken to the morgue, Texas Kid, the cause of this tragedy, callously "picked up another woman and / Went to bed" ("Death in Harlem"). All of the fun, all of the illusion have gone from this new and brutal night life world; and as a fitting symbol of the change which has come about, we find a little cabaret girl dying forlornly as a ward of the city ("Cabaret Girl Dies on Welfare Island").

There is seemingly only one bright spot in this new Harlem—the spectrum-colored beauty of the girls on Sugar Hill ("Harlem Sweeties"); but this is only a momentary lightening of the mood. The prevailing tone is one of depression and futility:

> Down on the Harlem River
>   Two A.M.
>   Midnight
>   By yourself!
> Lawd, I wish I could die—
> But who would miss me if I left?

We see here the spectacle of a city feeling sorry for itself, the most dismal and depressing of all spectacles. Hughes has given us a whining Harlem. It is not yet the belligerent Harlem of the 1943 riot, but it is a city acquiring the mood from which this riot will inevitably spring.

The Harlem poems in *Fields of Wonder* (1947) are grouped under the title "Stars Over Harlem," but they do not speak out as clearly and as definitely as former pieces on the theme have done. The mood, however, continues in the sombre vein of *Shakespeare in Harlem*, and the idea of escape is stated or implied in each of the poems. In the first of the group, "Trumpet Player: 52nd Street," we find a curious shift in the African imagery used. Practically all former pieces having an African background tended to stress either the white-mooned loveliness of jungle nights or the pulse-stirring rhythm of the tom-tom. But from the weary eyes of the 52nd Street musician there blazes forth only "the smoldering memory of slave ships." In this new Harlem even the jazz players are infected with the sectional melancholy, and this performer finds only a vague release and escape in the golden tones he creates.

In "Harlem Dance Hall" there is again an interesting use of the escape motif. The poet describes the hall as having no dignity at all until the band began to play and then: "Suddenly the earth was there, / And flowers, / Trees, / And air." In short, this new dignity was achieved by an imaginative escape from the close and unnatural life of the dance hall (and of Harlem) into the freedom and wholesomeness of nature and normal living.

Although it is rather cryptic, there is also the suggestion of escape in "Stars," the last of these poems to be considered here: "O, sweep of stars over Harlem streets . . . / Reach up your hand, dark boy, and take a star."

One-Way Ticket (1949) and *Montage of a Dream Deferred* (1951), especially the latter work, bring to a full cycle the turning away from the Harlem of *The Weary Blues.* The Harlem depicted in these two works has come through World War II, but has discovered that a global victory for democracy does not necessarily have too much pertinence at home. Although the Harlem of the 1949–51 period has far more opportunity than the 1926 Harlem ever dreamed of, it is still not free; and the modern city having caught the vision of total freedom and total integration will not be satisfied wih anything less than the ideal. It is therefore a critical, a demanding, a sensitive, and utterly cynical city.

In *One-Way Ticket,* for example, Harlem remembers "the old lies," "the old kicks in the back," the jobs it never could have and still cannot get because of color:

> So we stand here
> On the edge of hell
> In Harlem
> And look out on the world
> And wonder
> What we're gonna do
> In the face of
> What we remember.

But even though Harlem is the "edge of hell," it still can be a refuge for the black servant who works downtown all day bowing and scraping to white folks ("Negro Servant"). Dark Harlem becomes for him a "sweet relief from faces that are white." The earlier Harlem was a place to be shared with fun-seeking whites from below 125th Street; the new city is a sanctuary from them.

So deep is the unrest in this 1949–51 Harlem it may experience strangely conflicting emotions. Like aliens longing sentimentally for the "old country," it may feel momentarily a nostalgia for the South, even though it has bought a one way ticket from that region. In "Justice-Joint: Northern City," we find sad-faced boys who have forgotten how to laugh:

> But suddenly a guitar playing lad
> Whose languid lean brings back the sunny South
> Strikes up a tune all gay and bright and glad
> To keep the gall from biting in his mouth,
> Then drowsy as the rain
> Soft sad black feet
> Dance in this juice joint
> On the city street.

The deepest tragedy of a disillusioned city is the cruelty it inflicts on its own unfortunates, and this bitter Harlem wastes no pity on a poor lost brother who was not "hep":

Harlem
Sent him home
In a long box—
Too dead
To know why:
The licker
Was lye.

The longest and most revealing Harlem poem in *One-Way Ticket* is the thumping "Ballad of Margie Polite," the Negro girl who "cussed" a cop in the lobby of the Braddock Hotel and caused a riot when a Negro soldier taking her part was shot in the back by a white cop. In these thirteen short stanzas, Langston Hughes has distilled, as it were, all of the trigger-sensitiveness to injustice—real or imagined; all of the pent-up anti-white bitterness; and all of the sick-and-tired-of-being-kicked-around feelings which characterize the masses of present-day Harlem. It is indeed a provocative analysis of the frictions and the tensions in the black ghetto, this narrative of Margie Polite, who

Kept the Mayor
And Walter White
And everybody
Up all night!

In *Montage of a Dream Deferred*, Mr. Hughes' latest volume of poems, the Harlem theme receives its fullest and most comprehensive statement. Devoting the whole volume to the subject, he has touched on many aspects of the city unnoticed before. His undersanding is now deep and sure, his handling of the theme defter and more mature than in any of the previous works. In this volume, the poet makes effective use of a technique with which he has been experimenting since 1926—a technique he explains in a brief prefatory note: "In terms of current Afro-American popular music . . . this poem on contemporary Harlem, like be-bop, is marked by conflicting changes, sudden nuances, sharp and impudent interjections, broken rhythms, and passages sometimes in the manner of the jam session, sometimes the popular song, punctuated by the riffs, runs, breaks, and distortions [*sic*] of the music of a community in transition."

According to this scheme, we are to consider the whole book of ninety-odd pieces as really one long poem, marked by the conflicting changes, broken rhythms, and sudden interjections characteristic of a jam session. This "jam session" technique is highly effective because, tying together as it does fragmentary and otherwise unrelated segments in the work, it allows the poet, without being monotonous, to return again and again to his overall-theme, that of Harlem's frustration. Like the deep and persistent rolling of a boogie bass—now loud and raucous, now soft and pathetic—this theme of Harlem's dream deferred marches relentlessly throughout the poem. Hughes knows that Harlem is neither a gay nor healthy but basically a tragic and frustrated city, and he beats that message home. Because of the fugue-like structure of the poem, it is impossible for the reader to miss the theme or to forget it.

This 1951 Harlem is a full and many-sided community. Here one finds the pathos of night funerals and fraternal parades: "A chance to let / the whole world see / old black me!"; or the grim realism of slum-dwellers who like war because it means prosperity; or the humor of a wife playing via a dream book the number suggested by her husband's dying words. This is the Harlem of black celebrities and their white girl admirers, the Harlem of vice squad detectives "spotting fairies" in night spots, the Harlem of bitter anti-Semitism, and the Harlem of churches and street corner orators, of college formals at the Renaissance Casino and of Negro students writing themes at CCNY. It is now definitely a class-conscious Harlem, a community of dicties and nobodies; and the Cadillac-riding professional dicties feel that they are let down by the nobodies who "talk too loud / cuss too loud / and look too black." It is a Harlem of some gaiety and of much sardonic laughter; but above all else, it is Harlem of a dream long deferred; and a people's deferred dream can "fester like a sore" or "sag like a heavy load."

Whatever else it may or may not believe, this Harlem has no illusion about the all-inclusiveness of American democracy. Even the children know that there is still a Jim Crow coach on the Freedom Train.

> What don't bug
> them white kids
> sure bugs me;
> We knows everybody
> ain't free.

Perhaps the dominant over-all impression that one gets from *Montage of a Dream Deferred* is that of a vague unrest. Tense and moody, the inhabitants of this 1951 Harlem seem to be seeking feverishly and forlornly for some simple yet apparently unattainable satisfaction in life: "one more bottle of gin"; "my furniture paid for"; "I always did want to study French"; "that white enamel stove"; "a wife who will work with me and not against me." The book begins and ends on this note of dissatisfaction and unrest. There is "a certain amount of nothing in a dream deferred."

These then are the scenes that make up the Harlem of Langston Hughes' poetry. The picture, one must remember, is that of a poet and not a sociologist; it naturally lacks the logic and the statistical accuracy of a scientific study, but in its way the picture is just as revealing and truthful as an academic study. As one looks at this series of Harlems he is impressed by the growing sense of frustration which characterizes each of them. Whether it is in the dream fantasy world of *The Weary Blues* or in the realistic city of *Montage of a Dream Deferred*, one sees a people searching—and searching in vain—for a way to make Harlem a part of the American dream. And one must bear in mind that with Langston Hughes Harlem is both place and symbol. When he depicts the hopes, the aspirations, the frustrations, and the deep-seated discontent of the New York ghetto, he is expressing the feelings of Negroes in black ghettos throughout America.

Notes:

1. *The Dream Keeper* (1932) is not considered a major publication and will not be examined here. It is a collection of Mr. Hughes' poems edited by Miss Effie L. Powers and designed for young readers.

Jazz Poetry and Blues

Charles S. Johnson*

"Negro Poetry" has two meanings which are constantly confused: in one sense it is poetry of any mood and theme which happens to have been written by Negroes; in another it is poetry bearing a distinct and recognizable flavor of the Negro temperament and his life. All Negroes do not write "Negro poetry" in the sense of one definition, and there is much "Negro poetry" not written by Negroes, in the sense of the other. The confusion draws its strength from the intimate circumstances of social relations, with their cross-play of emotions and reticences. Out of it have developed, among other consequences, the expectation that there should be expressed by Negroes only those passions colored by the fact of race; the over-zealous efforts to sense the sombre rustle of the jungle in innocently unracial lines about nasturtia, the seasons, or trees at night; and, with a most tragic irony, the division of Negro ranks themselves into opposing philosophies on the social advantages of artistic themes. While unracial Negro poetry is doubtless as honest as any other, and, socially considered, is demonstrating that Negroes are capable of mastery of a familiar technique, and of expressing intricate emotions with the same grace of language as any

*Reprinted from the *Carolina Magazine* 58 (May 1928):16–20, by permission of the journal.

one else, the racial poetry strikes out boldly to extract a new romance and beauty from a homely life, scarcely noticed before and never understood; it is venturing into deeper corners of life as it is lived uncomplicated by conscious subtlety, life rich in human emotions, clouded and concealed by centuries of social tradition.

"Jazz Poetry" is, of course, a misnomer. Jazz itself is not so much music as method. The poetry which goes by the name is a venture in the new, bold rhythms characteristic of the music. And, although it has come, curiously, to express the fierce tempo of our contemporary life, it is also its vent. For jazz, more than being rhythm, is an atmosphere,— that of abandon and escape from the tedium of this "stepped-up" life, a fact which explains its fascination. It has its verve, which is a throbbing, sometimes cruel, ecstacy of release; it also has its victims, crushed lives dying slowly in the shadow of their illusions. That the poetry like the music is violently strange does not detract from its fundamental value, for all new poetry arises so. George Moore contends that art is merely the embodiment of the dominant influence of the age. That its subjects are commonplace is not inconsistent with the struggle of writers since the end of the 19th Century "back to the concrete," to the new fascination of "watching the strangeness of familiar things." It is a part of the revolt against a stiff conventionalism which has yielded fewer of life's most intimate moments, than of petty and incomprehensible sentences. Louis Untermeyer begins the *New Era in American Poetry* with Sandburg, apostle of the same freedom, searcher for beauty in forgotten lives. He was severely criticized for his lack of the finer sensibilities, his indifference to the classic rhythms, and for his interest in subjects held sordid. But his is the poetry of new America, recording its beauty in its own idiom.

The new racial poetry of the Negro is the expression of something more than experimentation in a new technique. It marks the birth of a new racial consciousness and self conception. It is a first frank acceptance of race, and the recognition of difference without the usual implications of disparity. It lacks apology, the wearying appeals to pity, and the conscious philosophy of defense. In being itself it reveals its greatest charm. In accepting this life it invests it with a new meaning. "The Negro" of popular conception is not the educated person of Negro blood; he is the peasant, the dull, dark worker or shirker of work, who sprawls his shadow over the South and clutters the side streets of northern cities. These are the forgotten lives that thread about within their circles, who run the full scale of human emotions without being suspected of feeling; who, like the hopelessly deformed in body face futility and abandon themselves to their shallow resources before they begin to live. They are not known, and yet no life is without its beauty. Who would know something of the core and limitations of this life should go to the *Blues*. In them is the curious story of disillusionment without a saving philosophy and yet without defeat. They mark these narrow limits of life's satisfactions, its vast treacheries and ironies. Stark, full human passions crowd themselves into an uncomplex expression, so simple in their power that they startle. If they did not reveal a fundamental and universal emotion of the human heart, they would not be noticed now as the boisterous and persistent intruders in the polite society of lyrics that they are.

Herein lies one of the richest gifts of the Negro to American art. Art is a form of escape, and the poet's art an emotional outlet for both poet and reader. And this is the clue to the richness of Negro folk life to which the conscious racial artists have now turned frankly. The religion of the Negro was an escape from the hopelessness and drudgery of slavery,—a profound otherworldliness, for he had least to expect, and asked least, from life; his folk tales were projections of personal experiences and hopes and defeats in terms of symbols; his music has been the distillation of these moods. What the spirituals were to slavery, the *Blues* are now to his later stages.

The poetry of Langston Hughes is without doubt the finest expression of this new Negro poetry. Like Sandburg he has shocked polite circles by daring to search for beauty in things and beings too commonplace for dignity and exaltation, and actually by finding this in the folk idiom as despised as its life. His subjects have been cabaret singers, porters, street walkers, elevator boys, the long range of "hard luck" victims, Beale street and Railroad Avenue, prayer meetings, sinners, and hard working men. What does life mean for them? There is no pleading for sympathy, or moralizing; there is a moment's blinding perception of a life being lived fiercely beneath the drunken blare of trombones, or in blank weariness of the Georgia roads. Jazz to Hughes is not the debauch that the social critics conceive it to be. It is a significant expression. Significant of what? The manner of telling of the answer is really the vital point of difference between him and the very self conscious Negroes. In his lines one gets the warm sweat and breath of these lives, their shallow joys, the echoing emptiness:

Strut and wiggle,
Shameless gal.
Wouldn't no good fellow
Be your pal?

Hear dat music . . .
Jungle night.
Hear dat music . . .
And the moon was white.

Sing your Blues song,
Pretty baby.

You want lovin'
And you don't mean maybe.

Jungle lover . . .
Night black boy . . .
Two against the moon
And the moon was joy.

Why do they dance and laugh? Here is the revolt against weariness that more than Negroes feel, but none so deeply as they; to use his own expression, "pain swallowed in a smile." They dance! And his music holds the rhythm and the abandon of the cabaret,—an abandon more to be pitied than censured:

Sun's going down this evening—
Might never rise no mo'.
The sun's going down this very night—
Might never rise no mo'—
So dance with swift feet honey,
    (The banjo's sobbing low)
Dance with swift feet, honey—
    Might never dance no mo'.

Tenderness and comprehension are here when he speaks of the black dancer in "The Little Savoy":

Wine maiden
Of the jazz tuned night,
Lips
Sweet as purple dew,
Breasts
Like the pillows of all sweet dreams,
Who crushed
The grapes of joy
And dripped their juice
On you?

The *Blues* always strike a note of despondency and yet they provoke laughter. Is not this a vital adjustment, that curious condition of survival so manifest in practically all social relations across the line of race? When the horizon is so near, troubles become racial when multiplied enough by persons. In the aggregate, there comes to be told a sort of racial history. These are the *Blues*, not of the Negro intellectuals any more than of the white ones, but, of those who live beneath the range of polite respect. But they touch the springs of all human emotion, or they would not be, with their brash notes, so universal in their appeal:

Did you ever wake up in de middle of the night wid de
blues all around you, de blues all around you, did you?
Ever wake up wid de blues all round yo' bed?
An' no one near, to soothe yo' achin' head!

Or this: "My man's got a heart like a rock cast in de sea." That is the motif of the *Blues.* But the despondency touches many facets of life. Hughes sums up more than one life in "Po' Boy Blues":

> When I was home de
> Sunshine seemed like gold.
> When I was home de
> Sunshine seemed like gold.
> Since I come up North de
> Whole damn world's turned cold.
>
> I was a good boy,
> Never done no wrong.
> Yes, I was a good boy,
> Never done no wrong.
> But this world is weary
> An de road is hard an' long'.
>
> I fell in love with
> A gal I thought was kind.
> Fell in love with
> A gal I thought was kind.
> She made me lose ma money
> An' almost lose ma mind.
>
> Weary, weary,
> Weary, early in de morn.
> Weary, weary,
> Early in de morn,
> I's so weary
> I wish I'd never been born.

There is a vast and wistful restlessness in "De railroad bridge's / A sad song in de air." What matters most in all of this is the fresh and glowing re-orientation of the poet himself, and when he speaks it is for a confident new generation:

> We younger Negro artists who create now intend to express our individual dark-skinned selves without fear or shame. If white people are pleased we are glad. If they are not, it doesn't matter. We know we are beautiful. And ugly too. The tom-tom cries and the tom-tom laughs. If colored people are pleased we are glad. If they are not, their displeasure doesn't matter either. We build our temples for tomorrow, strong as we know how, and we stand on top of the mountain, free within ourselves.

The "Madam Poems" as Dramatic Monologue

Dellita L. Martin*

The word *madam* has complimentary as well as pejorative connotations. When used without a name, it signifies respect or polite address, and when coupled with surname or a designation of rank or office, it means "mistress" (*Madam* Johnson, *Madam* President, or *Madam* Chairman). In other instances, it refers to one's wife, to the head of a household, or to the operator of a callhouse.[1] My purpose in this essay is to examine Langston Hughes' approach to portraiture in the "Madam Poems."

Hughes uses dramatic monologue to convey the point of view of the character Alberta K. Johnson. As the persona in Hughes' poems, Madam assumes several roles. She tells the reader of these roles in "Madam to You: The Life and Times of Alberta K. Johnson," Part I of *One-Way Ticket*.[2] As with her male counterpart, Simple, Madam dramatically illuminates the urban conditions of Afro-American life from 1900 to 1950. In contrast with Simple's prose dialogue, however, her literary form is the dramatic monologue, "a lyric poem which reveals 'a soul in action' through the conversations of one character."[3] Although the individual poems are self-contained examples of the genre, I wish to consider them as one unit, as an extended affirmation of the experience of urban black America.

Alberta K. Johnson is a "Jill-of-all-trades," so to speak, who has survived the Depression and who continues to live in spite of hardship and setbacks. She does not discuss the details of her life, origin, parentage, family background, or age. Her caution prevents complete self-revelation, but lyricism informs the poems in which she speaks. Madam is a type, a social dwarf (to others) in the machine age, a survivor from the American underclass. She is a fairly realistic portrait which Hughes endows with just enough ambiguity to transcend stereotype. Furthermore, her poems express a communal lyricism from the female perspective.

In keeping with the dramatic monologue, Madam addresses an identifiable but silent listener at various points of tension (dramatic moments) in her life. The twelve poems of the extended form correspond to twelve such moments. Although the identity of the auditor changes according to the circumstances implied, there are two categories of listener. The first is presumably a black person with whom Madam feels comfortable enough to talk about herself. This character might be a close friend, a lover, an authority figure, or an associate

*Reprinted from *Black American Literature Forum* 15 (Fall 1981):97–99, by permission of the author and Indiana State University.

whom Madam prefers to keep at arm's length. The second is more removed from Madam's personal relationships, but, nonetheless, controls her life. This persona is white society, represented by various players. The first listener interacts with Madam through familiar encounters and direct conversations; the second through impersonal meetings and reported conversation. By manipulating the two types of situations, Hughes reinforces the orality of the poems, whose power comes with performance.

The "circumstances surrounding the conversation, one side of which we 'hear' as the dramatic monologue, are made clear by implication in the poem, and a deep insight into the character of the speaker is given."[4] The context is worth considering, since Madam's is the first and most prominent of many voices which represent broken dreams and deferred promises of urban Afro-Americans. The initial hope that permeated the mood of the Great Exodus which began around 1915 is captured in the title poem of *One-Way Ticket.* The speaker of the poem says,

I pick up my life
And take it away
On a one-way ticket—
Gone up North
Gone out West
Gone!

The comedy and tragedy, hope and desperation, frankness and subtlety, simplicity and irony, earthiness and sophistication with which black people react to city life are rendered through the voice of the communal "I." But once in Canaan the migrants are overwhelmed by the familiar ring of Jim Crow, northern or western style. Many get enmeshed in the trappings of freedom, but they are determined to stay for better or worse. Their one-way ticket means closed doors, no turning back. They will have to survive.

And survival dramatizes character, as Alberta K. Johnson unequivocally informs her listener in the opening sketch, "Madam's Past History." In her conflict with American history, the character boldly affirms self: "My name is Johnson— / Madam Alberta K. / The Madam stands for business. / I'm smart that way." She reveals that she has the native intelligence and drive to try for success. First she opens a hair-dressing parlor and then a barbecue stand. But the Depression, an external force, and her involvement with a "no-good man," an internal weakness, hinder her. One principle of the Puritan Ethic, financial security (her insurance), bolsters the system's (WPA's) refusal to aid her in times of need. She is a free loader, they say, not a temporarily displaced entrepreneur. Nevertheless, Madam Johnson resolves to overcome ("I'll get along"), and reiterates her pride at being able to take care of business by asserting, "I do cooking, / Day's works, too! . . . / *Madam* to you." *Madam* means independence.

"Madam and Her Madam" illustrates that pride and self-reliance do not prevent Alberta K. Johnson from working at any job necessary to support herself. The episode also depicts the saga of the black woman, whose exploitation has known few limits. Although Madam appears as the image of the domestic so common in American literature, she rejects the role of mule which her employer attempts to thrust upon her. She confronts her "madam" with the awareness of the latter's motives ("Can it be / You trying to make a / Packhorse out of me?"). When Mrs. Liberal retreats behind the facade of sentimentality (". . . Oh, no! / You know, Alberta, I love you so!"), Madam forces the issue ("I said, Madam, / That may be true– / But I'll be dogged / If I love you!"). *Madam* means cynicism.

"Madam's Calling Cards" poses the dilemma of "I love you / I love you not." The love/hate relationship between black and white America historically assumes the form of ambivalence, the two-headed monster which threatens Du Bois' dark body and soul. Although Madam has a strong sense of self-worth, in spite of American oppression, she quickly asserts her Americanness when asked by a printer, "Shall I use Old English / Or a Roman letter? / I said, Use American. / American's better." The humor of the sketch lies in the pun achieved through the confusion of technical terms and Madam's off-beat sense of patriotism, for to be American then was to be the image of her exploiter. Yet she seeks to identify ("But I hankered to see / My name in print.").

Patriotic duty must go on the back burner when the rent is due and the money is not there. The classical drama of "blaxploitation" is reenacted in "Madam and the Rent Man," where Madam confronts the system. The catalogue of ugly, unsanitary conditions in which she lives (rats, a cracked window, a leaking attic) reflects the infinite broken promises of the deferred dream, summarily expressed in the statement, ". . . you ain't done a thing / You promised to've done." When the rent man tries to "pass the buck," Madam advises him sarcastically that he is "out of luck" anyway, because she cannot and will not pay. The clash of two historical perspectives culminates in the brief but charged comments of each: "He said, Madam, / I ain't pleased! / I said, Neither am I. / So we agrees!" They know that they inhabit mutually exclusive spheres that seem unlikely to interface amicably.

In "Madam and the Phone Bill," Madam Johnson defies another institution of American society, "Ma Bell," or Central. On the one hand, she is childish and irresponsible for having accepted "reversed charges" from Roscoe, an old flame, and for not wanting to face the consequences. On the other hand, Alberta K. is frustrated and rebels: "Unhumm-m! . . . Yes! / You say I gave my O.K.? / Well, that O.K. you may keep— But I *sure* ain't gonna pay!" She refuses to let the system intimidate her.

In "Madam and the Charity Child," Madam takes advantage of the opportunity to criticize a welfare worker. Here it is easy to see that a concerned, compassionate person lies underneath the gruff exterior. The foster children that Madam cares for are gobbled up by the concrete jungle (The girl "got ruint" and the boy "used a switch-blade for a toy."). By posing a rhetorical question, "What makes these charity / Children so bad?" she attempts to get to the root of the problem, namely uncaring parents and an unfeeling society. Her "report" to the social worker is concise and pointed: "Last time I told her, / Report, my eye! / Things is bad— / You figure out why!" The report symbolizes America's efforts to manufacture reality, to explain away child abandonment, especially when racism is at fault. Although official facts and figures simplify the social worker's job, they hardly touch on the dimension of human suffering. Madam's reply directs the burden to the dehumanizing system where it belongs. The irony underscores her compassion.

The last point of conflict with American life occurs in "Madam and the Census Man." Here Madam locks horns with one who tampers with her identity when queried about the meaning of the "K": "I said, K— / And nothing more. / He said, I'm gonna put it / K-A-Y. I said, If you do, / You lie." The census taker's ignorance of the black naming tradition and his arrogance combine to ignite Madam's temper. He does not know, or even care, that many black people choose to use initials in place of a full name because it signifies distinction, because it marks a privilege to name oneself or one's own, or because the combination merely sounds good.[5] Alberta K. reminds him in no uncertain terms that "My mother christened me / ALBERTA K. / You leave my name / Just that way!" To tamper with her name is to trample on her heritage, but the census agent wants what is convenient for him. In addition, he is impatient with her "uppity ways." Not only does he feel it ridiculous to write down a mere initial ("Just a K / Makes your name too short."), he also rejects the sense of equality that her title implies (indicated by his "snort"). The sarcasm is designed to bolster his feeling of superiority as well as to remind her indirectly that, like other Negroes, she should have a name which smacks of the mock-heroic (Booker Taliaferro Washington, Franklin Delano Roosevelt Brown, or Phillis Wheatley Jones). Not to be demeaned by anyone, Alberta K. keeps her identity intact with the sharp retort, "I said, I don't / Give a damn! / Leave me and my name / Just like I am!" To reduce him to the stature of man, to knock him from the throne of grace, she adds insult to injury: "Furthermore, rub out / That MRS., too— / I'll have you know / I'm *Madam* to you!" *Madam* stands for respect, dignity, and pride.

The personal dimension of the "Madam Poems" is evident in the six monologues which treat Madam's encounters with members of black society. In "Madam and the Number Writer," Alberta K. tries to "get a hit." The whispering hope that the numbers game offers the powerless is symbolized by the 6-0-2 / 7-0-3 combination she arranges with the numbers writer. But 3-2-6 comes out, forcing them both to return to "go" ("And we both was in / The *same* old fix."). When Madam resolves not to "play no more" until she reaches "the other shore," the numbers writer dispels such otherworldly notions from her head with a timely rejoinder: "That's all very well— / But suppose / You goes to hell?" The numbers writer shatters Madam's argument for his own benefit.

Disillusionment is sufficient to drive Madam to seek comfort in "Madam and the Fortune Teller," where Alberta K. discovers that she must defer to another "madam." Like many who seek the oracle, she fails to understand or to accept the simple truth of the message, "Your fortune, honey, / Lies right in yourself. / You ain't gonna find it / On nobody else's shelf." The concrete symbol of the shelf evokes the blues mood and theme since a number of traditional lyrics refer to putting one's troubles on the shelf. Unfortunately, Madam lacks either the insight or the desire to explore her inner regions and, thus, leaves herself open to exploitation by one of her own kind.

The fear of lowering one's guard in the harsh environment of the big city results in a basic distrust of one's fellow man, both literally and figuratively. Thus, Alberta K. laments her foolish decision to reject a sincere suitor whom she suspects of having ulterior motives: "When you grow up the hard way / Sometimes you don't know / What's too good to be true, / Just might be so." The reason for such paranoia comes through as urban pessimism, which she expresses in the phrase, "When you think you got bread / It's always a stone—." Suspicion and hostility grow out of a situation where people feel compelled to deceive and connive to survive, and in a society in which values are negotiated on a dollars-and-cents basis, the character feels justified in believing that "nobody loves nobody / For yourself alone." Her rejection of the man's unconditional love is, more than likely, based on her previous experience with her first two husbands. Determined not to be "burned" again, *Madam* demonstrates fear and loneliness. Through mistrust she has possibly victimized herself.

"Madam and the Minister" portrays Madam Johnson's battle with the Reverend Butler, a personification of the Church. Like many a nominal Christian, she thinks that her "old-time religion" is adequate to meet the Maker. She gets irritated when the minister asks her what she has done lately. Madam counters: "None of your / Business, friend." But she is sorry for her mockery of religion and is even humbled by the remnants of the preacher's warning when she meekly utters, "I ain't in no mood / For sin today." To the chagrin of her male friend, possibly the listener in the vignette, *Madam* expresses guilt and remorse.

Her brushes with religion remind her of her own mortality. Unlike the previous monologue, "Madam and the Wrong Visitor" illustrates a contest between unequal forces, Madam and Old Death. Although apprehensive, Madam does not succumb to her fears but fights bravely. She gladly awakens only to find that she has had not only a nightmare, but also a close call, for apparently she has been seriously ill. Yet she is determined to overcome: "I'm still here kickin'!"

Madam has the mark of an Amazon or Sapphire, quite the common images of the black woman in American literature. She is bold, loud, aggressive, rebellious, tough, cynical, independent, and proud. Yet, she is also ingenious, ambivalent, sharp-minded, weak, hard-working, cautious, compassionate, vulnerable, loving, and fearful. Her dialectical nature reveals the complexity of human nature. Langston Hughes is one of very few male writers to achieve complex female characterizations. The character, Madam, encompasses the heroic, comic, and tragic dimensions immortalized by Hughes' dramatic presentation of archetypal woman.[6] Madam speaks for herself; she represents the jubilance and pain of urban blacks, who laugh to keep from crying.

Notes:

1. *Webster's Seventh New Collegiate Dictionary* (Springfield, MA: G. & C. Merriam, 1965), p. 507.

2. Langston Hughes, *One-Way Ticket* (New York: Alfred A. Knopf, 1949), pp. 3–27.

3. C. Hugh Holman, *A Handbook to Literature* (Indianapolis: Bobbs-Merrill, 1972), p. 172.

4. Ibid.

5. Lewis Chandler, "Selfsameness and a Promise," *Phylon*, 10 (Summer 1949), 190.

6. R. Baxter Miller, " 'No Crystal Stair': Unity, Archetype, and Symbol in Langston Hughes's Poems on Women," *Negro American Literature Forum*, 9 (Winter 1975), 113.

"Some Mark to Make": The Lyrical Imagination of Langston Hughes

R. Baxter Miller*

W. R. Johnson, a superior theorist, illuminates the lyric well:

> We want the pictures, yes, but we also want the hates and loves, the blame and the praise, the sense of a living voice, of a mind and heart that are profoundly engaged by a life they live richly, eagerly. Art, then, any art, is not a reproduction of what is seen: it is a highly complex action (action both by artist and audience) in which what is outer and what is inner—things, perceptions, conceptions, actualities, emotions, and ideas—are gathered into and made manifest by emotional and intelligible forms. The artist cannot be undisciplined in searching for such forms; . . . he can no more be slovenly in his habits of feeling and thinking than he can be slovenly in his habits of looking and listening or of using the implements of his craft; but neither can he be dispassionate, emotionless, unconcerned. The lie in modern imagism is that no one snaps the picture. But the difference between a bad or mediocre photo and a good or great one is precisely who takes the photo—and the photographer, like any other artist, is defined not merely by his technique or his mastery of his instrument but also by the quality of his feeling, by the precision and vitality . . . which his composition captures and reveals . . . the thing that called his mind and heart into action. . . .[1]

The words describe well many poems by Langston Hughes, one of Black America's greatest lyricists. Over nearly sixty years one has hardly dared think so. While the Greeks believed the lyric to be a communal performance in song, the shared epiphany between the singer and the audience, the form implied the aristocratic elitism at court during the Middle Ages and the Elizabethan period. In the romantic and Victorian eras, the genre suggested privacy and isolation from the masses. Today, somewhat diminished in favor of the dramatic monologue, as poetry has possibly ebbed into esoterism, those who prefer personal lyric often disclaim the social rhetoric of direct address. Indeed, one might almost take Langston Hughes at his word and accept the distinction between the forms. But while the margins between genres are convenient, they are yet flexible and partly illusory. Literary forms really mean only variations in degree. "The Negro Speaks of Rivers" (*Crisis*, June 1921), Hughes's first published poem, displaces the personal reflection, or the narrative, through a sequence of shifts from ancient Egypt in 3,000 B.C.

*This essay is drawn from the working manuscript of the forthcoming book *For A Moment I Wondered: The Literary Imagination of Langston Hughes* and appears here for the first time by permission of the author.

to the United States in the nineteenth century. Through the speaker's placement in history, it leads back to the present. Drawing upon the narrative and the dramatic elements, the poem celebrates Black America and humankind.

But, ironically, Black American history complicates the appreciation of Hughes as a lyricist. In a personal voice the poet revises the tradition he inherited. Where Phillis Wheatley praised George Washington, he honors the Black Everyman and, indeed, Everyperson. Though his contemporary, Countee Cullen, depended on sources in the poetry of John Keats, Hughes relied on allusions to the folk ballads of 1830–50 and on the nature and prophetic poems of Walt Whitman. Hughes drew upon the more contemplative verse of Vachel Lindsay. Where Paul Laurence Dunbar had earlier accommodated himself to the Old South, Hughes revised the pastoral for the times. But, as regards the folk integrity, Hughes was less naive.

From *Weary Blues* in 1926, to "Daybreak in Alabama" at the end of *Panther and the Lash* in 1967, the lyric serves to open and close Hughes's literary life and work.[2] When other genres attract his attention, this one retains particular resilence. But the impulse wanes in the fifties and sixties. For Langston Hughes the lyric illuminates the graphic and timeless. Against the backdrop of time, he invokes dynamic feeling in order to subordinate and control personal loneliness, but he never excludes the communal response. In retrospection, he downplays the narrative of miscegenation ("Cross") and the allegorical tragedy ("Pierrot") into precise understatement. Or he sometimes disguises the lyrics themselves as dramatic performances through the blues song and the jazz instrument. What one finds ultimately in the lyricist concerns the sensitive self who speaks to Nature and the masses. In an epiphany the solo and the chorus face each other, at the height of the performance, itself timeless through intensity and will, but the personae live within three decades (1920–40), no matter how universal the writer dreams them to be. Whether in the twenties or the forties, one ultimately redescends from "The Negro Speaks of Rivers" or from "Oppression" to the fallen world.[3] From the poetic re-creation of Black American history in particular and the American South in general, the narrator inevitably returns to a certain death in Harlem. Sequential history is fact.

For Langston Hughes the lyric highlights the human and social dream. Incarnated in the blues singer and player, it signifies the artistic performance in general. It suggests the oral teller and the cultural priest, who recount the sacred story about experience and the past. From the history of 1855–65, the lyric records the poetic remembrance of the Civil War and the presence of one poet, Walt Whitman, who wrote it down.[4] Almost indifferent to the historical context, the speaker never mentions whom Whitman met, or when, or says why so. Including the death of Abraham Lincoln, the narrator overlooks the troubled circumstances. But what he manages yet involves a frozen moment in human and self-communion. Sometimes disguised as the blues performance, Hughes's lyric first subsumes social rhetoric into epiphany (*The Weary Blues*, 1926). Then it encourages inquiry into the technical means for the evocation of awe and wonder, for astonishment, and for the sublime.[5] Finally, the lyric demonstrates the compression and acrostic power in *Fields of Wonder* (1947). Over the years Langston Hughes abandons much lyricism to the use of dramatic monologue.

Largely to assess the significance of the change, it profits one to define the purpose and function of lyric.[6] The genre involves poetic emotion which, expressed in time, insists that time itself or, sequential thought, is illusion. Just as the lyric quality displaces the narrative poem on the grand scale, so it often represses from itself much analytic idea and dramatic action. Yet lyric situates itself in the dramatic context from which emotion emerges. Though drama takes place in history and time, the lyric distances itself from them. While the drama tends to move, the lyric remains still. The drama reveals the development of plot and character, but the lyric illuminates the progression of emotion. While the drama signifies the narrative and historical action, the lyric signifies the story of the self. At times Langston Hughes succeeds through the projection of the lyric personality into the narrator who speaks and feels truly. While the implicit dramatic action depends upon time and space, the particular situation, the lyric quality suspends them. And though a play such as *Mulatto* benefits from a precise setting, "The Negro Speaks of Rivers" reveals the permanency of memory and human existence.

However academic the overtones, any elitist assessment of Langston Hughes's lyrics must fail. Open to the range of human emotion, they express misanthropy, egoism, or cynicism.[7] In the display of the solo self, they reveal a concern for the choral one as well.[8] Here the individual talent speaks within cultural and racial tradition. So even Hughes's lyrics are covertly rhetorical. Where poetic images exist, as part of human language, they necessarily contribute to emotive and moral discourse. For the Black American and social poet, they intensely reconfirm the tension between the pictured world (American Dream) and the real one (racial lynching): "A totally unrhetorical poetry will be, as we have come to know all too well, a poetry void of passion, void of choosing, void of rational freedom—it will be in Paul Valery's metaphor, the rind of the orange without the pulp and the juice."[9] Even lyric distills the sublime, the humane and social spirit that informs figurative language: "In our technological societies, when the individual human began more and more to feel cut off from his fellows and from the world, when inwardness became less a matter of anger and terror, the modern choralists, in their different ways, attempted to countervail this process of alienation by reaffirming our kinship with each other and with the world that begets us and nourishes us, by denying that the exploitations of empire and the degradations worked by the machine had or would or could succeed. . . ."[10]

To recognize the covert rhetoric in lyric means to appreciate the overlap between emotive and discursive poetry.[11] Rooted in song, the lyric reestablishes the ritual of human communion. From the ancients who sang out the odyssey, to Woody Guthrie and Bob Dylan, to Roberta Flack and Lionel Richey, the flow contains an inspirational power nearly akin to religion. What one remembers, finally, concerns the double presence that allows Langston Hughes to speak at once within and without history, to participate in the dynamic story, yet inertly reflect upon it, to read as well as feel the meaning.

For Langston Hughes the lyric imagination bridges the prelapsarian and lapsarian worlds. Aware of the discrepancy between the American word and deed, he hardly mistakes the country itself for the ideal. The imagination and social mind separate only in the failure to impose the coherent vision upon the entire range of human experience. While the tragic *Mulatto*, or the comic *Semple Takes a Wife* represents the diverse sides present, the lyrics express the duality of the whole imagination. The poems convert fact into value, power into thought, and the "dualism of word and deed into an orphic unity."[12] While Hughes's speakers perform the historical rites from the Harlem Renaissance (1920–28), from the Great Depression (1930s), from World War II (1940s), and from the Civil Rights Movement (1954–68), they supersede historical sequence. They contain ideals that transcend time or, indeed, Time (human pattern): " 'words' and 'silence' denote two different states of feeling, the second higher and purer than the first. Words issue from time (*tempus*) and are vitiated by the penury of our daily concerns. However, they know enough to aspire to a higher and purer state, given in Eliot's lines as 'form' and 'pattern' in which the mere contents of form are not transcended but enhanced, fulfilled, redeemed. Silence is therefore a scruple which attends upon the local satisfaction of words, the voice which says that words are often self-delusions, trivial gratifications. Silence speaks against time to redeem time. Silence therefore corresponds to the fine excess of the imagination."[13] Hughes's lyric voice clarifies his own signature to Black American history. Shaped through words themselves become symbols,[14] it mediates between antonyms which are untranslatable, at least completely, into each other, including Black and White, Harlem and Africa, war and peace. However apparently private, the lyrics ultimately implode back into the folk center implied. Where the images suggest cultural beliefs and myths, the values are Black American: "Expressions cannot save us from temporality, but thanks to symbols, we can ascend to the realm of eternity."[15] While Hughes's lyricism displaces the drama and narrative of Black American history, it nevertheless signifies the passage from the Harlem Renaissance to the Civil Rights Movement. The lyrics imply the very drama which they displace, the advance from tragedy to peace.[16] While Hughes confines racial suffering and conflict to the half-light, he clarifies the need for reconciliation. Langston Hughes reclaims from American history the right to reimagine Black humanity and, indeed, humankind.[17]

A broad overview of *The Weary Blues* clarifies the thematic unity and diverse technique. Grouped according to seven romantic ideas, sixty-eight poems appear under seven headings. While the emphasis goes to the collective consciousness derived from African ancestry in particular and human history in general, other concerns are personal loneliness, isolation, and loss. Still signifying the Harlem Renaissance and the jazz age, a third set presents the cabarets, infusing interracial sex within overtones of the exotic. In a deftness often overlooked, Hughes uses anaphora to narrate an imperial self so as to sustain the blues stanza as countermelody and ironic understatement. What most complements the lyric skill concerns the dramatic movement of feeling. Through the impulse, he portrays the child's maturation into the state of the lost imagination and the transmutation of suffering into art. In narrative distancing his speakers achieve a double identification. While they situate themselves in the dramatic situation implied, they share the reader's historical consciousness. The lyric hardly represents all of the range, but the formal movement does counterplay to the dramatic tragedy suggested.

Indeed, the performance in the title poem completes the ritualistic conversion from Black American suffering into epic communion. On 1 May 1925, during a banquet at an "elegant" Fifth Avenue restaurant in New York City, the poem won a prize from *Opportunity* magazine, where it subsequently appeared. The thirty-five-line lyric presents a singer who plays one night on Harlem's Lenox Avenue. Having performed well in the club, the pianist goes to bed, as the song still sounds in the mind. In the dull pallor, and beneath the old gas light, he has played his ebony hands on the ivory keys. During the "lazy sway" from the bar stool, he has patted the floor with his feet, done a few chords, and then sung some more. Finally, he sleeps "like a rock that's dead," the artistic spirit exhausted.[18]

His performance clearly implies several dramatic actions. While one sets the dynamic playing, the Black self-affirmation against what fades, a second concerns a vital remaking of the Black self-image. A third shows the transcendence through racial stereotype into lyrical style. From the dramatic situation of the player, both musical as well as performed, the poem imposes the isolation and loneliness, yet the refusal to accept them. The song marks a metonym for the human imagination.

When Hughes's speakers step back from the dramatic performance into the lyric perception, they delimit the space of dream, sometimes in covertly sexual metaphor. At the detached distance from any dramatic situation, they even remake the iconography of Black and White, often revising and neutralizing the traditional code of culture, race, and value. Written in two stanzas, "Dream Variations" has nine lines in the first part and eight in the second one. While the persona longs for his dream, he sees the externalization in Nature, the place and the sun. What confronts him concerns the very duality of dream, which exists only in the lyric moment of timelessness. For the player within the concealed story, on the night in 1924, the performance must be completed in time to assure the customary paycheck.

While the lyric dream may therefore seem static, it finally has a meaning in the dynamic world of social change, where it would decay. In "Dream Variations" the Black self impregnates the lighted world and even Time itself. While the phallic drive into the Harlem Renaissance, the advance in chronological time, is finite, the vaginal response to sentiment, as the imaginative reassertion, remains infinite. Insofar as the Western world asserts the priority of linear time over the natural frontier, the view ultimately vanishes into darkness. Survival depends upon universal harmony with the world.

> whirl
> Till the white day is done
> Then rest at cool evening
> Beneath a tall tree
>
> . . . .
>
> A tall, slim tree
> Night coming tenderly
> Black like me

Here the speaker balances the double compulsion toward reason and light (white day) with the mythic sentiment which justifies life.

While the double identification with phallic time and vaginal timelessness appears perhaps most notably in "The Negro Speaks of Rivers" (*Crisis*, June 1921), a poem dedicated to the late W. E. B. Du Bois, it is more essential to the well-crafted and allegorical "Jester." "Rivers" presents the narrator's skill in retracting known civilization back to the source in East Africa. Within thirteen lines and five stanzas, through the evocation of wisdom and anagoge, one marks human consciousness. Then the speaker affirms the spirit distilled from human history, ranging from 3,000 B.C., through the mid-nineteenth century to the author himself at the brink of the Harlem Renaissance.[19] The powerful repetend, "I've known rivers. / Ancient, dusky rivers," closes the human narrative in nearly a circle, for the verse has subtly turned itself from an external focus to a now unified and internal one: "My soul has grown deep like the rivers." Except for the physical and spiritual dimensions, the subjective "I" and the "river" read the same.

So East Africa marks the source for both physical and spiritual humanity. When the Euphrates flows from East Turkey southeast and southwest into the Tigris, it recalls the rise as well as the fall of the Roman Empire. For over two thousand years, the water helped delimit the domain. Less so did the Congo which south of the Sahara demarcates the natural boundaries between White and Black Africa. The latter empties into the Atlantic Ocean, just as the Nile flows northward from Uganda into the Mediterranean. In the United States, the Mississippi River flows in the southeast from North Central Minnesota to the Gulf of Mexico. Whether north or south, east or west, the rivers signify in concentric half-circles the fertility as well as the dissemination of life. For the imaginative mind, the liquid externalizes the flow and depth. In suggesting the challenge to explore brave new worlds, Europe and the Americas, "The Negro Speaks of Rivers" reclaims the origins in Africa.

Just as the speaker in "The Negro Speaks of Rivers" stands outside of historical time, so the narrator in "Jester" distances himself from literary forms as well:

In one hand
I hold tragedy
And in the other
Comedy—
Masks for the Soul

Detached from the dramatic situation, the narrator makes a choral appeal without didacticism, not excluding the epigrammatic twist, abruptly closing the lyric in understatement and rhetorical question. Here appears the invocation to chorus through recovery of the solo:

Laugh at my sorrow's reign.
I *am* the Black jester
The dumb clown of the world,

. . . .

Once I was wise
Shall I be wise again?

What some would mistake for simplistic discourse is thoughtful reflection.

While the lyric dream in Langston Hughes suggests the personal solo, the sea implies the choral response in Nature. Sometimes the parts coalesce in an epiphany. "As I Grew Older" tells about the persona's loss of a dream and the subsequent disillusion. The poem opens with a memory of the ideal, but the rising wall eclipses it. In color the "dark hands" resemble the shadow. What challenges the speaker concerns the need to deconstruct the negative associations and to reimage himself as positive Black light.

While the social restrictions (the wall) exist during the 1920s, they ironically imply the dream that transcends Time. In the rise, the wall demonstrates the dynamic recurrence. The social eclipse appears as "dimming" and "hiding." When dynamism leads finally to stasis, the solo self invokes Nature:

Find my dream!
Help me to shatter this darkness,
To smash this night;
To break this shadow
Into a thousand lights of sun,
Into a thousand whirling dreams
Of sun!

Where color was descriptive ("my dark hands"), it becomes metaphorical, for any real "darkness" exists within.

Whatever the imminent dangers, the sea provides a means for lyric escape. Written in two stanzas, "Water-Front Streets" is simply a romantic ballad that shows a movement from external nature to the poetic mind. Hughes achieves the personal revision of the pastoral tradition in English. Evolved from Edmund Spenser, the genre was already decadent by the time of Alfred Lord Tennyson, but it subsisted in the lyrics of the Georgians near the turn of the century, just as it does today in confessional and neo-romantic poetry. While biographical and autobiographical sources generally note Lindsay and Lowell as the major influences on Hughes's verse, the diction and tone suggest Tennyson's "Crossing the Bar" (1889). The placement of life and death reverses itself, "But lads put out to sea / Who carry their beauties in their hearts / And dreams, like me." From Milton's "Il Penseroso" to Gray's "Elegy Written In A Country Churchyard," Gothic ascent and romantic isolation suggest the evolution of English lyricism. When the sailor (the poet) lifts anchor in "A Farewell," those on shore hardly miss him. Realists lack patience with dreamers. The gypsies and the sailors are metonyms, or the "wanderers of the hills and seas." Seeking the fortune, they leave "folk and fair." For Hughes's speakers, the invoked chorus provides only silence, for the "you" who live between the hills / And have never seen the seas." And they counterplay to the poet, the Black Odysseus. In "Seascape" Hughes's narrator redescends from lyric heights to sequential history. When a ship passes off the coast of Ireland, the seamen view a line of fishing ships etched against sky. Later, off the coast of England, the seamen ride ("rode") the foam where they observe an Indian merchant "coming home." Still, realism infringes upon the dreamworld. While the seascape is a revelation, the speaker rides in time as well, not merely toward his literal "home" but toward death.[20]

For Langston Hughes the lyric arrests the movement of the personal narrative toward extinction. "Death of an Old Seaman" portrays a persona who has returned home. Through alliteration and assonance, he appears against the background of the hill and sea. In facing the winds, he sets into relief all of the natural elements except fire, possibly because his life now ends. The musical recovery may exist as much within the narrative content as in the sentimental rhythm. Clearly a ballad more than a lyric, "Beggar Boy" dramatizes the mysterious performance of a black flute player. Despite the poverty, he incarnates the creativity that eludes all imagery. Distilled from Black American deprivation, the introspection tells: "And yet he plays . . . / As if Fate had not bled him. . . ." However much the final line bumps, the beggar boy remains a "shadow," but the narrator truly reads the "Fate." The story resembles the boy's "flute," the "sun." What the child feels but cannot articulate, the speaker understands well. As the signs for self-determination, the story and song oppose dark fate.

In *Fields of Wonder* (1947) Hughes disproves the critic's arbitrary and condescending claim: "His lyric poetry is no doubt of secondary importance in his work; yet, as usually happens with the minor work of great artists, this minor (lyric) poetry is high enough in quality and great enough in quantity to have sustained the reputation of a lesser poet."[21] Where the prescriptive critic favors the "social" verse, he accepts too readily the distinction between lyric and rhetoric.[22] But what generates the lyrical power in *Fields* conceals the real concern with community. While the persona feigns privacy, he addresses the men and women who would hear him, for the lyric, like the dramatic monologue, implies the respondent. Sometimes the hearer is anthromorphic Nature, almost elegaic in the counterplay and impervious to Time.

In *Fields* Hughes makes the external world (fields) parallel the personal sentiment (desire and tears). The language shows greater compression. Derived from the acrostic design, it displays alliteration as well as assonance. What sometimes begins as a skillful apostrophe ends in rhetorical and cryptic counterpoint.[23] Published originally in the *Christian Register* (May 1947), a twelve-line lyric, "Birth," signifies the artistic credo. Without direct address to the social mission, as does the "cool poet" in "Motto,"[24] it images the creative calling into the metonyms of stars, moon, and sun. Just as the lyric emotion subsides into the lyric process, so the pictorial frieze fades into the surge of dramatic action. Private feeling has become public deed. Where the social revolutionary seems displaced, he still speaks in undertone. Indeed, he imposes the signature and voice upon human history: "stroke / Of lightening / In the night / Some mark to Make / Some Word / to Tell." Indirectly, the persona partially confirms: "The imagination deals with feelings preferably wayward, congentially wild, and it wants to move them not into formulae but toward the state of value and purity for which Eliot's 'form' and 'pattern' at once moving and still. . . . The imagination makes nothing happen, but it lets things happen by removing obstacles of routine and providing a context of feeling from which they appear naturally to emerge."[25] But for Langston Hughes the lyrical imagination is dynamic and fertile.

"Carolina Cabin," a neglected poem, displaces lyricism into the dramatic situation. In twenty-two lines and four stanzas, two lovers take warm refuge near a fireplace. Viewed first as an imaginative landscape, the setting has hanging moss, holly, and "tall straight pine." The unfolding drama parallels the narrator's silent movement inward. Near the cracking fire and rare red wine, the narrator hears good laughter. When he looks then outward, the gloomy world has

> The winds of winter cold
> As down the road
> A wandering poet
> Must roam.

Still, the plot peacefully evolves itself in reinforced laughter. Where love's old story recurs, people make a home. The poem reveals the angle on post–World War II alienation in the United States. While the aesthetic world lures the narrator, he must eventually return to realistic commitment. The diction has both secular and religious connotations. As a participant in the racial narrative implied, the speaker achieves the mythic dimensions of the Wandering Jew. In the way, he perceives the limits of literary myth and historical reality.

"Old Sailor," far less dramatic and well-structured, subordinates the lyric quality to greater narrative. For twenty lines, a paralyzed mariner fancies women all over the world lament his absence. Indebted to Hughes's own days as a sailor (1923–24), the tragicomic poem completes the career vicariously. The literary work closes the frame on the historical life. In the first twelve lines, the narrator has "tasted" mysteries in Oriental cities. With Bohemian joy and international sorrow, he pursues the Dionysian urge. Then, in the last eight lines, he deteriorates into a poor dreamer. Unable to perform "heroic" deeds, he remembers from youth the sexual prowess and laughter. Yet while the mind itself faces decay, it "re-minds" itself of the spiritual recovery that resists physical death. Embodied in Time, the poetic urge remains timeless.

In twenty-four lines and four stanzas, "Sailing Date" tells the story of old mariners who face the fading years. Here are the twist, strangeness, and "bitter rage" of the lives. The sailors have deteriorated from youthful adventure ("salt sea water") to lushness ("whiskey shore"). While the decline marks the broken dreams and the imminent aging, the men narrate the past. Experienced in a thousand storms, they have survived world wars. Since the days when submarines once threatened them, they have mastered an ironic indifference.

For the tone Hughes draws heavily upon the poetry of England and the United States, especially from the nineteenth century, though the sources still merit original consideration.[26] In "O Captain! My Captain!" Whitman alludes to Abraham Lincoln (history) and to God (eternity). For "Crossing the Bar," on the contrary, Tennyson allegorizes God (the Pilot) alone. And Hughes himself celebrates Whitman in "Old Walt,"[27] a poem which appropriately reappeared in a chapbook called *The Pilot* (26 December 1954). Whether about the president during the Civil War or the God beyond, the narrator portrays events within historical time, but imaginatively projects himself beyond them. The implicit drama of history underscores Lincoln's death and Tennyson's life, but the lyric highlights the symbolic actions of mourning and faith. Thus in the repressed rhetoric Hughes's lyrics bridge the disparate worlds of fact and value.

In "Trumpet Player: 52nd Street," as in "The Weary Blues," the dramatic performance completes the lyrical impulse.[28] The quality implodes in the instrumental metaphor rather than in the choral rhetoric. During the forty-four lines, the player distills jazz from old desire and hardship. Then, with the trumpet at his lips, he blows against and through the ambivalence for acculturation, the paradox of racial identity. In the "tamed down hair," the straightened "process" he demonstrates more than style, for he would resemble Whites whose hair is naturally so. But what the player has accepted socially, he rejects artistically. The inner Black light, the implicit metaphor, "glows" brilliantly through the "process" and "gleams" as "jet [Black] were yet a crown."

What gives the image dramatic power concerns the lighted frieze in the counterplay to the persona's inner light and, indeed, to the musical time in the played song as well as to Time. The light on the player moves so fast as to feign no movement. But the music, the movement of which is clearly heard, sounds rhythmically. And the music reminds the reader that the temporal lapse between 1947 and 1985, indeed the future, is hardly the static illusion by which speeding light tricks the eye. Immediate in the challenge to lyrical experience, history and time are real. Distanced from them, the narrator focuses on different angles for the trumpeter and for the performance. Partly identifying with the sound and light, he narrates the communion of the dramatic performance. In the arrestment of time, both auditory (sound) and visible (light), the player mixes "honey" with "liquid fire," an oxymoron in flowing and "burning" sweetness. The dynamic performance merely plays out the inert desire. Though the scene gives the illusion of permanence, he expresses "longing for the moon" and "longing for the sea." In the reflection of the moonlight, from earth at night, he has resolved a paradox, for if fire can flow yet appropriate to itself the quality of the contrasting element, water, so the imagination might reverse the very racial terms through which poets image human experience. Literary light, like the trumpeted song, may well be Black. And the Black light exorcises the previous self-disillusion. When the repetend reinforces the dramatic performance, including the frieze, the player sports his "one-button roll" or jacket. In the convenient shift from the dramatic mode to the lyric one, the narrator wonders about the trumpeter's motivation.

While the performance obscures the lyric form itself, the latter subsides in the instrumental music. Herein modernity only appears to have displaced the pastoral world. Through rhetorical convention, the soloist delivers the song to the chorus but expects no answer. While any reaffirmations are silent from the poem, they are yet implied. Thus Langston Hughes, like Ezra Pound, "found that he loved and praised only what Pindar and Horace and Johnson and Whitman had loved and praised: perfection of good order, the kinship of earth, the earth herself in her epiphanies of fertility, Nature, and culture, the paradises of earth and the unearthly paradises that engender them, the dignity of humankind and of the universe. Like his predecessors in choral, he had also blamed what offered to harm or destroy what he loved and praised, but he had spent too much time in blaming. And the joy and celebration survived even that."[29]

Even the sensitive insight implies the illusions that Western critics impose upon human history. At least three thousand years before Pindar, the lyric in Africa must have made for the communal recitation during which the original humans listened to history from the oral teller. Today the lyric still marks the ritual through which the self and society collectively reaffirm community. Whether the song is vocal or instrumental, the writer's narrators merely displace the racial history that the speakers inevitably signify. The lyric implies both the social narrative and the dramatic event. Never completely detoured into aristocratic and private poetry, Langston Hughes helps restore the ancient form to rhetorical timelessness.

Notes:

1. W. R. Johnson, *The Idea of Lyric* (Berkeley: University of California Press, 1982), 23.

2. See R. Baxter Miller, " 'A Mere Poem'; 'Daybreak in Alabama,' Resolution to Langston Hughes's Commentary on Music and Art," *Obsidian* 2 (1976):30–37.

3. I am mainly concerned here with *The Weary Blues* (1926; reprint, New York: Alfred A. Knopf, 1945) and *Fields of Wonder* (New York: Alfred A. Knopf, 1947).

4. See Donald B. Gibson, "The Good Black Poet and the Good Gray Poet: The Poetry of Hughes and Whitman," in *Modern Black Poets*, ed. Donald B. Gibson (Englewood Cliffs, N.J.: Prentice-Hall, 1973), 43–56; reprinted from *Langston Hughes: Black Genius*, ed. Therman B. O'Daniel (New York: William Morrow, 1971).

5. Edmund Burke, *The Philosophy of Edmund Burke*, ed. Louis I. Bredvold and Ralph G. Ross (Ann Arbor: University of Michigan, 1967), 256–67.

6. See Felix E. Schelling, *The English Lyric* (Boston: Houghton Mifflin, 1913), 1–2; Barbara Hardy, *The Advantage of Lyric* (Bloomington: Indiana University Press, 1977), 1–3.

7. The position disagrees with Schelling's (*The English Lyric*, 5–12).

8. The distinction is Johnson's (*The Idea of Lyric*).

9. Ibid., 23.

10. Ibid.

11. Ruth Finnegan, *Oral Poetry* (London: Cambridge University Press, 1977), 25–29; Thomas R. Edwards, *Imagination and Power: A Study of Poetry on Public Themes* (New York: Oxford University Press, 1971), 6.

12. Denis Donoghue, *The Sovereign Ghost* (Berkeley: University of California Press, 1976), 221–22.

13. Ibid., 228

14. Seiichi Hatano, *Time and Eternity*, trans. Ichiro Suzuki (Tokyo: Ministry of Education, 1963), 20.

15. Ibid., 20, 148.

16. See Albert William Levi, *Literature, Philosophy, and the Imagination* (Bloomington: Indiana University Press, 1962), 274.

17. See Peter Conrad, *Imagining America* (New York: Oxford University Press, 1980), 5.

18. See Faith Berry, *Langston Hughes: Before and Beyond Harlem* (Westport: Lawrence Hill, 1983), 61.

19. See Chancellor Williams, *The Destruction of Black Civilization* (Chicago: Third World Press, 1976), 139.

20. "Home," the metaphor of death, occurs in "Soul Gone Home," in *Five Plays by Langston Hughes*, ed. Webster Smalley (Bloomington: Indiana University Press, 1963).

21. Onwuchekwa Jemie, *Langston Hughes* (New York: Columbia University Press, 1976), 139.

22. See Johnson, *The Idea of Lyric*, 1–23.

23. The groupings are Fields of Wonder, Border Line, Heart of the World, Silver Rain, Desire, and Tearless.

24. Arthur P. Davis, "Langston Hughes: Cool Poet," *CLA Journal* 11 (June 1968):276–83.

25. Donoghue, *The Sovereign Ghost*, 226–27.

26. Though Gibson ("The Good Black Poet") deals satisfactorily with the sources in Whitman, nearly everyone overlooks the Victorians.

27. "Old Walt," *Beloit Poetry Journal*, no. 5 (1954):10.

28. For a folk reading, see Richard K. Barksdale, "Langston Hughes: His Times and Humanistic Techniques," in *Black American Literature and Humanism*, ed. R. Baxter Miller (Lexington: University Press of Kentucky, 1981), 23–25.

29. See Johnson, *The Idea of Lyric*, 195.

Prose

Old John in Harlem: The Urban Folktales of Langston Hughes

Susan L. Blake*

"If you want to know about my life," says Simple in the story that introduces him to readers of *Simple Speaks His Mind* and *The Best of Simple*, "don't look at my face, don't look at my hands. Look at my feet and see if you can tell how long I been standing on them." In the well-known catalogue of things Simple's feet have done—the miles they've walked; the lines they've stood in; the shoes, summer sandals, loafers, tennis shoes, and socks they've worn out; and the corns and bunions they've grown—Langston Hughes characterizes Jesse B. Simple, Harlem roomer, as the personification of the accumulated black experience. But what is especially significant about Simple is that he not only acknowledges his past, but uses it to shape his present. When his bar-buddy Boyd challenges him to name one thing his feet have done that makes them different from any other feet in the world, Simple points to the window in the white man's store across the street and replies that his right foot broke out that window in the Harlem riots and his left foot carried him off running, because his personal experience with his history had taught him, as he says, "to look at that window and say, 'It ain't mine! Bam-mmm-mm-m' and kick it out."[1]

In creating the Simple stories, Hughes has done the same thing with the black folk tradition that his character does with black history—made it live and work in the present. It is easily recognized that Hughes has a relationship to the folk tradition. He wrote poetry in vernacular language and blues form. He edited *The Book of Negro Humor* and, with Arna Bontemps, *The Book of Negro Folklore*, which includes several of his own poems and Simple stories as literature "in the folk manner." Simple himself has been called a "folk character" on the basis of half a dozen different definitions of the term: sociological average,

*Reprinted from *Black American Literature Forum* 14 (Fall 1980): 100–104, by permission of the author and Indiana State University.

composite of Southern folk types, epic hero, ordinary man, wise fool, blues artist.[2] But Simple is more than vaguely "folk," and Hughes's relationship to the folk tradition is direct and dynamic. Simple is the migrant descendant of John, the militant slave of black folklore, and the fictional editorials that Hughes wrote for the *Chicago Defender* from 1943 to 1966[3] function as real folktales in the political storytelling tradition of the John-and-Old-Marster cycle. Not only do they follow the pattern of the John tales in characterization and conflict, not only do they include traditional motifs, they also recreate on the editorial page of a newspaper the dramatic relationship between storyteller and audience that characterizes an oral storytelling situation.

The principal difference between folk and self-conscious literature is in the relationship between the work and the audience. Generally speaking, self-conscious literature, usually written, isolates the experience of individuals; is addressed to individuals, who may or may not share either personal or social experience with either the author or the characters; and is experienced by the individual as an individual. Folk literature, usually oral, isolates the experience of a socially-defined group; is addressed to all members of the group; and is experienced by a group, even if it consists of only two members, as a group. The self-conscious artist tells a story to suit himself, and the audience takes it or leaves it. The folk storyteller chooses and adapts a traditional text according to the occasion and the audience. The folk audience, therefore, participates in the storytelling and, in a sense, is also part of the story told. The story is told by, to, and for the people it is about; it is part of their lives as they are part of it. The Simple stories close the gap between story and audience created by the medium of print in several ways. They, too, adapt traditional materials from black folklore, the Bible, U.S. history, and popular culture. They, too, are occasional, as they deal with current events and social conditions. Their consistent subject, race, is the one experience that unites and defines the folk group to which they are addressed. Their principal character is an avid reader of the very publication in which the audience encounters him. Their story-within-a-story structure creates a dialogue between characters and audience. And their purpose is to function in the social conflict in which both characters and audience are engaged.

The typical Simple story is narrated by Boyd, who reports an encounter with Simple in which Simple has narrated an experience of his own. Each story contains two conflicts—one expressed in Simple's confrontation with an outside antagonist, the other in the conversation with Boyd in which he narrates it. Both conflicts are based on the consequences of race, which Simple defines in this exchange:

> "The social scientists say there is *no* difference between colored and white," I said. "You are advancing a very unscientific theory."

> "Do I look like Van Johnson?" asked Simple.
>
> "No, but otherwise–"
>
> "It's the *otherwise* that gets it," said Simple. "There is no difference between me and Van Johnson, except *otherwise*. I am black and he is white, I am in Harlem and he is in Beverly Hills, I am broke and he is rich, I am known from here around the corner, and he is known from Hollywood around the world. There is as much difference between Van Johnson and me as there is between day and night. And don't tell me day and night is the same. If you do, I will think you have lost your mind."[4]

The *otherwise* that Simple is talking about—the social, political, and economic disparity between blacks and whites—generates other disparities: between Christianity and racism, legislation and application, "race leaders" and black folks, "say-ola" and "do-ola," *ought* and *is*, the American Dream and the American Dilemma. These in turn produce the psychological disparity, the twoness that Du Bois classically defined, between being black and being American. In general, the story Simple narrates addresses the social disparity; his dialogue with Boyd addresses the psychological. The dual structure of the stories makes Simple both actor and storyteller; it makes Boyd actor, teller, and audience. It enables Hughes to explore all the implications of American race discrimination and to bring them home to the audience that experiences them.

In the inside story, Simple follows the model of John, the insubordinate slave in the cycle of folktales about the perpetual contest between John and Old Marster. John is Old Marster's favorite slave, his foreman, his valet, his confidant, his fortune-teller, his alter ego. When Old Marster throws a party, John plays the fiddle; when he gambles with his neighbors, he bets on John; when he goes on a trip, he leaves John in charge. John is as close to Old Marster as a slave can be, but he is still a slave. He spends his life trying to close the gap between himself and Old Marster, between slavery and manhood. In the words of Julius Lester, John does "as much living and as little slaving" as he can.[5]

He does so by effectually swapping places with Old Marster. At every opportunity, he puts himself in Old Marster's shoes: throws a party in the big house when Old Marster takes a trip, appropriates Old Marster's hams and chickens, "borrows" his clothes and his best horse, copies his manners, kisses his wife, and generally assumes the prerogatives of manhood that Old Marster takes for granted. He also shows Old Marster what it is like to go barefoot. When Old Marster and Old Miss sneak back from their trip in ragged disguise to spy on his party, John sends them to the kitchen like white trash. When Old Marster sends John out at night to guard his cornfield from a bear,

John ends up holding the gun while Old Marster plays ring-around-the-rosy with the bear.

John is neither big nor strong, and he is more than clever. He is a political analyst. When he wins a round with Old Marster, his victory is the result of an objective understanding of the political and psychological principles of slavery that enables him to turn those principles back upon the institution. In one version of a popular tale called "The Fight," for example, John bluffs his opponent into forfeiting a fight on which Old Marster has staked his entire plantation by slapping Old Miss across the face. Since John has saved the plantation, Old Marster is reduced to diffidence when he inquires why John has violated the rock-bottom rules of slavery. When John explains, "Jim knowed if I slapped a white woman I'd a killed him, so he run," there is nothing further Old Marster can say.[6] Even when John himself loses, the tale contains the analysis of slavery that represents the teller's and audience's intellectual control over their situation. Whether he wins or loses, John is the personification of this control.

Simple, the character in his own stories, like John, has the circumstances of a slave and the psychology of a free man. Although he works for a wage instead of for life, it's a subsistence wage, as evidenced by his chronic inability to save the One Hundred and Thirty-Three Dollars and Thirty-Four Cents to pay for his share of his divorce from Isabel so he can marry Joyce. Although he doesn't need a pass to leave Harlem, as John needs a pass to leave the plantation, Simple knows that there are barber shops, beaches, and bars outside Harlem where he would be unwelcome or in danger. Although his antagonists are as various as newspaper reporters, hotel clerks, Emily Post, and Governor Faubus, they all represent institutions of a society that excludes him, just as Old Marster represents slavery. But just as John refuses to behave like a slave, Simple refuses to be restricted by race: "What makes you think I'm colored?" he demands when told a factory is not taking on any "colored boys." "They done took such words off of jobs in New York State by law."[7]

As a storyteller, Simple points out the same kinds of disparities that concerned the tellers of John tales. First, there are the practical disparities between life uptown and life downtown. The folk storyteller points out that John sees chicken on Old Marster's table and fat bacon on his own. Simple observes that Joyce buys her groceries downtown because "everything is two-three-four cents a pound higher in Harlem";[8] that he could get a hotel room if he asked for it in Spanish, but not if he asked for it in English;[9] that white folks Jim Crow and lynch him "anytime they want to," but "suppose I was to lynch and Jim Crow white folks, where would I be?"[10] Second, there is the disparity between stated and practiced values. Two of the themes that Simple returns to most frequently are also common themes in folk literature: the difference between Christian doctrine and Christians' doing, and the reversed status of people and animals when the people are black. In "Cracker Prayer," a variant of a traditional type of satiric prayer of which there is an example in Hurston's folklore collection *Mules and Men,* Simple impersonates a pious bigot who prays to the "Great Lord God, Jehovah, Father . . . to straighten out this world and put Nigras back in their places."[11] In "Golden Gate," he dreams a dream based on the traditional tale of The Colored Man Barred From Heaven, in which he arrives at the gate of Heaven and finds "Old Governor of Mississippi, Alabama, or Georgia, or wherever he is from," telling him to go around the back.[12] Black folklore compares the lot of the black man, often disadvantageously, to that of the mule. Simple does the same thing with dogs. "Even a black dog gets along better than me," says Simple. "White folks socialize with dogs—yet they don't socialize with me." The army "Jim Crows me, but it don't Jim Crow dogs."[13] In slavery days, Simple recalls, "a good bloodhound was worth more than a good Negro, because a bloodhound were trained to keep the Negroes in line."[14] And dogs are still, he observes, more carefully counted than Negroes, better fed, sometimes even better clothed.[15]

As an actor, Simple, like John, endeavors to resolve the disparities he has pointed out. His most common method is the folktale expedient of swapping places. He dreams that he is the one "setting on the wide veranda of my big old mansion with its white pillars, the living room just full of chandeliers, and a whole slew of white servants to wait on me, master of all I surveys, and black as I can be!"[16] He turns himself into a general in charge of white troops from Mississippi: "They had white officers from Mississippi in charge of Negroes—so why shouldn't I be in charge of whites?"[17] He sets himself up in the Supreme Court, where he uses the principle of swapping places to enforce the laws he promulgates: "For instant, 'Love thy neighbor as thyself.' The first man I caught who did not love his neighbor as hisself, I would make him change places with his neighbor—the rich with the poor, the white with the black and Governor Faubus with me."[18]

Just as John not only seats himself at the head of Old Marster's table, but uses the opportunity to treat Old Marster as Old Marster has treated him, Simple insists not simply on integration, but on "reintegration": "Meaning by that, what?" asks his white boss. "That you be integrated with *me,*" replies Simple, "not me with you."[19] If a white reporter from one of the downtown newspapers were to interview him about life in Harlem, for example, Simple would suggest that they swap apartments for thirty days: " 'By that time, you will have found out how much the difference is in the price of a pound of potatoes uptown and a pound of potatoes downtown, how much the difference is for what you pay for rent downtown and what I pay for rent uptown, how different cops look downtown from how cops look uptown, how much more often streets is cleaned downtown than they is uptown. All kinds of things you will see in Harlem, and not have to be told. After we swap pads, you would not need to interview me,' I would say, 'so let's change first and interview later.' "[20]

The circumstance that makes Simple act as John acts is the same one that makes Simple experience what John experiences. Slavery and Jim Crow are both manifestations of the idea that race determines place. The society dictates the theme of swapping places by creating places:

> "You talk just like a Negro nationalist," I said.
> "What's that?"
> "Someone who wants Negroes to be on top."
> "When everybody else keeps me on the *bottom*, I don't see why I shouldn't be on top. I will, too, someday."[21]

What Simple really wants is not for top and bottom to be inverted but for there to be no top or bottom, no "place," to swap:

> "Anyhow," said Simple, "if we lived back in fairy tale days and a good fairy was to come walking up to me and offer me three wishes, the very first thing I would wish would be:
>
> THAT ALL WHITE FOLKS WAS BLACK
>
> then nobody would have to bother with white blood and black blood any more."[22]

But Simple does not live back in fairy-tale days, so he tries to combat racism by showing how unfair it would look if the tables were turned. The principle of swapping places is literally the principle of revolution. But the elimination of places is equally revolutionary. Hughes's purpose in Simple's stories is to make revolution look simple.

To the extent that inside and outside plots can be separated, the inside plot of a Simple story is addressed to the problem of Jim Crow and the outside plot to the people who suffer from it. The narrator of the Simple stories, identified in the later stories as Boyd (though "Boyd" in the earlier stories is the name of another roomer in Simple's house), is both the immediate audience of Simple's narrative—and, thus, a stand-in for the newspaper audience—and one of Simple's antagonists. For although Simple and Boyd are both black, and in full agreement on what *should* be, they disagree about what *is*. Because Boyd views reality in terms of American ideals and Simple views it in terms of black experience, their friendly disagreements focus on the psychological disparity between being black and being American.

Boyd talks American. He is a romantic, an idealist, one of the two hundred ninety-nine out of a thousand people, as George Bernard Shaw figured it, who recognize the conventional organization of society as a failure but, being in a minority, conform to it nevertheless and try to convince themselves that it is just and right. Simple talks black. He is Shaw's realist, the one man in a thousand "strong enough to face the truth the idealists are shirking."[23] The truth he faces and Boyd shirks is the importance of race. Though Boyd is black, rooms in Harlem, listens to Simple nightly, sees the evidence of race discrimination all around him, he keeps trying to believe that what ought to be is. The police are there to "keep you from being robbed and mugged"; "violence never solved anything"; "bomb shelters will be for everybody"; "Negroes today are . . . advancing, advancing!"[24] "I have not advanced one step," counters Simple, getting down to cases, "still the same old job, same old salary, same old kitchenette, same old Harlem and the same old color."[25] "You bring race into everything" complains Boyd. "It is in everything," replies Simple.[26]

Boyd considers Simple's race-consciousness provincial, chauvinistic, and un-American. He repeatedly encourages Simple to "take the long view," "extend a friendly hand," get to know more white people, try some foreign foods.[27] But Simple insists on his Americanness as much as his blackness. In his imaginary encounters with representatives of all the institutions that exclude him because he is black, he replies, "I am American." The difference between Simple's and Boyd's assumptions about what it means to be American is dramatized by their response to a folk joke Simple tells about an old lady who enters a recently-integrated restaurant, orders various soul-food specialties, is politely but repeatedly told "we don't have that," and finally sighs, "I knowed you-all wasn't ready for integration":

> "Most ethnic groups have their own special dishes," I said. "If you want French food, you go to a French restaurant. For Hungarian, you go to Hungarian places."
>
> "But this was an American place," said Simple, "and they did not have soul food."[28]

To Boyd, as to the hotel clerks and employers Simple encounters, "Negro" and "American" are mutually exclusive; "American" identity is an achievement upon which "Negro" identity may be put aside. To Simple, they are mutually necessary. America is not American *unless* it has room for him, "black as I can be," "without one plea." From Simple's point of view, Boyd's is not American at all, but white. Though Boyd voices the ideals of freedom, he represents the influence of racist conventions in his interpretation of them. The repartee between Simple and Boyd puts a contemporary conflict of attitudes into the context of the historical conflict beween John and Old Marster. Through Boyd, Hughes shows that to deny the reality of racial oppression is actually to support it.

Since Boyd, as Simple's audience, also represents the reading audience, Simple's argument with him becomes an argument with his audience as well. The framework conversation with Boyd applies the meaning of Simple's narrative to the audience and anticipates their objections. Through it Simple the folk narrator confronts the legacy of Old Marster in the audience as Simple the folk hero confronts Jim Crow. Folktales could not free the slaves who told them, but they could keep the slaves from being tricked into believing they were meant to be slaves; the tales could keep the distinction between living and slaving clear. The Simple stories do the same for the distinction between American ideals and black reality. The principle of the Simple stories is that the way to overcome race discrimination is to confront it, and they keep their audience confronted not only with the principle of confrontation but also with the evidence of discrimination. In the words of Ellison's definition of the blues, they keep alive the painful details and episodes of black experience and transcend them—keep them alive in order to transcend them—just as Simple remembers his past in order to free his future.

The similarity between Simple's conflict and John's makes the Simple stories resemble folktales, but the active engagement in the audience's social and psychological experience makes them be to an urban newspaper-reading folk what the John tales must have been to a rural storytelling folk: a communal affirmation of the group's own sense of reality. Like the folk storyteller, Hughes speaks of and to the group. He speaks of their immediate experience, by commenting on current events, and puts it into the context of their historical experience and the fundamental fact of their group identity, race. He uses the medium, the newspaper, that draws the largest audience, and a narrative form that not only simulates narrator-audience exchange in the dialogue between Simple and Boyd, but stimulates it by making Simple and Boyd personify conflicting attitudes he knows his audience—individually as well as collectively—holds. The Simple stories seek to show that, though the forms of life in mid-twentieth-century Harlem are different from those on the ante-bellum plantation, the fundamentals are the same. The stories themselves are written and published on this same principle; and the adaptation of their form to the realities of an urban, literate, mass society is what in fact allows them to function as folktales.

Implicitly in the Simple stories, Hughes has redefined the notion of black folk tradition. Most of the writers who consciously used black folk materials in the first half of the twentieth century located "the folk tradition" in the South, in the past, in a pastoral landscape. They either employed it—as did Toomer, Hurston, O'Neill in *The Emperor Jones*, Heyward in *Porgy*—or rejected it, as did Wright, as a retreat from the social complexities of modern life into either pastoral simplicity or the individual psyche. But Hughes's definition of black folk tradition is dynamic. Limited by no time, place, or landscape, it is simply the continuity of black experience—an experience that is "folk" in that it is collective and a "tradition" in that it defines the past, dominates the present, and makes demands on the future.

Hughes asks his audience to recognize their place in this tradition and use it as Simple uses the history stored up in his feet. The force and purpose of his writing is to project his understanding of the folk tradition out among the folk, to bind black people together in a real community, united by their recognition of common experience into a force to control it. Modestly, like a relay runner, Langston Hughes picks up the folk tradition and carries it on toward the goal of social change in the real world.

Notes

1. "Feet Live Their Own Life," *Simple Speaks His Mind* (New York: Simon and Schuster, 1950), pp. 3–7.

2. Blyden Jackson, "A Word about Simple"; Harry L. Jones, "Rhetorical Embellishment in Hughes's Simple Stories"; Eugenia W. Collier, "A Pain in His Soul: Simple as Epic Hero," in *Langston Hughes, Black Genius: A Critical Evaluation*, ed. Therman B. O'Daniel (New York: Morrow, 1971). Arthur P. Davis, "Jesse B. Semple: Negro American," *Phylon*, 15 (1954), 21–28. Lawrence E. Mintz, "Langston Hughes's Jesse B. Semple: The Urban Negro as Wise Fool," *Satire Newsletter*, 7 (Fall 1969), 11–21. Phyllis R. Klotman, "Langston Hughes's Jesse B. Semple and the Blues," *Phylon*, 36 (1975), 68–77.

3. Subsequently collected in *Simple Speaks His Mind; Simple Takes a Wife* (New York: Simon and Schuster, 1953); *Simple Stakes a Claim* (New York: Rinehart, 1957); *The Best of Simple* (New York: Hill and Wang, 1961), an anthology which draws from the first three volumes; and *Simple's Uncle Sam* (New York: Hill and Wang, 1965).

4. "Night in Harlem," *Wife*, p. 133.

5. *Black Folktales* (New York: Grove Press, 1969), p. 94.

6. Richard M. Dorson, *American Negro Folktales* (Greenwich, CT: Fawcett, 1967), No. 38c, pp. 134–35. The foregoing composite picture of John is based on the folktale collections of Dorson, J. Mason Brewer, Zora Neale Hurston, Portia Smiley, and others.

7. "Four Rings," *Wife*, p. 234.

8. "Must Have a Seal," *Wife*, p. 169.

9. "Puerto Ricans," *Claim*, p. 73.

10. "Simple Prays a Prayer," *Mind*, p. 15.

11. *Uncle Sam*, pp. 124–26; *Mules and Men* (1935; rpt. New York: Harper, 1970), p. 120.

12. *Uncle Sam*, pp. 94–97.

13. "Equality and Dogs," *Mind*, pp. 152, 153.

14. "Dog Days," *Uncle Sam*, p. 105.

15. "Dog Days," p. 105; "Equality and Dogs," p. 154; "Letting Off Steam," *Mind*, p. 77.

16. "Rude Awakening," *Uncle Sam*, p. 127.

17. "Simple Pins on Medals," *Mind*, p. 194.

18. "Promulgations," *Uncle Sam*, p. 160.

19. "Coffee Break," *Uncle Sam*, p. 82.

20. "Interview," *Uncle Sam*, p. 89.

21. "A Toast to Harlem," *Mind*, p. 34.

22. "That Powerful Drop," *Wife*, pp. 85–86.

23. George Bernard Shaw, *The Quintessence of Ibsenism* (New York: Brentano's, 1912), pp. 23–26.

24. "The Law," *Mind*, p. 171; "Pray or Flay," *Uncle Sam*, p. 119; "Radioactive Red Caps," *Claim*, pp. 53, 54.

25. "Radioactive Red Caps," p. 53.

26. "Bop," *Wife*, p. 56.

27. "Present for Joyce," *Wife*, p. 209; "A Toast to Harlem," *Mind*, p. 34; "There Ought to Be a Law," *Mind*, p. 114; "Swinging High," *Uncle Sam*, p. 4.

28. "Soul Food," *Uncle Sam*, pp. 113–14. A traditional example of the joke may be found in J. Mason Brewer, *Worser Days and Better Times: The Folklore of the North Carolina Negro* (Chicago: Quadrangle, 1965), pp. 105–106.

"Bodies in the Moonlight": A Critical Analysis

James A. Emanuel*

The forty-five year literary career of the late Langston Hughes (1902–1967) is represented by notable work in many genres; stories, poems, novels, plays, essays, and other forms of literature originated at his typewriter in a third-floor apartment overlooking a back yard near the center of Harlem, U.S.A. "Bodies in the Moonlight," the first of sixty-six short published narratives written by Hughes, appeared in Harlem's *The Messenger* in April, 1927. The story is also the first in a trilogy which I named the West Illana Series in a dissertation I wrote for Columbia University ("The Short Stories of Langston Hughes," 1962). The other tales are "The Young Glory of Him" and "The Little Virgin," published in *The Messenger* in June and November, respectively, of 1927. In July, 1961, Hughes said: "The stories were commercial. [Editors Wallace Thurman and George Schuyler] said they would pay for them, and I needed the money, being here [in New York] for

*Reprinted from *Readers and Writers* 1 (November–January 1968):38–39, 42, by permission of the author.

the summer, so I wrote them." Each story concerns the freighter *West Illana*, with its crew of Greeks, West Indians, Irish, Portuguese and Americans, plying between New York and the West Coast of Africa. The trilogy reflects Hughes' own trip from June to the fall of 1923 as mess boy on the S.S. *Malone*, which with a crew of forty-two and with six passengers, visited at least thirty-two ports, from Dakar in Senegal southward to Loandra.

"Bodies in the Moonlight" and the rest of the sea trilogy combine with "Luani of the Jungles," which appeared in the magazine *Harlem* in November, 1928, to form a group of stories distinctive among all the productions of Hughes. The trilogy evokes the factual world of sailors. They spin tall tales on balmy evenings in the glow of a lantern hung over the stern; from their bunks they brag about port town girls enjoyed all over the world and display poignant and colorful remnants of their amours.

The concrete African environment is seldom pictured for its own sake. It is justifiable that Africa be seen by Hughes through a sailor's eye, for these stories present life at sea, not the indigenous life of West Africa.

The Africa of his fiction comes alive mainly through sailors disporting themselves in Africa. Scenes at Dakar in "The Young Glory of Him" are characteristic: urchins soliciting sailors for whores, and Jerry dancing a hornpipe on the edge of a fountain, are more vivid than the sketchy African background. To understand how stringently Hughes subordinated his real feelings for Africa to the needs of his themes, one should consider the closing passages of the first chapter of his autobiography, *The Big Sea*, which describe his poignant responses to what he calls "My Africa, Motherland of the Negro peoples!"

One of the most important themes common to the trilogy is that of innocence. Although innocence is the most emphatically thematic in "The Young Glory of Him," it is also a trait significantly assigned to the narrator of "Bodies in the Moonlight." Four times he recalls his own simplicity as a boy: once with nostalgia (at eighteen the world was "wonderful"), three times with regret (over the soft bodies and beauty of women "one can be a fool"). Symbols enhance the theme of innocence in this story of flower-like Nunuma. The reader who recalls Herman Melville's sea-going narrator in *White-Jacket* will attach that youth's symbolically deepened innocence to the white mess boy jacket of Hughes's narrator, and to the white shirt blood-stained in the knife fight that ends his innocence about the permanence and inviolability of beauty like that found in "Bodies in the Moonlight." Throughout the story Nunuma's beauty is posed between the experienced, hard-shelled character called Porto Rico and the boy. At the end, when she has disappeared like "a dart of Moonlight," and when the boy, weakly crying "Keep your damn dirty hands off her," has fallen "face forward in the grass," the collapse of the boy is emblematic of the fate of innocence.

The West Illana Series, then, is Hughes's presentation of the theme of initiation into the practical world, an initiation which began in his own life in 1923, with his confessedly melodramatic dumping of his large box of books into the ocean off Sandy Hook on his first trip to sea. The author relives that symbolic event in the third paragraph of "Bodies in the Moonlight," where the narrator throws his school books overboard, ceases communication with his parents (Hughes's correspondence with his father had ended in the spring of 1922), and welcomes the sea as his mother and the *West Illana* as his home. The three trips to sea in this trilogy become voyages of innocence in the Fever Coast of practical life. The truth of existence, in each case, takes violent shape, hostile but strangely and even cruelly indifferent to man. The lack of malice behind his knife thrust makes Porto Rico, in "Bodies in the Moonlight," an almost mechanical agent, as indifferent and swiftly instructive as the blazing African sun.

A practical world against which this innocence gives futile battle is reflected in the sea, the image of which tells something of young Hughes's attitude toward the world. Some passages objectify the sea. Others, in which the author reaches for its spirit, generally find it quiet and indifferent. The sea is more complex in "Bodies in the Moonlight" than in the other stories: it is not only weary, but "deep and evil"; it has a pernicious effect upon beauty like that of Nunuma, the "lovely flower growing too near the sea." Predominantly either beneficent or neutral, the sea appears evil to Porto Rico and the boy only when they are tired or homesick; and its malevolent inroads upon feminine beauty are made less by the sea than by the sailors who cross it. Veritably a part of the sea, the ships themselves, a composite reflection of the *Malone*, accentuate this slightly deistic view: each of the adjectives "solemn," "slow," and "calm" is twice applied to them, coupled with single uses of the subjective terms "languid," "quiet," and "restful."

Besides Hughes's recollections of the sea, these stories have a higher proportion of specific autobiographical references than do his later tales. Hughes, like many beginning authors, apparently relied as much on actual experiences and people as on his own imagination.

"Bodies in the Moonlight" has its share of characters based upon men who sailed with him on the *Malone*. A number of events, too, reflect the author's experiences.

These earliest stories contain traits of style characteristic of much of Hughes's later fiction. The Chief Mate's "Christ, mess, I'm tired o' this damn place" is typically individualized and realistic dialogue. It compares to the Greek fireman's complaint in "The Little Virgin," as he says, "What a hell you tell da kid to hit me for? You would ain't do it yourself," followed by "He's no you brother." There are some unusually slow-moving pictures drawn with sentence fragments. As the two tired friends in "Bodies in the Moonlight" are being paddled ashore, for example, Hughes writes: "Under the stars, the ocean deep and evil. The lights of the 'West Illana' at our stern." The paragraph in the middle of "Bodies in the Moonlight" beginning with "Porto Rico and I were ashore every night" shows how the author's expository passages sometimes mix tenses, mix sentences and fragments, stop for exclamations, and employ repetition. A different, thematic kind of repetition, not only sounding within a passage, but running like an incremental strain throughout the pages, is found in the same story: recurrent of the name Nunuma and of her image, slender and brown like a flower. Added to the delirium-ridden refrain of the Little Virgin, in the story named after him, is an especially important technique: the inclusion of song lyrics, a forerunner of Hughes's later style. Foreshadowing is another of his typical, early stylistic devices.

The West Illana Series, then, led by "Bodies in the Moonlight," provides a small but active picture of sailors plying the West Coast of Africa in the 1920's, with adaptations of that life, one poetic ("Burutu Moon") and one exotic ("Luani of the Jungles"), added at opposite ends of the trilogy. Using a narrator to recall the crew frolicking in port towns, the author employs occasional, brief word-pictures to evoke the Africa that he felt to a depth not revealed in the tales. In the restricted, nautical world of these stories, the reader is not led far below the decks of human experience; yet the author infuses such universal themes as innocence, beauty, love, and manhood. Later stories like "Red-Headed Baby," a favorite of Hughes's, and "Sailor Ashore" reveal the somber thinking sometimes enforced upon a seafarer during that brief ride from ship to shore.

It is less important to assess a writer's first works qualitatively than it is to discover in them the reaching for style, the manner of shaping experience, and the themes which first attract him. Although the stories of the crew of the *West Illana* have never been discussed in published criticism, they are important for the ways in which they prefigure the later methods of this American author whom much of the world has read and admired.

Jesse B. Semple and the Narrative Art of Langston Hughes

Phyllis R. Klotman*

Jesse B. Semple is certainly no romantic hero, protest victim or militant leader, no charismatic character for the young to emulate. Yet according to Professor Blyden Jackson, "it is highly probable that Langston Hughes reached his most appreciative, as well as his widest, audience with a character whom he names, eponymously and with obvious relish, Jesse B. Semple."[1] Simple reached a wide, appreciative black audience because he appeared in newspapers readily available to black readers,[2] and he reached white readers when Hughes began to publish the tales in book form. What is Simple's appeal? My contention is that the popularity of the tales is based on the narrative technique of the artist; that is, on the artistic devices used by Langston Hughes, a writer who not only knew his medium, but also knew the people whom he addressed through that medium: 1) the sure-fire appeal of the skit technique, 2) an apparent artlessness and simplicity in the development of theme and character, 3) reader identification and 4) the intermittent sound of the blues in prose.

The skit technique, adapted to the demands of the newspaper column, is a natural form for the tales. The oral tradition of the Afro-American was carried on in the vaudeville and burlesque routines which were so popular in the twenties and thirties. Those routines had elements that we also see in the Simple stories: two stand-up comics playing against and to each other, fast-paced dialogue and a quick exit. Each of the tales is self-contained and is almost entirely in dialogue; each gives Simple a chance to make some comment, flavored with his unique malapropisms, about the world of Harlem or the world in general. Hughes' persona, Boyd, is the straight man, the foil to Simple's wit, and his educated language is juxtaposed to Simple's Black English, rich in the folk idioms of Harlem.[3] They come on stage, make the point of the story quickly and then move off. "Weight in Gold" is this kind of short skit, and in it Simple explains to Boyd what he would do if he were rich enough to be kidnapped. Boyd responds:

> "In other words, you would be Harlem's Ford Foundation . . . on a really big scale."
>
> "Yes," said Simple, "because on my scales, every kid in Harlem is worth his weight in gold." (*Simple's Uncle Sam*, p. 170)

That the tale is brief is aesthetically appropriate to the teller and to his special wit—itself the soul of brevity. It consists not only of delib-

*Reprinted from the *Journal of Narrative Technique* 3 (January 1973):66–75, by permission of the author and the journal.

erate fractures (a few samples of these: "Negro hysterians" who plan "interracial seminaries"; "inconptemptible" and "touchous" women like Joyce, Zarita or Isabel; Simple's admonishment to Boyd, his "colleged" friend, to "listen fluently" while he reads his "poetries," etc., etc.), but also of verbal pyrotechnics with simple props, in this case "up" "down" and "out": "And if they got locked up a few times, them signs [WHITE and COLORED] would come down! White folks do not put up with whatever they don't like. Just let a white man get turned down when he goes in a restaurant hungry. He will turn the joint out. If I get turned down, all they do is turn me out" ("Duty Is Not Snooty," *Simple Stakes A Claim*, p. 31). In this, "face" and "race": "that is what I am always coming face to face with—race. I look in the mirror in the morning to shave—and what do I see? *Me.* From birth to death my face—which is my race—stares me in the face" ("Present for Joyce," *The Best of Simple*, p. 173).

Such seeming artlessness in the verbal and situational irony redolent in the tales is also reflected in the development of theme and character. This is belied, however, by the artful way we learn of Simple and of the characters who touch his life. Some recur, like Isabel, his first wife, Zarita, his "goodtime" friend, and Joyce, the girl he wants to and finally does marry. Others wander in, like cousin Minnie and Simple's nephew F. D.; they stay for an episode or two and then depart. Yet in almost every case, the characters and experiences are filtered through Simple's singular vision. These are tales, after all, not plotted short stories, and there is little description or exposition. We learn of Simple's past and present life from the experiences he shares with us and with Boyd, and of some of the actions as they take place. Characteristically, Simple begins his history from the ground up—in "Feet Live Their Own Life" (*Simple Speaks His Mind*). From that episode we learn that he was born in the South, in Virginia, that he was "raised up" with three brothers, two sisters, seven cousins, one married aunt, a common-law uncle, and the minister's grandchild—all in a four room house—and that he was hungry much of the time. We learn more as the tales progress and Simple ruminates about how he feels and how he looks. Blyden Jackson remarks that Simple "is a black man, highly visible with skin too dark, facial features too African, and hair too anything but lank, to be mistaken for Aryan. . . . After childhood in which he was, in his own words, 'passed around' among his relatives—for, of his actual parents, he clearly never had much knowledge—he has gravitated to Harlem, with intermediate stops."[4] One of those stops was Baltimore, and there he "picked out the wrong woman," married and separated from her. Isabel not only recurs in his speech but also in his nightmares. Until she, Simple *and* Boyd finally put together enough money for a divorce. Simple is plagued by his "once in a wife-time" past which is the major hindrance to his "brand new tomorrow" with Joyce. (That finally does come about by the end of *Simple Takes A Wife.*) In the meantime, on the corner, in the Wishing Well or Paddy's Bar, or at his landlady's establishment, he tells Boyd of some experience he's had and that experience inevitably leads to some deceptively simple conclusion. When Jess gets caught out with Zarita, he bemoans his fate ("telephone, telegraph, tell-a-Negro—and the news is out"), and Boyd responds with apparent relief that someone has finally taken Simple's mind off the color problem:

> "Sometimes I wonder what made you so race-conscious,"
> "Sometimes I wonder what made me so black," said Simple. (*Simple Takes A Wife*, p. 222)

On another occasion Simple's brush with the law leads him to the conclusion that there are two kinds of justice, one for black men and one for white. The last two lines, like the concluding couplet of a sonnet, are often an exchange between Boyd and Simple, with the latter always having the last word:

> "You look at everything, I regret to say, in terms of black and white."
> "So does the Law," said Simple. (*Simple Speaks His Mind*, p. 172)

In "Vicious Circle" Simple explains: "If the first colored family did not move into a white neighborhood, the second one couldn't. But as soon as one Negro moves in, here comes another. After a while, they tell me, we're right back where we started from—in a slum. . . . That is what Mrs. Maxwell-Reeves [Joyce's exclusive "dicty" friend] calls a vicious circle, when Negroes move in." He asks Boyd—"are Negroes vicious?"

> "Do you think Negroes are vicious?"
> "No," said Simple, "it must be the circle." (*Simple Stakes A Claim*, p. 117)

Not all of the tales end with the two line finale, nor are they all of the short-skit variety; on occasion Simple even waxes eloquent. Nonetheless, the large majority do reflect a deceptive simplicity in theme and character which may in part explain the "seduction" of both black and white readers. Arthur Davis suggests one possible clue to black reader appeal: "as we read these dialogues, we often find ourselves giving lip-service to the sophisticated Hughes side of the debate while our hearts share Simple's cruder but more realistic attitude."[5] And it may be possible that at the time the tales first reached the wider public, some white readers embraced what they thought to be a shuffling, word-mangling Rastus at whose antics they could chuckle comfortably, as they nurtured their illusions of intellectual superiority while, at the same time, missing the subtleties of Simple's barbs.

The serio-comic nature of Simple's wit, as well as the black idiom in which it is expressed, is an immediate locus of identification for the black readers who know that without "mother wit," which Simple has in abundance, life in America would be unendurable. Imagine the laughter of the black reader when the white census taker, in all seriousness, writes down that Simple is here "in spite of all" but that he expects to die by "uglying away" ("Census," *Simple's Uncle Sam*, p. 3).[6] Or the response to Simple's "in-group" explanation of the color question—"Where was us Negroes when the Lord said, 'Let there be light'?": "Late as usual. . . . old C. P. Time. We must have been down the road a piece and did not get back on time" ("Temptation," *Simple Speaks His Mind*, p. 39). And black readers undoubtedly recognize in Simple's "complaint"[7] catalog a slice of black life:

> I've been fired, laid off, and last week given an indefinite vacation, also Jim Crowed, segregated, barred out, insulted, called black, yellow, and red, locked in, locked out, locked up, also left holding the bag. I have been caught in the rain, caught in raids, caught short with my rent, and caught with another man's wife . . . but I am still here! . . . My mama should have named me Job instead of Jess Simple. I have been underfed, underpaid, undernourished, and everything but undertaken. . . . In this life I have been abused, confused, misused, accused, false-arrested, tried, sentenced, paroled, blackjacked, beat, third-degreed and near lynched! ("Final Fear," *Simple Speaks His Mind*, pp. 112–113)[8]

Inherent in Langston Hughes' philosophy, throughout all of his works, is his recognition of, and pride in, the fact that the Afro-American has developed (or perhaps had innately) the ability to endure—to endure not only all of the sorrows to which man is heir, but also all of the racial calumnies devised by white society to defame its black citizens. Simple suggests that the assault of racism is comparable to the lethal attack of an atom bomb, but assures his friend Boyd that black people like himself will be able to survive even such an attack:

> "Negroes are very hard to annihilate. I am a Negro—so I figure I would live to radiate and, believe me, once charged, I will take charge."
>
> "In other words come what may, you expect to survive the atom bomb?"
>
> "If Negroes can survive white folks in Mississippi," said Simple, "we can survive anything." ("Radioactive Red Caps," *Simple Stakes A Claim*, pp. 46–47)

Robert Nemiroff puts Simple "in the full blown, freewheeling tradition of Huck Finn and Mr. Dooley, Harlem's Everyman—an authentic folk philosopher hero, capable of safeguarding that which is best in the human spirit through his perverse capacity to remain undaunted by the most insuperable forces arrayed against him."[9] But enduring also means recognizing the folly of martyrdom—or what Simple calls "bending over too far," like the washerwoman who got her breasts caught in the wringer. "There is such a thing as bending over too far—even to get your clothes clean. Certainly there is plenty of dirty linen in this U.S.A., but I do not advise nobody to get their breast caught in a wringer" ("Swinging High," *Simple's Uncle Sam*, p. 8). The wringerless washer may have made this Simple-ism passé, but there are still plenty of black women to whom taking in washing is far from history.

If the black reader's identification with Simple's characteristically black experience in America is ultimately successful, how is it possible for the white reader (who may often find himself on the butt end of a joke) to identify positively enough to keep reading?[10] For one thing, the appeal of the "common man" who rises above the exigencies of everyday life is essentially raceless, as are a number of Simple's predicaments with which we identify *as though* we had been in such situations ourselves. It is our common lot as human beings that we share with Simple. Any man may be caught in the rain, caught in raids, caught short with his rent and caught with another man's wife. And many men have had a childhood like Jess', which was not happy but not without love: "When peoples care for you and cry for you, they can straighten out your soul," he says about his "Last Whipping," administered by old Aunt Lucy, one of the few relatives who "took her duty hard" but loved him enough to cry over him. "That was my last whipping. But it wasn't the whipping that taught me what I needed to know. It was because she cried—and cried" (*Simple Speaks His Mind*, p. 116). It is therefore Simple's basic humanity with which the larger audience identifies. Boyd (although functioning on one level as Hughes' persona) is, according to Harry L. Jones, "representative of Simple's wider audience, and he reflects Hughes' assumptions that people of the United States and of the world subscribe to Simple's ideas about peace, freedom, and brotherhood; in a word, that the world constitutes an audience which is consubstantial with Simple, a world which is, therefore, able to appreciate Simple's essential humanity."[11]

Hughes also achieves a delicate balance in the satiric view of life reflected in Simple's philosophy. We may hear him rail against such heinous crimes and flagrant injustices as lynchings, segregation, job discrimination and bigotry (of both northern and southern extractions), while at the same time we hear him considering the universal problems of war and peace, death and immortality, love, hate, and sympathy:

> "Some people do not have no scars on their faces . . . but they has scars on their hearts. Some people have never been beat up, teeth knocked out, nose broke, shot, cut, not even so much as scratched in the face.

> But they have had their hearts broke, brains disturbed, their minds torn up, and the behinds of their souls kicked by the ones they love. It is not always your wife, husband, sweetheart, boy friend or girl friend, common-law mate—no, it might be your mother that kicks your soul around like a football. It might be your best friend that squeezes your heart dry like a lemon. It might be some ungrateful child you have looked forward to making something out of when it got grown, but who goes to the dogs and bites you on the way there. Oh, friend, your heart can be scarred in so many different ways it is not funny," said Simple. ("Sympathy," *Simple's Uncle Sam*, p. 171)

This is not to to assume that Jess B. Semple is anything but a "race man" first; he may ridicule the foibles of black people (as he does their pretentiousness in "Banquet in Honor"), but white racism—in all its forms, whether mild or virulent—is the main target for his sharpest criticism.[12] When Boyd argues that "there are many nonracial elements common to humanity as a whole that create problems from the cradle to the grave regardless of race, creed, color or previous condition of servitude," Simple replies: "But when you add a black face to all that . . . you have problem's mammy" ("God's Other Side," *Simple's Uncle Sam*, p. 19). Wars are terrible for everyone, Simple readily admits: "To be shot down is bad for the body . . . but to be Jim Crowed is worse for the spirit." When Boyd accuses him, in effect, of singing the "color problem" blues, he says, "Facts is . . . my problem is ME. I am colored, Afro-American, black, sepia, jet, ebony, whatever you want to call me. Until I am right in this world, and this world is right by me, I got to talk about my problems. Is there anything wrong with that?" ("Color on the Brain," *Simple Stakes A Claim*, p. 107).

Simple is, in LeRoi Jones' terms, one of the Blues People.[13] There are of course many kinds of Blues, most of which Hughes fits into such categories as: family blues, loneliness blues, left-lonesome blues, broke-and-hungry blues, and the desperate, going-to-the-river blues. In the family blues, the man and woman have quarreled and there's no way to patch up the quarrel, but in the loneliness blues, there's no one to quarrel with. If you can't sleep, can't eat and your baby's "gone away," you've got the left-lonesome blues, and if you're a "stranger in a strange town" with no job and no prospects, you've got the broke-and-hungry blues. But if you have the going-to-the-river blues, you're at the point of desperation. One important characteristic of the blues, however, is that it was created by a people determined, like Simple, to survive, and one method of survival is humor: "For sad as the Blues may be, there's always something humorous about them—even if it's the kind of humor that laughs to keep from crying."[14]

It is not too far afield then to listen for the sound of blues in a number of Simple's tales. The opening one, which gives us his history from the feet up, might be expressed, for example, as the "Sore 'n Achin Foot Blues" with lines like these:

> My feets achin so's I cn hardly stan,
> My feets achin, yeah, so's I cn hardly stan,
> But ah ain't gonna trade em
> Cause they done saved me from the man.

In "The Atomic Age" Simple sings the "Last Hired First Fired" Blues, in "Manna from Heaven" the "Carry and Clean" Blues. Several of the tales are specifically about the blues; in one with that title (from *Simple's Uncle Sam*) we have Simple's own explanation of the blues and how he is himself connected with the blues tradition: "The blues can be real sad, else real mad, else real glad, and funny, too, all at the same time. I ought to know. Me, I growed up with the blues. Facts is, I heard so many blues when I were a young man, and left Virginia and runned away to Baltimore, behind me came the shadow of the blues" (p. 17). In *Simple Takes A Wife* one of the tales is called "Shadow of the Blues," but after Jess marries Joyce he gets rid of that "left-lonesome" feeling, a feeling which takes in a whole category of the blues, as Langston Hughes defined them. Of course, women figure prominently in the blues as singers and subjects to be sung about (Boyd can remember all three Smiths, Bessie, Clara, and Mamie, the great blues singers; Simple even admits that he's heard Ma Rainey).[15] "So many blues is about womens," Simple says. Perhaps Hughes had that in mind when he began Simple's life story with a "woman"—Virginia.

> "And who is Virginia? You never told me about her." [Asks Boyd]
> "Virginia is where I was borned," said Simple. "I would be borned in a state named after a woman. From that day on, women never give me no peace." (*Simple Speaks His Mind*, pp. 3–4)

And when he does wish he was a "singerman," it's so that he can sing the blues:

> The blues ain't nothing
> But a good woman on your mind
> I say, blues ain't nothing
> But a good woman on your mind.
> But your potatoes is gone
> When the frost has killed the vine.
> If you see Corinna,
> Tell her to hurry home.
> Simple ain't had no loving
> Since Corinna's been gone.
> Blues, blues, blues, please
> do not come my way.

Gimme something else, Lord,
Besides the blues all day!
("The Blues," *Simple's Uncle Sam*, pp. 17–18)

Jesse B. Semple, the Bluesman, has himself become as classic as the blues.

Notes

1. Blyden Jackson, "A Word about Simple," *Langston Hughes: Black Genius, A Critical Evaluation*, edited by Therman B. O'Daniel for the College Language Association (New York, 1971), p. 110.

2. Langston Hughes has remarked that the "Negro press was his favorite reading"—that it kept him in touch with the real world of black people. "In my time I have been all around the world and I assure you there is nothing printed in the world like the American Negro Press. It is unique, intriguing, exciting, exalting, low-down and terrific. It is also tragic and terrible, brave, pathetic, funny and full of tears. It's me and my papa and my mama and Adam Powell and Hazel Scott and Rev. Martin King, Eartha Kitt, and folks who are no blood relation of mine but are brothers and sisters in skin." (Foreword to *Simple Stakes A Claim*, pp. 9–10).

In a way, the description sounds much like Hughes' own writings: the poetry, the prose, the drama.

3. Arthur P. Davis considers Simple and Boyd as two sides of Langston Hughes: "Insofar as an author may be his own creations, Langston Hughes is the earthy, prejudiced, and race-conscious Simple as well as the urbane, tolerant, and sophisticated 'straight man' in the sketches" ("The Cool Poet," *Langston Hughes: Black Genius*, p. 19). Harry Jones, on the other hand, suggests that there are *three* voices in the stories: Hughes's, Boyd's and Simple's ("Rhetorical Embellishments in Hughes' Simple Stories," in the same volume, p. 136).

4. Blyden Jackson, "A Word about Simple," p. 111.

5. Arthur P. Davis, "Jesse B. Semple: Negro American," *Phylon* XV (Spring, 1954), p. 22.

I'm reminded here of Alberta K. Johnson's brush with the census man:

The census man,
The day he came round,
Wanted my name
To put it down.

I said, JOHNSON,
Alberta K.
But he hated to write
The K that way.

He said, What
Does K stand for?
I said, K——
And nothing more.

He said, I'm gonna put it
K-A-Y,

I said, If you do,
You lie.

My mother christened me
ALBERTA K.
You leave my name
Just that way!

He said, Mrs.?
(With a snort)
Just a K
Makes your name too short.

I said, I don't
Give a damn!
Leave me and my name
Just like I am!

Furthermore, rub out
That MRS., too—
I'll have you know
I'm *Madam* to you!

6. Davis aptly refers to Alberta K. in the series, "Madam to You" or "The Life and Times of Alberta K. Johnson" (*One Way Ticket*, 1949) as "almost as great a creation as Simple, whom she resembles in some respects. Like Simple, she shows Mr. Hughes's humorous yet profound understanding of the Negro urban character" ("The Cool Poet," p. 35).

7. The complaint, as we know, was a lyric form popular during the Renaissance in England. Several are found earlier in Chaucer, one very humorous one in fact, in which he upbraids his purse for lightness ("The Complaint of Chaucer to his Purse"). Simple's complaint reflects Hughes's skill in the use of alliteration, consonance, repetition and parallel structure—all of which are consistent with Simple's verbal style and double-edged wit.

8. Eugenia Collier (in "A Pain in his Soul: Simple as Epic Hero," *Langston Hughes: Black Genius*, p. 128) cites this Simple truth as one example of the black realities that are reflected in Simple's conversations.

9. See Nemiroff's record jacket, *Langston Hughes: Simple Stories* read by Ossie Davis (Caedmon TC 1222).

10. The number of editions through which the tales have gone, including those published in other countries (e.g., *Simple Speaks His Mind* was published in an English Edition in 1951, a Danish Edition in 1954, and a German Edition in 1960), should offer objective and affirmative proof, although the tales themselves furnish the best evidence.

11. Harry L. Jones, "Rhetorical Embellishment in Hughes's Simple Stories," *Langston Hughes: Black Genius*, p. 139. The "conception of the Negro as a symbol of Man," according to Ralph Ellison, "was organic to nineteenth-century literature." Huckleberry Finn is one of the examples he cites. In it Jim "is not simply a slave, he is a symbol of humanity . . .". "Twentieth-Century Fiction and the Black Mask of Humanity," *Shadow and Act* (New York, 1966), p. 49.

12. Hence my disagreement with Donald C. Dickinson who says that "while white behavior often fills Simple with wrath, Negro misdeeds bring down his utter scorn," *A Bio-bibliography of Langston Hughes* (New York, 1968), p. 98.

13. In his book, *Blues People* (New York, 1963), LeRoi Jones (Imamu Amiri Baraka) discusses the genesis of the blues: "Blues was a music that arose from the needs of a group, although it was assumed that each man had his own blues and that he would sing them. . . . If someone had lived in this world into manhood, it was taken for granted that he had been given the content of his verses . . ." (p. 82). Simple has grow to manhood "in the shadow of the blues," and his blues-in-prose tales echo Louis Armstrong's familiar rhetorical question:

What did I do
To be so black
And blue?

14. *The Langston Hughes Reader* (New York, 1958), p. 160

15. According to Jones, "singers like Gertrude 'Ma' Rainey were responsible for creating the classic blues style. She was one of the most imitated and influential classic blues singers, and perhaps the one who can be called the *link* between the earlier, less polished blues styles and the smoother theatrical style of the later urban blues singers." See his chapter, "Classic Blues," in *Blues People*, p. 89.

Drama

Miscegenation on Broadway: Hughes's *Mulatto* and Edward Sheldon's *The Nigger*

Richard K. Barksdale*

On 4 December 1909, at Broadway's New Theatre, the curtain went up on a new three-act play written by Edward Sheldon. Although it bore the somewhat inflammatory title *The Nigger* and dealt with the intriguingly controversial topic of racial miscegenation, the play was apparently well received by the playgoing public—so well received, indeed, that it was published in book form by Macmillan in 1910, with a reprinted edition following in 1915.[1] In 1909 Broadway enjoyed a lively season, and the competition was vigorous and stimulating. *The Nigger*'s big competition was *The Fortune Hunter* starring that scintillating star of the stage (and later the screen), John Barrymore. As far as race relations in America were concerned, 1909 was also an interesting year. For this was the year that a group of concerned white northern liberals—Oswald Garrison Villard, Joel Spingarn, and Mary Ovington White—met to form the National Association for the Advancement of Colored People. Joining them in this enterprise was the young black scholar, William E. B. Du Bois, whose Niagara Movement in 1905 and 1906 became a model for the NAACP. The NAACP's founders were motivated to organize their association because of the ever-increasing turbulence in race relations throughout the nation. They were particularly concerned about preventing further race riots like those in Brownsville, Texas, in 1906 and in Springfield, Illinois, in 1908. So Sheldon's play's title blended with the racial climate of the times and evidently reflected white America's interest in this aspect of black-white relations.

Almost twenty-six years later, on 24 October 1935, Langston Hughes's *Mulatto* opened at Broadway's Vanderbilt Theater. Like Sheldon's play, Hughes's two-act play dealt with the theme of miscegena-

*This essay was written for this volume and appears here by permission of the author.

tion and enjoyed a relatively long Broadway run (270 performances) and then successfully toured the nation for eight months. This was considered to be a fairly remarkable achievement for a play in the middle of the depression. However, *Mulatto*'s publication history was quite different from that of *The Nigger*. Hughes's play was not published in English until 1963, twenty-eight years after its first Broadway run. Ironically, during this time, the play was translated into three foreign languages—Italian, Japanese, and Spanish—and the play proved popular in Italy, Japan, and Argentina. But there was no American publication of *Mulatto* until Webster Smalley's *Five Plays by Langston Hughes* was published by Indiana University Press in 1963.

Between 1909 and 1935, some conditions and circumstances in America had changed and some had remained agonizingly constant. America's racial climate had changed little. Blacks in the South were still voteless, powerless, and legally segregated; and blacks in the North lived, in the main, in poverty-stricken ghettos. In other words, although by 1935 Booker T. Washington had been dead for twenty years, the conditions about which he had prophesied blacks and whites could be as separate "as the fingers on the hand" still existed. One interesting item of evidence attesting to this state of affairs was that, in 1935, Hughes was not given complimentary orchestra seats to attend the opening of his play at the Vanderbilt because the theater management had "reservations" about seating blacks in the orchestra section.[2]

Some things had changed. In New York City proper, blacks no longer lived in the Tenderloin and San Juan Hill areas in mid-Manhattan where they were to be found in 1909. After the infamous Tenderloin District riot in 1902, they had begun moving over into Brooklyn and then, after World War I, they had moved in great numbers into Harlem. By 1935 this area of Manhattan housed over 360,000 blacks and had become the most populous black metropolis in the world. In the early 1920s it had been a heavenly refuge, but by 1935 the refuge was rapidly becoming a ghetto. Another interesting change of circumstances occurred on Broadway. In 1909 there were no black playwrights on Broadway, whereas in 1935 at least one enjoyed a somewhat tenuous status on the Great White Way.[3] Hughes's status is termed "tenuous" because the production and staging of *Mulatto* proved to be a traumatic and discouraging experience for him. Indeed, the story of how *Mulatto* found its way to Broadway is evidence of the bizarre nature of a black playwright's lot in the 1930s.

According to Faith Berry, Hughes, just prior to his departure for the Soviet Union in June 1931, gave Blanche Knopf a manuscript copy of *Mulatto*.[4] At that time the author had no idea that four years would elapse before he could return to New York City and inquire about his manuscript. He returned to the States in the summer of 1933, but he came back to California via Vladivostock, Shanghai, and Tokyo. In California, Hughes stayed with friends in Carmel in order to complete his first volume of short stories, *The Ways of White Folks.* From Carmel, he traveled to Reno, Nevada and thence, in December 1934, to Mexico to assist in settling the estate of his father who had died in November 1934. Unfortunately, once in Mexico Hughes found himself stranded; his wealthy father had left him nothing, and he found himself without funds to return to the States. So he stayed in Mexico with friends until May 1935. Even then, he did not return to New York to inquire about the *Mulatto* manuscript. Instead, he accepted an invitation from his friend Arna Bontemps to visit with the Bontemps family in Los Angeles in the summer of 1935. As a consequence, Hughes did not return to New York City until late September 1935.

To his amazement, he found upon his return that *Mulatto* was not only in rehearsal but was scheduled for an October 1935 opening. He also discovered something else. When he attended his first rehearsal, he found that Martin Jones, *Mulatto*'s producer, had drastically revised the brief two-act plot. For instance, where Hughes had Sallie, Cora's illegitimate mulatto daughter, leave to attend a northern college early in act 1, Jones, in order to retain a sex-*cum*-violence emphasis, canceled Sallie's departure in act 1 so that she could be raped in act 2 to climax the racial violence at the end of the play. As a consequence, Hughes's emphasis on the tragic consequences of miscegenation was somewhat diluted in the acted version of *Mulatto.* For there is no doubt that Hughes had intended to probe the psychological impact of miscegenation in his play just as he had done in his poetry (*Cross, Mulatto*) and in his short story, *Father and Son.* In other words, his emphasis had consistently been on the vitiating aftereffects of miscegenation and its accompanying evil, black concubinage. The South's penchant for racial violence was certainly an important area of concern, but Hughes was primarily interested in the emotional stress and psychological insecurities of children born of forced interracial liaisons. In his view, they developed identity problems which, in turn, adversely affected their social behavior and their personal self-esteem.

Ironically, the changes introduced by Martin Jones in Hughes's play script to gratify the tastes of Broadway playgoers reflect, in some respects, the story line of Sheldon's *The Nigger.* That play, too, has an interracial rape scene and an off-the-set lynching. It also has an overly romantic love plot. The major difference, among several to be noted later, is that *The Nigger* is a tawdry melodrama with a happy ending; *Mulatto* is a tautly written drama with an unhappy ending.

A difference of less significance is that in Sheldon's play the social and moral collapse of the Old Plantation South is writ large. This is in contrast to Hughes's pointed analysis of a small unit of that South.

Also, Hughes in his character portraits strives to avoid stereotyping his principal black characters. In *The Nigger*, on the other hand, all of the major characters are white stereotypical middle- or upper-middle-class landowners. Indeed, Sheldon's characters are almost nauseatingly "Southern" in their often mannered pomposity and their social posturing. They represent a storybook South that presumably ceased to exist after the Civil War. In contrast, Hughes's *Mulatto* presents only brief glimpses of the South and its regional idiosyncracies. The play's focus is on the intense father-son conflict between Robert and his white father, Colonel Norwood, and on how deeply Cora was emotionally and psychologically lacerated by her experiences as Norwood's concubine.

The plot of Sheldon's play may be summarized as follows. The principal male character or protagonist is Philip Morrow, a young, well-bred Southern aristocrat who presides over "Morrow's Rest," a stately antebellum plantation mansion that has been in his family for generations. "Morrow's Rest" is described as an old-fashioned "colonial mansion fronted by four great white Doric columns" and festooned by "luxuriant" honeysuckle vines and rambling crimson roses; and, of course, magnolia trees, redolent with fragrance, are everywhere. Completing the picture of tranquil beauty is a cluster of white rose bushes circling a moss-grown live oak. Sheldon seems to be saying that it is only in such a setting, reeking with heavily scented beauty, that heinous crimes can be committed and dark sins remembered. Philip Morrow's character foil is Clifton Noyes, a young man who, but for a lost wager, would have inherited a life of indolent gentility as the master of "Morrow's Rest." Instead, he has been forced to take the low road and become the owner of a whiskey distillery. And there is, of course, Georgiana Byrd, a beautiful but appropriately modest young Southern belle who is charmingly gracious, ladylike, and, fortunately, unmarried. She exudes that rare quality of soft virginal innocence and saccharin purity found in 1909 only among ladies who reside south of the Mason Dixon line.

To complete the cast of characters, there are the "colored" servants —Jinny, "an ancient quadroon woman" who was Philip Morrow's mammy and Philip's father's mammy; Sam, the butler who is also ancient, slow of foot, but loyal to Mastah; and Jim, Jinny's grandson. This last is shiftless, "no-count," obsequious, and, of course, immoral and given to strong drink. Eventually, he is lynched (in act 2) for committing the South's most outrageous and unpardonable crime—the rape of a pristinely pure white woman.

The action of the play reaches an exciting climax when Philip Morrow proposes marriage to "Georgie" on the eve of his election to the governorship of the state. Extensive plans are being made for the wedding when Clifton Noyes, "pale" with jealousy, reveals what Jinny, Philip's black mammy, already knows—that Philip's father's mother was really not white but a very light-skinned slave girl with whom his grandfather had had a "secret" affair just before he left to be killed in the Mexican War. Thus Sheldon revealed a South that northern playgoers in 1909 expected to find—a land full of dusky lovers and sexual guilt, or, as Langston Hughes wrote in "Mulatto," one of the poems in *Fine Clothes to the Jew* (1927):

> Silver moonlight everywhere
> . . . .
> Sharp pure scene in the evening air
> A nigger night
> A nigger joy
> A little yellow
> Bastard boy[5]

Philip is naturally overwhelmed to learn the dark secret hidden in his family's festered past, for death is to be preferred to the curse of blood that is tainted by blackness. And when he is compelled by gentlemanly honesty to tell his beloved betrothed, she shrinks from him with loathing and disgust and runs screaming from the room. As a white Southern lady, she cannot bear the touch of a lover who has suddenly become, because of his mulatto grandmother, "a nigger."

This highly dramatic scene occurs at the end of act 2, and act 3 is devoted to resolving the complex situation that had developed. The fact that a white Southern governor has suddenly metamorphosed, through irrefutable historical evidence, from white to black is tragic, and something must be done to restore the protagonist's good fortune. This Sheldon does with all of the melodramatic finesse that was so popular on pre–World War I Broadway. First, Georgiana changes her mind about her lover's racial background and announces that love will triumph over all—over race, over bad luck, over evil. She "bursts out": "I jus love you so much, Phil, that I won't let anything come between us—not even—*that*!"[6] And about "that," she goes on, "it's only such a little! Just a trace—that's all!" (245). To this Phil, the recently elected governor of a sovereign Southern state, replies as a Southern gentleman should: "Black's black, and white's white. If yo not one, you the othah, Geo'gie" (245). But when he states further that his racial identity should not remain a secret and that he will reveal all in a speech from his office balcony to a huge crowd gathered to honor him, Geo'gie is horrified: "Yo gon to stand up an say a thing like that—befo the whole city?" (248). When Phil insists on full disclosure of his racial identity, Geo'gie finally relents and makes her final speech as a fully redeemed heroine should: "Theah's only one thing I know I understand and that is—I love you. . . . I don't care who you are or what you do—I don't care if ev'rybody in the world goes back on you, I'll stick all the closah, you can't get rid of me" (251).

At this point, one can almost hear violins sobbing beautifully in the background. But Sheldon is not through; and, after a few moments of well maneuvered suspense, he serves up, at the play's end, his melodramatic pièce de résistance. The crowd has gathered before the Capitol Building, and Phil goes out to announce to all and sundry that he is a "nigger." But the cheering crowd and the band's playing of the national anthem drown out his words. In vain, he raises his hands for silence, but "the band crashes through the national anthem and the roar of voices still rises from below" as the curtain falls.

So Sheldon's *The Nigger* suggests two truths about miscegenation. The first is that miscegenation could be borne and accepted especially if the race-mixing had occurred during slavery time—a time when the superordinate white male master held full sway over his black female slaves to use and abuse as he wished. The second truth suggested is that there always existed the possibility that white men of high position and status could have "tainted" blood as a result of a grandfather's sexual *mésalliance.* Undoubtedly, a play with these implications in 1909 reflected a Northern liberal bias and could not have been presented in Charleston or Richmond or Atlanta.

As has been suggested above, Hughes's *Mulatto* differs from Sheldon's play in many respects. It is shorter, has a more restricted focus, and is much more concerned with the psychological consequences of miscegenation from the black perspective and not with the sociological consequences from the white perspective. Moreover, *Mulatto* is much more than a "sociopolitical statement," as Webster Smalley suggests.[7] The father-son conflict is intense throughout; in fact, the miscegenation theme is almost lost when Robert Lewis, the black illegitimate son, in a scene of Oedipal fury slays his white father, Colonel Norwood. At this point, race seems to be of little concern.[8] Rather, the emphasis is on an aborted filial love and a callous and inhumane rejection of the offer of that love.

So Hughes's play castigates a system that turned father against son, son against father, and made a mockery of the family as a unit. Slavery left blacks, once they were freed, poor, fearful, and illiterate; but, in Hughes's view, slavery's worst heritage was the psychological damage done to the mulatto boy or mulatto girl whose mother, like Cora in *Mulatto*, was forced to be her master's concubine. Hughes could have explored the full dimensions of concubinage in slavery, had he written a third act in which Sallie, Cora's daughter by Colonel Norwood, would also have been forced to become her own father's concubine. Had Hughes devoloped his plot in this direction, his play would have revealed how incest was the most sordid aspect of the sexual victimization and depravity inherent in American slavery.[9] But even without any mention of incestuous concubinage, Hughes's play does stress the fact that white men often felt constrained by custom and tradition from recognizing their mulatto children.

It is also appropriate in this context to state that Hughes's emphasis on the father-son conflict in *Mulatto* strongly suggests his own conflict with his father. The son of parents who divorced when he was a boy, Hughes had a harried childhood living with his poverty-ridden mother. When he went to live with his father in Toluca, Mexico, following his graduation from high school in Cleveland, Ohio, he found that he and his father were not compatible. According to the author's own report in his 1940 biography, *The Big Sea*, his father had become a hard-driving, profit-seeking businessman who had no patience with his poetry-writing son and no sympathy for the plight of his fellow blacks in the States. Thus, when the young Hughes, in compliance with his father's wishes, left Toluca to enroll, with considerable reluctance, as a first-year engineering student at Columbia University, the father-son relationship was tense and embittered. And when the year at Columbia proved to be an academic disaster, Hughes eventually got a job on an Africa-bound freighter and never saw nor corresponded with his father again.

Another difference between Sheldon's *The Nigger* and *Mulatto* is that Hughes's play places considerable emphasis on the psychological dilemma of Cora, Colonel Norwood's concubine and the mother of his three mulatto children—William, Robert, and Sallie Lewis. The longtime partner of the Colonel's bed but never the wife of his bosom, Cora is torn between her mother's love for her self-assertive and aggressive son Robert and her respect for the Colonel who is angered by his bastard son's attitude and life-style. In the Colonel's eyes, Robert does not behave the way a black bastard should behave; where he should have been obsequious and humble, Robert is aggressive and demanding. In fact, he demands the recognition that he is a Norwood who can walk into the Norwood front door and do anything that a white man can. Caught in a cross-fire of anger between father and son, Cora tries unsuccessfully to serve as peacemaker. Then, when the actual physical struggle takes place between Norwood and Robert and the son strangles the father, Cora's first thought is to help her son escape the lynch mob that she is sure will be formed to track her son down. Scene 1, act 2, closes with Cora's highly emotional soliloquy in which she converses with the Colonel's corpse:

> Don't you come to my bed no mo'. I calls for you to help me now, and you just lays there. I calls for you to wake up, and you just lays there. Whenever you called me, in de night, I woke up. When you called for me to love, I always reached out ma arms fo you. I borned you five chilluns and now one of 'em is out yonder in de dark runnin' from yo people. Our youngest boy out yonder in de dark runnin'. (*Accusingly*) He's runnin' from you too. You said he

> warn't your'n—he's just Cora's little yellow bastard. But he *is* your'n, Colonel Tom. (*Sadly*) And he's runnin' from you. You are out yonder in de dark, (*Points toward the door*) runnin' our chile, with de hounds and de gun in yo' hand. . . . I been sleepin' with you too long, Colonel Tom, not to know that this ain't you layin' down there with yo' eyes shut on de flo'. You can't fool me. . . . Colonel Thomas Norwood, runnin' my boy through de fields in de dark, runnin' ma po' lil' helpless Bert through de fields in de dark to lynch him. . . . Damn you, Colonel Norwood! Damn you, Thomas Norwood! God damn you! (27)

As the play draws to a close and the sounds of the lynch mob pursuing her Bert grow louder, Cora, in another long soliloquy, bitterly recalls how her concubinage with the Colonel began: "Colonel Thomas Norwood! . . . Thirty years ago, you put yo' hands on me to feel my breasts, and you say, 'Yo' a pretty little piece of flesh, ain't you? Black and sweet, ain't you?' An' I lif' up my face, an you pull me to you, an we laid down under the trees that night, an' I wonders if yo' wife'll know when you goes back up da road into de big house. . . . An' ah loved you in de dark, down thuh under dat tree by de gate, afraid of you and proud of you, feelin' yo gray eyes lookin' at me in de dark" (32). And at one point, she observes: "White mens, and colored womens, and lil' bastard chilluns—tha's de ol' way of de South—but it's ending now" (30).

Mulatto ends when Robert takes his own life rather than be taken by the lynch mob. The last person on the stage is Cora. She stands quietly and does not move or flinch when Talbot, the white overseer, vents his frustration by slapping her. Her personal slavery as a white man's concubine has come to an end, and *Mulatto*'s message also seems to be that no black person is truly free as long as one black woman is kept as a white man's concubine.[10]

Obviously, Hughes's 1935 statement on miscegenation is far more psychologically penetrating and direct than Sheldon's 1909 statement. The principal cause for this difference is not that the intervening twenty-four years bred a greater awareness in the body politic of the social and psychological implications of miscegenation and black concubinage. Rather, the difference in approaches stems from the fact that Hughes's view is a racially interior view and Sheldon's is the racially exterior view commonly held by Northern liberals in appraising Southern mores and racial practices. Indeed, Sheldon, in the end, presents miscegenation as just another regional foible bespeaking the legendary moral turpitude of the sinful South. Hughes, on the other hand, had, like many of his fellow blacks, some experiential proximity to the problem. His father, like Colonel Norwood, had abandoned him for selfish and appetitive reasons. Moreover, Hughes had had a much-revered great uncle, John

Mercer Langston, who, like many other black race leaders of the nineteenth century (P.B.S. Pinchback, Francis and Archibald Grimke, Frederick Douglass, Booker T. Washington, William Wells Brown, and others) had a slave-master father (Ralph Quarles, a wealthy planter from Louisa County, Virginia). One can therefore conclude that because Hughes, in his own life and career, had been close to the problem, his play has an emotional tautness and psychological intensity lacking in *The Nigger*. Sheldon had aesthetic distance from his subject, but this very fact robbed his play of the emotional intensity that differentiates good drama from melodramatic entertainment.

Notes

1. Edward Sheldon, *The Nigger* (New York: Macmillan, 1910). Sheldon was a moderately popular pre-World War I playwright. His *Salvation Nell* (1908) and *Romance* (1913) enjoyed good runs on Broadway.

2. Faith Berry, *Langston Hughes: Before and Beyond Harlem* (Westport, Conn.: Greenwood, 1983), 241.

3. Black musicals–*Clorindy, In Dahomey, Lode of Coal*–were popular on and off Broadway at the turn of the century, and Wallace Thurman's *Harlem* had enjoyed a good season's run on Broadway in 1929.

4. Berry, *Langston Hughes*, 240–41.

5. *Fine Clothes to the Jew* (New York: Knopf, 1927), 71–72.

6. Sheldon, *The Nigger*, 242; hereafter cited in the text.

7. Webster Smalley, ed., *Five Plays by Langston Hughes* (Bloomington: Indiana University Press, 1963), xi; hereafter references to *Mulatto* will be to this edition.

8. This is an interpretation that I think best coheres with the play's plot action. Another interpretation could be that Robert's action symbolizes a subconscious Freudian wish of all black males.

9. It is now general knowledge that incest of this kind was widely prevalent during slavery. Fiction writers as widely separated as Faulkner and Gayl Jones mention it in their writings, Faulkner in his stories about some of the slave families in Yoknapatawpha County and Jones in her account of the old Brazilian slave holder, Corregidora. Also, in *Young Frederick Douglass: The Maryland Years* (Baltimore: Johns Hopkins University Press, 1980), Dickens J. Preston confirms that Captain Aaron Anthony, Douglass's white father, also fathered Harriet Bailey, Douglass's mother.

10. The sexual slavery of the black woman is described with brutal directness in Gayl Jones's *Corregidora* when Ursa Corregidora recalls what her Great Gram had said occurred when she had been a slave on the Portuguese Corregidora's plantation in Brazil. A female slave had one major function–to "breed well or make a good whore. Fuck each other or fuck them" (*Corregidora* [New York: Bantam Books, 1976], 145).

INDEX